BUILDING AN AUSTRIAN NATION

BUILDING AN AUSTRIAN NATION

THE POLITICAL INTEGRATION OF A WESTERN STATE

BY WILLIAM T. BLUHM

NEW HAVEN AND LONDON, YALE UNIVERSITY PRESS, 1973

Published with assistance from the foundation
established in memory of Philip Hamilton McMillan
of the Class of 1894, Yale College.

Library of Congress catalog card number: 72-91288
International standard book number: 0-300-01585-2

Designed by Sally Sullivan
and set in Linotype Times Roman type.
Printed in the United States of America by
The Colonial Press Inc., Clinton, Mass.

Published in Great Britain, Europe, and Africa by
Yale University Press, Ltd., London.
Distributed in Canada by McGill-Queen's University
Press, Montreal; in Latin America by Kaiman & Polon,
Inc., New York City; in Australasia and Southeast
Asia by John Wiley & Sons Australasia Pty. Ltd.,
Sydney; in India by UBS Publishers' Distributors Pvt.,
Ltd., Delhi; in Japan by John Weatherhill, Inc., Tokyo.

For Mother and Charlotte

Those who dare to undertake the institution of a people must feel themselves capable, as it were, of changing human nature, of transforming each individual, who by himself is a perfect and solitary whole, into a part of a much greater whole, from which he in some measure receives his being and his life. . . .

To these conditions for establishing a people we must add one more which cannot take the place of anything else; but without which all the others will be of no effect: the enjoyment of peace and abundance; for the time of forming a State is, like that of forming a battalion of soldiers, the very moment when the body is weakest and most easily destroyed. Men make a more powerful resistance in a state of absolute disorder than at the busy crisis of a new arrangement, when the attention of each person is engaged by his own position and not by the general danger. If either war, famine, or sedition assail them at such time of crisis the State is inevitably overturned.

Jean Jacques Rousseau, The Social Contract

Love of country is what I do not feel when I am wronged, but what I felt when secure in my rights as a citizen.

Alcibiades at Sparta
Thucydides, Pelopennesian War

CONTENTS

TABLES

MAP

CHART

PREFACE

My interest in Austrian nation building arose out of a study of corporatism that I did as a graduate student. Examining the experience of the Dollfuss-Schuschnigg *Ständestaat,* I was struck by the banality of corporative theory but found the Austrian corporative experiment fascinating on another level. Corporatism, together with a collection of other traditionalist ideas, served a coalition of conservative elites as an ideological myth with which to inspire a national political identity in the people of the rump Danubian-Alpine republic that was left over when the Habsburg Empire collapsed. The ideology that these elites spun and manipulated was clumsy and ambivalent, designed to distinguish Austrians from Germans, and yet not to do so. And the mobilization politics for which it furnished the watchwords was marvelously inept. Four short years after its inception the Austrian *Ständestaat* was swallowed up by the "Thousand Year Reich." The thousand years lasted only until 1945, however, when Austrians were given a second try at establishing an independent republic. In 1965, the twentieth anniversary of the new beginning, I set to work to discover how they had proceeded and what success they had had this time in creating a viable national consciousness to give substance to their nation-state institutions. This book contains the results of that inquiry.

The basic research for this study was supported by a Fulbright Fellowship in Austria during 1965–66. I wish to thank the Austrian-American Educational Commission, which administers the Fulbright program in Vienna, and especially its executive director, Dr. Anton Porhansl, for invaluable assistance. Thanks are also due to the National Science Foundation for two summer grants which freed time for me to write up my findings. I also wish to thank the

University of Rochester for supporting my research during 1968–
69. The Austrian friends who helped me with information and contacts are too numerous to mention individually; I am grateful to
them all. I should also like to thank Rodney Stiefbold and John
Dreijmanis for helpful suggestions, and Bingham Powell, who read
part of the manuscript, for his useful critique. A special thanks is
due to Arend Lijphart, who read the entire manuscript and whose
trenchant criticisms and advice have been extremely helpful to me.
To my wife Elly I am grateful for sure and honest judgment, as
well as for her loving encouragement. To my patient secretary, Peg
Gross, I owe a special debt for managing so capably with my un-
tidy copy.

Translations from the German are my own, unless otherwise
noted. I have used the expression "Pan-German" throughout the
text in a broad cultural sense, rather than as a historical political
concept, to designate all *deutschnationale* tendencies and ideas.

Rochester, New York   W. T. B.
January 1, 1973

INTRODUCTION

This is a book about nation building. Unlike most of the burgeoning literature on this subject, however, the data it examines are not African, Middle Eastern, Asian, or Latin American, but European. The book tells the story of the development of Republican Austria out of the wreckage of the Habsburg Empire. The beginnings of that story in 1918 present a striking parallel to the experience of those states which since 1945 have been emerging from the wreckage of other empires. And it may be that the pattern of Austrian success in the republic's second incarnation contains useful information for statesmen engaged in the enterprise of nation building in the non-Western world.

Austria emerging from the ruins of dynastic empire in 1918 and the typical post–World War II "developing state," rising from the ruins of colonial empire, both stood at the beginning of the nation-building process. Both had the exterior form, but neither had the psychological substance of the nation-state (i.e., a spirit of citizenship); nor did they have the political and economic institutions "which can translate into policy and programs the aspirations of nationalism and citizenship." [1] Even the exterior form was an arbitrary foreign creation rather than an indigenous growth. The boundaries of Republican Austria were determined not by Austrians but by the triumphant democracies of World War I. In similar fashion, the boundaries of new states like the Congo and Nigeria were drawn by and for the power and convenience of colonial regimes, not by the inhabitants. Nor were the governmental systems adopted at the outset a native growth; rather, they were imported from abroad. In a similar way Austrian parliamentary democracy, within a republican frame of reference, though inaugurated by domestic forces, was patronized and sanctioned by foreign powers—the

---

1. Lucian W. Pye, "The Concept of Political Development," in Jason L. Finkle and Richard W. Gable, eds., *Political Development and Social Change* (New York: John Wiley, 1966), p. 86.

1

Western democracies that won the war. In the background was an indigenous authoritarian structure that had been "democratized only partially and at a late date." [2]

A lack of fit between group identity and state boundaries made for instability in the First Austrian Republic as it does in the developing state today. For a while parochial loyalties posed a threat of absolute fragmentation. Immediately following the dissolution of the empire 80 percent of the residents of the Vorarlberg, the westernmost province of Austria, voted in a plebiscite for absorption by Switzerland (which refused their overtures), and at another point the citizens of the Tyrol were thinking of going it alone as a Tyrolean free state before it was clear that the southern portion of the Tyrol was irrevocably lost to Italy.[3] In similar fashion tribal particularism threatened to detach Biafra from the rest of Nigeria in the late 1960s. Pan-German sentiment, which pulled the entire Austrian republic toward anschluss with the German-speaking neighbor to the north, finds some counterpart in the Pan-Arabism that threatens the tiny, fragile Middle Eastern sovereignties of today.

Parochialism and Pan-Germanism as politically centrifugal forces in post–World War I Austria were combined with a certain cultural pluralism, just as in the modern emerging state political conflicts are linked with cultural differences. Vienna, as the capital of an ethnically and linguistically conglomerate empire, had developed a conglomerate culture, which mingled Slavic with its German components. This was manifest in the very names of its inhabitants, who were Hawliceks, Schusseks, Csokors, Preradovics, Kokoschkas, and Wotrubas, as well as Meinrads, Böhms, Werners, and Holzmeisters. (To this day the Viennese have close family ties across the borders to the east and south, in Czechoslovakia, Hungary, and Yugoslavia.) The mixed quality of Viennese culture was also mani-

2. "In many underdeveloped countries governmental systems are foreign imports little related to their societies. . . . The African elite inherited an authoritarian structure, which was democratized only partially, and at a late date." Joseph S. Nye, Jr., *Pan-Africanism and East African Integration* (Cambridge, Mass.: Harvard University Press, 1965), p. 21.

3. Walter Goldinger, "Der geschichtliche Ablauf der Ereignisse in Österreich von 1918 bis 1945," in Heinrich Benedikt et al., eds., *Geschichte der Republik Österreich* (Vienna: Verlag für Geschichte u. Politik, 1954), pp. 67, 70, 73.

fest in language, especially in the dialect of the common man, which was (and is) a remarkable potpourri of German, Czech, Polish, Hungarian, and other words and stems. Even the high German spoken in Vienna had a Slavic lilt to it. The dialects of the western provinces—Salzburg, Tyrol, Vorarlberg—were all more recognizable as German.

Linguistic divisions became class-based as well as region-based. Leopold von Andrian-Werburg, in a 1937 volume entitled *Österreich im Prisma der Idee,* has shown how the imperial Austrian aristocracy failed to beget a united Austrian nation because of its failure to dominate the language of the western crown lands.[4] Their Viennese speech, he writes, was not destined to become the common property of all Austrians because the court nobility kept itself too much apart from the middle classes to allow its culture to influence them. Channels of communication between the classes were few and narrow. "A higher Austrian speech had been created, but it did not penetrate the middle class nor the literature dominated by this class." As a result "the beginnings of crystallization of an Austrian nation in the crownlands of the monarchy, the territory of the present Austrian state, came to a standstill." [5]

As the Austrian middle class began to develop during the nineteenth century, Andrian argues, instead of aping its own elite it looked for models to the north. The practical, commercial, and technical spirit developing there fit much better with the mentality of these classes than did the traditional, more aesthetic culture of the Austrian aristocracy. In addition, the exaggerated modesty and self-doubt that were becoming typically Viennese characteristics in the nineteenth century, as the political power of the empire declined and the old forms ossified, added to the impetus to seek cultural models abroad rather than at home. As a result the spoken language and the literature over which the middle class presided became more and more north-German in spirit and mentality. When the hour of political reckoning came

> the Austrians of the crown lands, who had been kept in constant conflict with the other peoples of the empire, who had remained

4. Leopold Andrian-Werburg, *Österreich im Prisma der Idee* (Graz: Verlag Schmidt-Dengler, 1937).
5. Ibid., pp. 343, 352.

in continued dependence, both political and cultural on Germany, and who had swung to and fro between an Austrian and a German consciousness which could no longer be reconciled with one another, finally had to choose between the two ideals, since human nature requires a certain unity of feeling. . . . The double ideology of the Austrian middle class was dead and set aside. For the first of its substrata, Great Austria, in the midst of which the crown lands were embedded, had been destroyed.[6]

During the long years when Vienna gradually extended its sway to the east, the other crown lands proudly maintained their independence. They were as old as the capital, and had their own assemblies of estates. In them the Habsburg ruler was not emperor, but count or duke of the locality. Willy Lorenz writes of Salzburg, Innsbruck, and the other western towns as "sister cities" to Vienna —cities which experienced all the jealousy and independence that that phrase implies. Very different were the "daughter cities," Budapest, Brno, Sarajevo, Lwow, Zagreb, which even now resemble Vienna in their architecture, while the principal cities of Republican Austria do not. It is interesting that the western half of the empire had no official name. Officially there were only "the duchies and lands represented in the Federal Council." [7]

The myth of blood also made for a certain looseness of cultural order in the Austria of 1918. If the Viennese were slavicized Germans, the Salzburgers saw themselves as pure-blooded *Bayuvaren,* and the Vorarlbergers boasted of their Alemannic descent (and still do). These are the names of two of the historic German *Stämme* (a word for which it is difficult to give a good English equivalent, but which translates literally as "tribes"). A comparison of differences between Ibo and Yoruba with these differences can be framed in terms of degree rather than kind.

The reality of the parochial spirit even today is dramatized by Hans Weigel, a Viennese litterateur, in a sprightly volume entitled *O Du Mein Österreich!,* a cultural vignette of modern Austria. Two-

6. Ibid., pp. 363–64.
7. See Willy Lorenz, *AEIOU, Allen Ernstes ist Österreich Unersetzlich* (Vienna: Herold, 1961), pp. 50–51. See also Gordon Shepherd, *Dollfuss* (New York: St. Martin's Press, 1961), p. 1.

thirds of the book is about Vienna—its music, its literature, its history, its manners and mores. In the last third the peoples of the other states are briefly characterized, seriatim. Each is introduced with precisely the same paragraph, designed to emphasize its separateness from Vienna, and from the others:

The Tyroleans [Salzburgers, Carinthians, Styrians, Vorarlbergers, etc.] are a rude and obstinate people, imagine themselves superior to the other federal states, maintain and cultivate proudly and jealously their independence as self-governing [*selbstherrlich*] communities, and are full of scorn when the talk is about "those Viennese." [8]

Added to the pluralism of language and blood (if only subjective) and manners were religious antagonisms. Despite a common nominal Catholicism, Austrians were divided religiously into three groups. In Vienna the close association of throne and altar had made bitter anticlericals of the growing working class and its Socialist leaders. In the provinces, staunchly Catholic areas, where Christian Social politics and Austrian feeling were strong, alternated with large islands of anticlericalism, where Pan-Germanism and Liberal politics held sway. The beginnings of the division lay in the Protestant Reformation, when all the estates of the Austrian crown lands went over to the new faith. Only by political coercion did the Habsburgs win them back to Catholicism. In the places that held out most stubbornly against the Counter-Reformation— Carinthia, parts of Styria, the Waldviertel of Lower Austria—a Crypto-Protestantism flourished until the reign of Joseph II. [9] Always strongly Pan-German, these places became, during the First Republic, centers of nazism, a pseudo religion both anti-Austrian and anti-Catholic. Thus religious rivalry, regional antagonisms, and political-ideological differences all reinforced one another, as in so many of today's emerging states.

Austria in 1918 also resembled the post–World War II emerging nation in its condition of economic dislocation, underdevelopment, and lopsidedness. Predominantly rural, the tiny state con-

8. Hans Weigel, *O Du Mein Österreich!* (Vienna: Donauland, 1963), p. 280.
9. Erika Weinzierl, "Das österreichische Staatsbewusstsein," in idem, ed., *Der Österreicher und sein Staat* (Vienna: Herder, 1965), pp. 15–16.

tained one vast urban area, sprawling Vienna, now cut off from her traditional economic hinterland to the east by new political boundaries and trade barriers. How like this is to Philip Hauser's description of the single sprawling metropolis, swollen with a population unjustified by the level of economic development of the region, as a chief mark of the underdeveloped non-Western state of today.[10] One Austrian writer recognizes the aptness of such comparisons by stating that "the First Republic was born . . . amid economic strains and stresses characteristic of a developing area" (*in der wirtschaftlichen Spannung eines Entwicklungslandes*).[11]

Another Austrian publicist, who takes frequent part in an ongoing polemic about the existence and character of the "Austrian nation" makes an overall comparison between the experience of Austria and that of the developing non-European state. "Large segments of the population," writes Walter Jambor, "have already declared their allegiance to Austria as a nation. There are still, however, political and pseudo-scholarly elements who want to prevent us from taking the last step to true nationhood. They want to keep Austria in the condition of a developing country that can't get beyond the 'Lumumba' phase." [12]

After more than fifty years of turmoil, disintegration, and reconstruction, Austria today has acquired most of the characteristics that students of nation building assign to developed nation-statehood. Her leaders fit the picture of the "modern man" described by Daniel Lerner and display the problem-solving, moderate pattern of behavior emphasized by Lucian Pye. The polity exhibits the fourfold system of functional capabilities stressed by Gabriel Almond (integration, international accommodation, participation, and welfare). The society manifests the social mobility and egalitarian class system underlined by Robert Chin.[13] The present book de-

10. See Philip M. Hauser, "Some Cultural and Personal Characteristics of the Less Developed Areas," in Finkle and Gable, *Political Development*, p. 54.

11. Ernst F. Winter, "Der Staat ohne Eigenschaften, oder, Die Suche nach der nationalen Identität," Norddeutscher Rundfunk, Third Program, Hamburg, October 24, 1965 (mimeographed transcript).

12. Walter Jambor, interviewed in *Express am Wochenende,* May 15, 1965.

13. Lerner's "modern man" loves change and sees the future as manipulable. He is ambitious in an instrumentally rational, calculating way. He is

scribes the processes by which ultimate success was won in the face of an apparently hopeless beginning.

The causal pattern revealed in this case study constitutes one test of a number of contradictory hypotheses about nation building and political development that have been put forward by leading students of these phenomena. One set of contributors to the literature of political development holds that cultural integration is a precondition of political integration. Thus M. G. Smith, a student of African politics, presents the thesis that

> Integration rests on common values. . . . It presupposes cultural homogeneity. . . . Cultural diversity or pluralism automatically imposes the structural necessity for domination by one of the cultural sections. It excludes the possibility of consensus, or of institutional integration, or of structural balance between the different sections, and necessitates nondemocratic regulation of group relationships.[14]

Similarly, Karl Deutsch and his coauthors, generalizing from European data in their study of the North Atlantic area, specify the mutual compatibility of main values in a society and a distinctive way of life as essential conditions for the growth of political community.[15]

---

empathic and can put himself in another's shoes. He is oriented to the larger rather than to the parochial world, likes urban living, and is happy amid mundane values. See *The Passing of Traditional Society* (New York: Free Press of Glencoe, 1958), pp. 47–75. Pye's image of modern rationality involves "an avoidance of reckless actions which threaten the vested interests of significant segments of society, some sense of limitations to the sovereignty of politics, an appreciation of the values of orderly administration and legal procedures, an acknowledgment that politics is rightfully a mechanism for solving problems and not an end in itself, a stress on welfare programs, and finally an acceptance of mass participation." Lucian W. Pye, "The Concept of Political Development," in Finkle and Gable, *Political Development*, p. 84. Almond's integrative capability means the ability to create national unity and a centralized bureaucracy. Participation capability means the capacity to create a political culture of civic obligation and one which supports a democratic political structure. The other two capabilities are self-explanatory. See also Robert Chin, "The Utility of Systems Models and Developmental Models," in Finkle and Gable, *Political Development*, p. 25.

14. Leo Kuper, Introduction to Leo Kuper and M. G. Smith, eds., *Pluralism in Africa* (Berkeley: University of California Press, 1969), p. 14.

15. Karl W. Deutsch et al., *Political Community and the North Atlantic Area* (Princeton, N.J.: Princeton University Press, 1957), p. 58.

Amitai Etzioni, on the other hand, argues that writers like these put too many variables together under the heading of "cultural homogeneity" or "shared culture" to make such concepts useful. They combine with elements of background culture—language, religion, and ethnic composition—the ingredients of political culture. Such concepts, he believes, are of no explanatory value and also lead to tautological argument. Indeed, he tells us, there is a "limited set of values and symbols directly related to unification including legitimation of the new power center, a sense of identity, shared political rituals, and the like," which are plainly requisite to political integration. But we must keep in mind that "it is the emergence of these shared values that the study of unification has to explain; their existence is part of our definition of integration. If we view that same factor as our dependent variable (integration) and as our independent one (culture) we are spinning tautologies." [16] It may be the case, Etzioni suggests, that most cultural values are politically irrelevant. In any event, background culture and political culture should be separately treated.

It is interesting that Austrians, in attempting to understand and come to grips with their integration problem, have conceived of it as one of relating the concepts "political nation" and "cultural nation" to one another, a distinction and a problem implied by Etzioni's analysis. They have produced an entire literature that seeks to answer the question, "Is there an Austrian nation?"—some identifying Austria as a political nation, others as a cultural nation, others as neither one. And they inquire whether politics and background culture can be kept separate from one another. Chapter 5 will review the highlights of this literature.

Hans Kohn, in his important seminal work, *The Idea of Nationalism,* has presented a precise definition of the two concepts of "nation" that figure so prominently in the debate that Austrians carry on with one another, and a statement of the circumstances under which each of the concepts emerged and obtained currency in modern political culture. The following excerpts from his book

16. Amitai Etzioni, *Political Unification* (New York: Holt, Rinehart & Winston, 1965), pp. 23, 35–36. Deutsch, however, recognizes the problem of specifying the content of "main values." See *Political Community,* pp. 46–47, 197.

should be useful for clarifying the terms of reference of the political discussion we are about to study:

In the Western world, in England and in France, in the Netherlands and in Switzerland, in the United States and in the British dominions, the rise of nationalism was a predominantly political occurrence; it was preceded by the formation of the future national state, or, as in the case of the United States, coincided with it. Outside the Western world, in Central and Eastern Europe and in Asia, nationalism arose not only later, but also generally at a more backward stage of social and political development: the frontiers of an existing state and of a rising nationality rarely coincided; nationalism, there, grew in protest against and in conflict with the existing state pattern, not primarily to transform it into a people's state, but to redraw the political boundaries in conformity with ethnographic demands.

Because of the backward state of political and social development, this rising nationalism outside the Western world found its first expression in the cultural field . . . a venture in education and propaganda rather than in policy-shaping and government.

Two main concepts of nation and fatherland emerged in the intertwining of influences and conditions. . . . The one was basically a rational and universal concept of political liberty and the rights of man, looking towards the city of the future. . . . The other was basically founded on history, on monuments and graveyards, even harking back to the mysteries of ancient times and of tribal solidarity. It stressed the past, the diversity and self-sufficiency of nations. . . . These two concepts of nationalism are the poles around which the new age . . . will revolve.[17]

The starting point of the Austrian debate is in the 1930s, when the Central European concept of "nation" as "cultural nation" predominated in Austria, and it was assumed on all sides (with a few notable exceptions) that polity depended on culture. The result was

17. See Hans Kohn, *The Idea of Nationalism* (New York: Macmillan, 1951), pp. 329–30, 574. Louis Snyder has digested Kohn's dichotomous theory and arranged its central elements in a two-column chart. See *The Meaning of Nationalism* (New Brunswick, N.J.: Rutgers University Press, 1954), pp. 118–20.

totalitarian warfare, as in so many of the developing states of today. It was only after World War II that the Western concept of the nation as a preeminently political community gained currency, and with it the idea that the "political nation" can have a certain independence of its cultural background. Though not universally agreed to, this is the common opinion of the leaders who built and now govern the Second Austrian Republic. They have, in a sense, moved away from Smith to embrace Etzioni in exchanging the Central European for the Western conception of "nation." Indeed, by their successful construction of an Austrian political nation these leaders have also demonstrated the superiority of Etzioni's hypothesis, at least as it applies to the Austrian case today.

Another area of debate in the nation-building literature concerns the relationship between economic factors and political integration. Ernst B. Haas claims that "generally shared expectations of economic gains are constituents of the process of integration found to recur with monotonous regularity." [18] But Claude Welch, in a study of African unification movements, argues in qualification of this thesis that "the successful operation of economic factors requires a relatively stable, long-established political system, in which economic interest groups play a recognized role in political life. Where political systems are in flux and the growth of nationalism signals the start of ideology . . . it may be misleading to base arguments for unification solely on economic grounds." [19] Welch thus suggests that economic well-being is an effect rather than a cause of political integration. Joseph S. Nye, Jr., in a study of East African integration, also tells us that the primacy of economic motives as integrating factors can be overrated. "To study integration in areas like East Africa," he says, "less attention should be paid to [economic interest groups] . . . more attention should be given to ideology." [20]

In this area, too, our discussion of nation building in Austria constitutes a test of conflicting theories. We shall show that the experience of the Second Republic bears out the thesis of scholars

18. Ernst B. Haas, "The Challenge of Regionalism," *International Organization* 12 (1958), cited in Claude E. Welch, Jr., *Dream of Unity* (Ithaca, N.Y.: Cornell University Press, 1966), p. 343.
19. Ibid.
20. Nye, *Pan-Africanism*, p. 18.

like Haas that political loyalties follow economic interests. The demonstration by a pragmatic leadership of Austrian economic viability and the development of a mature industrial economy which could produce affluence accounts, perhaps more than any other factor, for the present strong Austrian attachment to the state. Dollfuss and Schuschnigg, following in the 1930s a prescription like that of Nye, which stresses ideology, failed. And contrary to the arguments of writers like Welch that "the successful operation of economic factors . . . requires a relatively stable, long-established political system," the Austrian economic miracle was produced by a brand new political arrangement, the contractarian coalition of 1945, not by an old and stable polity.[21]

21. For a succinct discussion of the importance of economic development as a stimulus to the growth of national consciousness see Mostafa Rejai and Cynthia Enloe, "Nation-States and State-Nations," *International Studies Quarterly* 13, no. 2 (June 1969).

1. THE POLITICS OF DISINTEGRATION: THE MIRAGE OF AN "AUSTRIAN NATION" 1808-1938

A National Empire?

It is indeed remarkable that an effort to create a single Austrian nation out of the myriad ethnic and language groups of the empire should ever have been made. Yet there are on record numerous attempts by the imperial intelligentsia and bureaucracy to fashion a Great-Austrian ideal to supplement the weakening principle of dynasticism before it was completely undermined by the particularist nationalisms of the Czechs, Poles, Slovenes, Croats, and Hungarians.

In the aftermath of the Reformation, religion continued to be a focus of political community, though no longer of one community with its center in Rome. It was Protestant Britain that rallied around the centralizing Tudors and Catholic France that crushed the Fronde in the name of their "Most Christian King." In Central Europe, also, the Habsburgs were busy constructing a centralized polity on a religious foundation out of the loosely knit Holy Roman Empire. One writer maintains that unless they had smashed the power of the Protestant Estates, the Habsburgs would have been unable to avert the Turkish threat. Confessional unity strengthened their claim to sovereignty and furnished the power to wage successful war against the Turks, who mounted repeated and determined invasions.[1]

A second unifier of the Renaissance and Baroque state was the charisma of the absolute monarch, who ruled by divine right. In

1. Weinzierl, *Der Österreicher*, p. 16.

12

the soldiers' song about Prince Eugene, composed by an unknown folksinger to extol the great Savoyard's exploits against the Turks, the prince is represented as winning back "the city and fortress of Belgrade" not for the empire or for Austria, but "for the emperor." *State* and *monarchy* were interchangeable terms. After the Pragmatic Sanction of 1713 the identity had a legal basis.[2]

An idea of the state as such, apart from the person of the ruler and independent of the community's religion, begins to emerge in the Habsburg Empire during the last part of the eighteenth century. In a decree issued by Maria Theresa in 1775, which brought into being the public high school, the expression "national education" is employed, indicating an identification of the idea of "nation" with political community and recognizing the importance of education as a device for political socialization. Even earlier Charles VI, the father of the great empress, had said that his policy was directed "to the end one *gens* emerge." [3]

It was during the Napoleonic Wars that the first extensive and systematic efforts were made to rebuild the conception of the Austrian political community on the national idea by generating a concept of an Austrian nation. "Österreich über Alles," the title of Heinrich Collin's military anthem of 1809, reminds us of the later German nationalist watchword. Actually it was a revival of a slogan coined by Philipp von Hornigk in 1684, during the Turkish Wars: "Austria above all, if only she wills it!" And from the pens of Friedrich von Gentz, Ignaz Franz Castelli, Johann Nepomuk Passy, and others flowed a stream of similar patriotic songs, poems, and manifestos to inspire the soldiers of the liberation wars with patriotic fervor.[4]

In 1808, historian Josef Freiherr von Hormayr founded a journal devoted to "patriotic papers" for the Austrian Imperial State, through which he hoped to inculcate the love of Austria as fatherland in the educated elites of the empire and provide a vehicle for the exchange of ideas on patriotic themes across ethnic and cultural boundaries. His method was to glorify Austrian history, to create

2. Ibid., pp. 16, 17.
3. Ibid., p. 17; Peter Berger, "The Idea of an Austrian Political Nation Down to 1938," lecture at the Austrian National Library, Vienna, May 1966.
4. Weinzierl, *Der Österreicher*, p. 19; Rudolph Till, *Pax Austriaca* (Vienna: Babenberg Verlag, 1948), pp. 32–35.

national feeling by the emotional recollection of the empire's heroes and triumphs. In an 1814 work, *Österreich und Deutschland,* Hormayr actually calls the empire a nation, speaking of "sins against the Austrian nation." And he again sounds Hornigk's motto, "Austria above all, if only she wills it!" As early as 1809 Count Stadion thought the work of ideological and administrative renovation substantially complete, declaring: "We have made ourselves into a nation" (*Wir haben uns als Nation konstituiert*).[5] Moreover, it appears that in most of these cases "nation" was conceived in the Western sense of "political nation," rather than in the sense of "cultural nation," which was later to become the accepted Central European usage.

The strategy of the imperial intellectuals and bureaucrats was to beat the French by domesticating their most powerful political idea, the "nation." The feats of the citizen armies which had carried revolution to every part of Europe were an adequate testimony to the potency of the national ideal. As conditions for its reception, the Austrian elite thought administrative centralization and uniformity together with state control of education would be sufficient. Perhaps Emperor Francis, who discouraged the strategy, understood politics better than the bureaucrats and intellectuals did, however. He seems to have sensed that a whole new form of political community and a whole new conception of authority—in which he could play no part—lay hidden in the words *nation* and *fatherland.* For he struck from the military *levee* of 1813 the word *fatherland* and replaced it with the word *emperor.*[6] He may have decided that fraternity ultimately implies liberty and equality and that acceptance of one meant acceptance of all. It is certainly true that in the prototypical experience of France, "nationalization" had proceeded most vigorously and extensively under the Jacobins. And though *la grande Nation* returned subsequently to monarchical forms, Napoleon was not a legitimate hereditary king but a plebiscitary tribune of the people. His authority did not look backward to the Holy Roman Empire, but forward to the modern dictator. The concepts of political development which were discussed in the introduction include notions of liberty, equality, and national fra-

5. Till, *Pax Austriaca,* p. 32.
6. Ibid., p. 34.

ternity. They allow also for the role of dictator in the abnormal case. But the idea of a divine right monarch does not belong anywhere in the package.

The order created at the Congress of Vienna was the temporary graveyard of the new order and its symbols. Political development was arrested for more than thirty years. Europe awoke from its dream of universal liberty and equality to the restored realities of old-fashioned dynasticism. In Austria, Metternich seemed to sense the need for some sort of state ideology to support the personal authority of the emperor, but he mistrusted the notion of an Austrian peoples' state (*Völkerstaatsidee*) as dangerous to the dynastic principle. There seemed to be no Austrian idea separable from the dynastic idea, which might have served as an object of allegiance to the house of Habsburg.[7]

In the 1850s there were new experiments in formulating and cultivating the idea of an Austrian nation. Notable was the work of another historian, Josef Alexander Freiherr von Helfert, undersecretary of state in the Austrian Ministry of Education, who in 1853 published *Über die Nationalgeschichte und den gegenwärtigen Stand ihrer Pflege in Österreich,* in which he imposed the Western European political nation concept on Austrian history.[8] His object was to stimulate the development of the idea of Austria as a *Staatsnation.* Believing that the neglect of historical instruction in the colleges was responsible for the paucity of Great-Austrian patriots, he founded an institute for Austrian historical research at the University of Vienna in 1854; he hoped this would stimulate the growth of a Great-Austrian historical consciousness. His model was the Parisian Ecole des Chartes which he believed had played a large role in the fashioning of the French national historical consciousness. As it turned out, however, the energies of the people at the institute, under the directorship of Theodor Sickel, came to be focused on the creation of an academic research method rather than on writing Great-Austrian history.[9]

Helfert's work took place in a political climate that was abso-

7. Ibid., p. 35.
8. *Über die National-geschichte und den gegenwärtigen Stand ihrer Pflege in Österreich* (Prague: Tempsky, 1853).
9. Till, *Pax Austriaca,* p. 60.

lutely antithetical to its success. During the neoabsolutist period of the 1860s the suppression of constitution, parliament, and freedom of the press, prizes of the Revolution of 1848, turned the liberal middle class, the very stratum to whom the national idea has the greatest natural appeal, against the monarchy and its works. The military defeats of 1859 and 1866 at the hands of the Prussians did nothing to enhance Austrian patriotism. Middle-class nationalism in Austria was soon to develop around the Hohenzollern-sponsored concept of *Deutschtum* rather than around a Habsburg *Deutschtum* or *Österreichertum*.

In some parts of the imperial structure a genuine attachment to the state as such developed during the nineteenth century, despite the failure of efforts to have that state conceived as a nation. The army and the bureaucracy were Great-Austrian elements as were the clergy of the Catholic church, especially after the conclusion of the Concordat of 1855. And with the beginnings of political democracy the Christian Social party emerged as a carrier of the Great-Austrian mentality.

The origins of the Christian Social party are found in the 1888 secession of middle-class and peasant elements from an earlier conservative alliance with aristocrats and church prelates. One of the party's founders was Karl Lueger, a pragmatic politician who, as mayor of Vienna, based his power position on the petite bourgeoisie. Another was Baron Karl von Vogelsang, an ideologue whose romantic corporatist doctrines appealed to the artisan and peasant classes threatened by the rapid development of a capitalist economy under liberal auspices. Lueger's pragmatism prevented the party from adopting a pure anticapitalist line. But Vogelsang's corporatism and his authoritarian state doctrine introduced an element of ideological rigidity and exclusiveness into the party creed. During the First Republic, when the identity question became crucial, this was to produce a restricted Austrianism incapable of becoming a consensual belief system embracing a cross section of the Austrian population.[10]

10. Edgar Alexander, "Church and Society in Germany: Social and Political Movements and Ideas in German and Austrian Catholicism, 1789–1950," trans. Toni Stolper, in Joseph N. Moody, ed., *Church and Society, Catholic Social and Political Thought and Movements, 1789–1950* (New

Monsignor Ignaz Seipel, a Christian Social leader who was to be a chancellor of the First Republic, has left us a book from the final days of the empire which represents one of the last futile attempts to find an adequate verbal expression of the Great-Austrian mentality within the imperial context. The book, *Nation und Staat,* first published in 1916, is important because it grapples with conceptual and psychological dilemmas that were to be posed over and over again by Austrians in the tiny republic that succeeded the empire in 1918, dilemmas which are only now approaching solution.[11]

Groping for a Via Media: *Seipel's* Nation und Staat

Ignaz Seipel was born in Vienna on July 19, 1876, ten years after Königgrätz. Under the terms of the peace treaty imposed by Prussia after that disastrous battle, Austria was required to withdraw from the German Confederation. This withdrawal constituted one step in Prussia's construction of an empire in the north on a purely German national basis; the final step was taken just four years later in the Hall of Mirrors at Versailles after Prussia had proven her youthful vigor a second time by beating the French at Sedan.

For Austria the whole period from Königgrätz to 1918 was an extended phasing out, both organizationally and ideologically. The complicated *Ausgleich* of 1867 with Hungary pointed toward organizational collapse. With the name *German Empire* now preempted by an assertive nation-state to the north, the word *German* could no longer have a specifically Austrian meaning, as it had when, prior to 1806, there was only the Holy Roman Empire of the German Nation. Yet many German-speaking Austrians were unwilling to acknowledge that the values of the northern neighbor summed up everything in their own idea of "Germandom" (*Deutschtum*) and that the empire they loved had lost its meaning in the world. This was especially true of a Catholic cleric like Seipel.

Seipel opens his book with definitions of *state* and *nation.* Using a traditional scholastic rubric he tells us that the state is a pluralist society, the broadest of all human associations, an association of

York: Arts, Inc., 1953), pp. 477–79; Franz Borkenau, *Austria and After* (London: Faber and Faber, 1938), p. 150.

11. Ignaz Seipel, *Nation und Staat* (Vienna: Wilhelm Braumüller, 1916).

associations. The well-being of family, tribe, people, nation, parish, and all organizations to which men belong by nature or choice is confided to the state. It is an organization that rests on a community of interests broader than mere national interests, and one in which the power of all the individual members is joined together and subordinated to a common authority, whose job it is to promote the common good, the many-faceted well-being of its members. The state possesses all means necessary to accomplish this task, without itself being subordinated to another organization of the same order. Moreover, it is an organization of coercive power and wields the joint force of its members.[12]

Seipel's conception of the nation is cultural and historical. But he explicitly rejects all racist definitions. His nation is not a blood community, a kind of middle term between tribe and race. Tribal kinship is by no means decisive for nationality in any historically created people, he asserts. Nations have in the past, in fact, been created by the commingling of different tribes or blood groups. Nor can similarity of speech, taken alone, be considered a decisive criterion of nationality. Irishmen speak English, as do Americans, but neither are members of the English nation. Living together in a common territory for a long period of time defines a "people" (*Volk*) but not a nation. Only when such a people is also a cultural community can it be called a nation. "A number of men develop for themselves a common treasure of spiritual goods; gradually the entire group becomes aware of this joint possession and learns to distinguish its values from the spiritual goods of others. It loves its values as its own, seeks to defend and increase them—such a group is a nation." [13]

For Seipel, cultural nationalism does not imply political nationalism, however. To demand that each nation form a separate state carries the love of nation too far, "as though nationality were the highest good of man." A rigid political delimitation of nations would only increase international hatred and produce a regression of human culture.[14]

The synthesis of cultural nationalism with political international-

12. Ibid., pp. 52, 56, 78–80.
13. Ibid., pp. 5, 55.
14. Ibid., pp. 17, 95.

ism that Seipel attempts resembles the formulas of liberal national-ism. Witness, for example, the following Kantian-sounding passage:

> The old Imperium is dead and will never be resurrected, but its idea lives on. The modern form, in which it can and must be realized if the idea of an eternal peace on earth is to be fulfilled, can only be a system of confederations which form indestructible communities, be they national, economic, or of another kind. Within such federations the social and economic aspirations of all peoples can be realized. May the federation of the central powers bring the fulfillment of that goal which Austria alone attempted but could not realize.[15]

But Seipel's theory of the stages by which the world is to arrive at this confederal order differs considerably from that of the Liberal Nationalists. Mazzini, for example, believed that the path to world organization lay through the disruption of such great multinational agglomerations as the Habsburg Empire. Political independence for all nations and their democratization had to precede their regroup-ing into federal systems. Seipel denied this. To the nation-state, where it was already established, he was willing to concede a place in the divine plan. But where multinational units existed, they ought to be maintained; the way to the federal future lay not through their dismemberment but through their liberalization.[16]

Description is one thing but persuasion is quite another. For his theory of the multinational state Seipel needed an emotional sup-port stronger than the dying appeal of dynastic benevolence. He tried to create it by extending the messianic language of national-ism, such as the concept of "mission," from the nation to the state. Thus he writes that the function of each state in God's plan for the world should be considered its divine mission; if a state can find no mission for itself it has no right to exist. And he expressly de-nies the Fichtean equation of "state mission" with "national mis-

15. Ibid., p. 140.
16. A liberal plan for Austrian imperial reform was presented by Seipel as a six-point proposal to the Constitutional Committee of the Christian Social Parliamentary club in February 1918. See summary in Robert A. Kann, *The Multinational Empire* (New York: Columbia University Press, 1950), 2:216 ff.

sion." [17] Austria had "a special, indeed a divine mission" for the world. The organization of the Austrian state was "the ground (*Boden*) on which two great problems [could] be resolved: the greatest security for national autonomy combined with practice in national unselfishness (*Entselbstung*), with the ordering of the nationalities according to a higher organizational principle." [18] Just as in typical nationalist ideology the idea of the community takes the place of the divine right ruler, so in Seipel's theory of the multinational state the idea of the state replaces the charismatic person of the dynast. Just as to French nationalists devotion to *La Patrie* meant devotion to spreading the ideas of liberty, equality, and fraternity, or a *mission civilisatrice,* so to Seipel the Austrian Fatherland had the mission of being a bridge among and mediator of peoples. Seipel also named love of a common land and a common pride in the deeds of the forefathers, two other ingredients of modern nationalism, as ingredients in the patriotism of the multinational empire.[19]

In effect Seipel's book of 1916 was an attempt to propagate a Great-Austrian nationalism like that of Stadion, Hormayr, and Helfert. Its weakness lay in the fact that Seipel, unlike his nineteenth-century predecessors, could not apply the word *nation* to Austria because of the strength that particularist cultural nationalism had attained by 1916. He thought of himself, for example, as a German in national terms. Seipel's attempt to construct a principle of political community without calling his resultant organization a "nation" was both artificial and emotionally weak.

Reformulations of Identity in Other Camps

Of the political parties that proliferated in Austria as the democratic ideal began to take hold during the nineteenth century, and especially after the emperor created a representative Imperial Assembly (Reichstag), the Christian Social party was the most attached to the empire and the dynasty, the most Austrian-minded. Liberals, German Nationalists and Pan-Germans, while for the

17. Seipel, *Nation und Staat,* p. 17, n. 18.
18. Ibid., quoting Friedrich Wilhelm Förster, *Das Österreichische Problem,* 2d ed. (Vienna: H. Heller, 1916), p. 14.
19. Ibid., pp. 7, 8.

most part not openly disloyal to the state, idolized the Hohenzollern Reich as the shrine of all virtue and strove to enhance the leading position of the Germans in the Habsburg state, prevent all concessions to the Slavs, and establish a close alliance with the northern Reich in foreign policy. Only a small extremist group around Georg von Schönerer, however, pursued a policy aimed at detaching the German-speaking crown lands from Austria and at accomplishing their anschluss with Germany.

Socialists occupied a third position in the spectrum of identities. From the year of its founding (1889) the Austrian Socialist party represented a life style completely alienated and isolated from the values and structures of the Dual Monarchy. In insulating its members from the life of the surrounding society, the party created in a very strict sense a totalitarian organization dominating the entire lives of its members.

> They . . . laboured to build up Social Democratic societies which would cover all a member's activities from the cradle to the grave. His intellectual and physical needs were all catered for within the party. The party provided him with his flat; built kindergartens for his children, organized sport clubs, literary clubs, political clubs, and social clubs for himself and his wife; took charge of his economic life, . . . and even provided burial clubs for his death.[20]

In building a political party the Austro-Marxists in effect created a state within a state, a self-centered and self-contained community.[21] The result of this policy, taken together with Christian Social ideological exclusiveness, was to create an armed-camp (*Lager*) mentality which was to characterize Austrian political life down to the very recent years of the Second Republic. An ideological gulf was dug which would militate for years to come against the integration of Austro-Marxists into a larger Austrian polity.

Strangely enough, ideological division did not make impossible practical politicking by the Socialist party within the imperial de-

20. Mary MacDonald, *The Republic of Austria, 1918–1934* (London: Oxford University Press, 1941), p. 72.

21. Ibid.; Kurt Shell, *The Transformation of Austrian Socialism* (New York: State University of New York Press, 1962), p. 10.

cision-making system. Behind the language of separateness and
revolution there continued to operate the Austrian penchant for
bargain and compromise, a tradition of great age in an empire built
as much on marriage as on military conquest. And though their
leaders talked about proletarian dictatorship, the practice of the
party was consistently within developing liberal democratic lines of
behavior. Franz Borkenau has summed up the Austrian Socialist
policy as "totalitarian within the working class, democratic towards
the other classes; advanced in ideas and propaganda, moderate and
compromising in practical policy." [22]

Viktor Adler, ther Socialist party's founder, who entered politics
as a supporter of Schönerer, remained an enthusiastic Pan-German
after his conversion to socialism, though he did not reject the multinational Habsburg state. Otto Bauer, leader of the radical revolutionary wing of the party who after 1918 was to assume and
retain a strong Pan-German position, during the last years of the
Dual Monarchy actually defended the maintenance of the established order on pragmatic grounds. In 1907 in a work entitled *Die
Nationalitätenfrage und die Sozialdemokratie* he wrote:

> It is an irresponsible and catastrophic policy to persuade the
> working class to set their hopes on the fall of this Empire. . . .
> The fall of Austria would bring with it the triumph of imperial-
> ism in Germany, in Russia and in Italy. But the victory of Im-
> perialism would mean a defeat for the working class in all these
> countries. . . . Therefore the proximate goal of the workers of
> all the nationalities of Austria cannot be the realization of the
> nation-state, but only national autonomy within the established
> political order.[23]

Karl Renner, the outstanding representative of right-wing, revisionist socialism in Austria and father of the two republics to come,
defended the empire with utilitarian arguments of another sort. His
views are most fully set forth in *Österreichs Erneuerung (The Renewal of Austria)*, a counterpart to Seipel's study. Published the

22. Borkenau, *Austria and After*, pp. 215, 171
23. Otto Bauer, *Die Nationalitätenfrage und die Sozialdemokratie* (1907),
cited in Ernst Hoor, *Öesterreich, 1918–1938* (Vienna: Österreichischer
Bundesverlag, 1966), p. 30.

same year as *Nation und Staat,* it was based on an earlier pamphlet
of the same name. "If the once historically given, but thereafter
organically developed economic territory of the Danube Monarchy
is the internal common interest of the Peoples which form her population," Renner writes, "so is the compelling necessity of defense
the external common interest." [24] Socialists, much less than Christian Socialists, were able to write in emotional, heartwarming terms
of the dying empire and confined themselves to a patriotism of
calculated interest.

The State That Nobody Wanted

The debate about "nation" and "state" was destined to go on not
only until the demise of the Dual Monarchy, but also beyond it. For

24. Karl Renner, *Österreichs Erneuerung* (Vienna: Verlag der Wiener
Buchhandlung, 1916), 1:35. The following titles are only a small portion of
the literature on imperial reform and the nationalities question which appeared during the last decades of the Habsburg Empire. Richard Kralik in
several works tried to build an "Austrian idea" around the notion of justice
for the peoples (*Völkergerechtigkeit*). Robert Sieger in a series of works
tried to show how its geographical position, which bound several peoples
together in a community of interest, required the maintenance of the empire:
Die geographischen Grundlagen der österreichischen Monarchie (Leipzig:
B. G. Teubner, 1915), and *Der Österreichische Staatsgedanke und seine
geographischen Grundlagen* (Vienna: C. Fromme, 1918). Other important
works are Richard Charmatz, *Der demokratisch-nationale Bundesstaat Öster-
reich* (Frankfurt a/M: Neuer Frankfurter Verlag, 1904); Friedrich Tezner,
Die Wandlungen der österreichischen Reichsidee (Vienna: Manz, 1905);
Aurel C. Popovici, *Die Vereinigten Staaten von Gross-Österreich* (Leipzig:
B. Elischer Nachf., 1906); Otto Bauer, *Die Nationalitätenfrage und die
Sozialdemokratie* (Vienna: Wiener Volksbuchh., 1907); Oswald Redlich,
Österreich-Ungarns Bestimmung (Vienna: C. Strache, 1916); A. Dopsch,
Österreichs geschichtliche Sendung (Vienna: C. Fromme, 1918); Friedrich
Wilhelm Förster *Das Österreichische Problem* (Vienna: H. Heller & Co.,
1916); and Joseph Redlich, *Das Österreichische Staats- und Reichsproblem*
(Leipzig: Der Neue Geist Verlag, 1920). During the war, an Austrian Library was founded whose purpose was to inculcate an appreciation of the
value of the empire in its citizens. And in 1917 a periodical entitled *Österreich* was established with the objects of explaining the life of the state in
terms of its development, propagating the idea of Austria as a cultural concept, and popularizing Austrian history. A vast periodical literature on the
problem of the empire also appeared at this time. The works cited are
drawn from the lengthy bibliography in Till, *Pax Austriaca,* pp. 65–67. Also
see Kann's comprehensive and definitive study of the nationality question,
Multinational Empire.

the abdication of the emperor and the territorial dismemberment
of the empire still left an extant Austrian state with an identity
problem. Restösterreich, the diminutive republic born in the imperial ashes of 1918, consisted of sprawling, cosmopolitan Vienna, its
breadbasket of Lower Austria, and a motley collection of Alpine
valleys.

Economically and culturally the new state was a loose bundle of
centrifugal forces. Allied charity might stave off hunger in the short
run, but how could the tiny republic adequately repair by domestic
reorganization and trade agreements with the succession states the
disruption of the imperial economic complex of which her states
(Länder) had been the hub? Everything seemed to point to a need
for integration into some kind of a larger political unit. Heavy industry, the foundation of a healthy modern economy, was virtually
nonexistent. The centers of the empire had been in Bohemia and
Moravia, which now were foreign territory. Only in Styria could
one find the beginnings of a heavy industrial plant. The Vienna
Basin was given primarily to light and finishing industries. The empire had not formed or accumulated capital to anything like the
degree typical of western European industrial states during the second part of the nineteenth century, so that the capital legacy to
the successor states amounted to very little.[25]

With no capital-building resources to be found at home and few
obtainable abroad, the Austrian republic, fifteen years after its inception, found itself with a structural unemployment problem; there
was a labor force of two million but only 1.4 million jobs. The un-
employed were congregated in the eastern three states, with the
largest number in Vienna, the seat of government, and in a mood
to use their power in anarchic ways. An impoverished middle class
and an elite cadre idled by the disappearance of the civil and military bureaucracy of the empire were willing and eager to engage
in civil conflict.[26]

With the dynasty gone, what principle might promote unity and
common meaning among this congeries of disparate territories?
The only thing the inhabitants of the republic obviously had in

25. Alexander Vodopivec, *Die Balkanisierung Österreichs* (Vienna: Molden, 1966), pp. 22, 23.
    26. Ibid

common was the German language, but this could hardly support a specifically Austrian state. The Austrian leaders (or "receivers") could find no better way of giving sense and meaning to their land than by attaching the republic, the moment it was proclaimed, to an injured but still living Germany. On November 12, 1918, the Provisional National Assembly unanimously voted a constitutional law declaring that "German Austria is a part of the German Reich."

All parties from Socialist to Christian Social were agreed on this move, some as a rational expedient, others out of their emotional fervor as Germans, which had been growing both at and below the political surface for fifty years. "We are one tribe (*Stamm*) and one community of destiny (*Schicksalsgemeinschaft*)," intoned Karl Renner, and then he could not continue because of the din of excited shouts and applause that filled the chamber. The Herrenhaus had become a "witches' cauldron of enthusiasm." [27] The political formula of the new order had taken form some days earlier when Field Marshal Adolf von Boog, receiving the office of commander in chief of the army from Karl Seitz, president of the Provisional State Council (not from the Kaiser) had solemnly sworn "to fulfill [his] duties loyally as a German with burning love for [his] German people and for [his] beloved fatherland, German-Austria." [28]

Faced at St. Germain with the adamant refusal of the Allies to allow anschluss with Germany, the Austrian leadership thought chiefly of the practical side of the question. "If German-Austria is compelled to sign this peace treaty," said Karl Renner, "it should be made known as quickly as possible to the Entente leaders that they endanger their victory, for they are inviting a corpse to climb up on their triumphal chariot." Writing in the *Reichspost* on July

27. Hellmut Andics, *Der Staat den Keiner wollte, Österreich 1918–1938*, (Vienna: Herder, 1962), p. 35.
28. Ibid., p. 17. Barbara Ward explains the vote for anschluss as "a perfectly natural and spontaneous reflection of the belief that the new Austria, consisting of an imperial city with two million inhabitants surrounded by a small group of mountainous provinces was an economic impossibility. But it was more. It was the answer of the *German* nation in Austria to the challenge of the Czechs, the Poles, and the Serbs, the Croats. It was the acceptance of the principle of nationality, the demand of the Austrian Germans to exercise the right which appeared among the war aims of the Allies, the right of national self-determination." Barbara Ward, "Ignaz Seipel and the Anschluss," *Dublin Review*, July 1938, p. 38.

11, 1920, Leopold Kunschak, editor of the Christian Social newspaper, outlined the positions of the three tendencies within his
party: the anschluss group; those looking for salvation in a Danubian confederation; and those favoring a Catholic South German
state. Missing was any group that would project a future for the
Austria of St. Germain.[29] This Austria was considered incapable of
sustaining life (*lebensunfähig*); it was a state that nobody wanted.[30]

Seipel as Chancellor:
Second Thoughts about "Nation" and "State"

When Seipel wrote *Nation und Staat* he was still teaching moral
theology at the University of Salzburg. Shortly thereafter he was
drawn into the political world and remained active in politics until
his death. In 1918 he was appointed minister of social welfare in
the Lammasch cabinet, the last imperial Austrian government. At
the collapse of the monarchy, Seipel returned briefly to his university work, but he retained the position of adviser to the Christian
Social party which he had recently accepted. He stood as a candidate in the first Austrian republican elections and won a seat as a
representative of a Vienna district in the Constituent National Assembly. By 1920 he was the acknowledged leader of the Christian
Social party, which became, as a result of the election of that year,
the strongest party in the parliament. From that time until his death
in 1932, Seipel held the office of Chancellor of the Austrian Republic four times.

What was Seipel's attitude toward rump Austria? He vacillated,
and this posture, coming from the most authoritative political figure of the 1920s, was symbolic of the tenuous position of the new
state. It was also testimony to the importance of economic viability
for national feeling. In a *Reichspost* article of November 18, 1918,
Seipel came close to despairing, as did most Austrians, of the viability of an independent Austria. "The German Austrians have been
members of a great state for so long that they cannot suddenly confine their spirit to the narrow interests of a small state." [31] In addi-

---

29. Andics, *Der Staat den Keiner wollte,* p. 91.
30. This is the translation of the title of Andics's book.
31. Quoted in Ward, "Ignaz Seipel," p. 39.

tion, the economic problem seemed insuperable—how to feed the inhabitants of a rump state politically severed from its former food supply areas. Membership in a large state seemed imperative for German Austria. The anschluss seemed the obvious solution, but Seipel was against an immediate decision in this direction. The economic situation should be given time to clarify, and further he did "not yet know in which position we can best serve the German people." [32] The devoted servant of the ancient Habsburgs was reluctant to join the upstart northern Reich.

During the 1920s Seipel as chancellor sought to save the situation through foreign economic policy. A liberalized trading system with neighboring states and with the Western powers might prove an adequate substitute for anschluss. Through "well-considered treaties" Austrians might "break through the terribly narrow confines with which our frontiers encircle our economic life," he argued.[33] These efforts bore little fruit, however, and as the decade wore on the idea of a German nation-state grew more attractive to him. In a lecture at the University of Vienna in January 1925 Seipel told his audience that "nation and state are two independent forms of human community life both of which prosper most the more the state is filled with national life and the more the nation is supported by its own state." [34] In 1916, still living in the broad Habsburg Reich, he had maintained precisely the opposite view.

By 1928 Austria's economic situation had deteriorated badly, and its decay had spawned a polarization of left and right. The paramilitary forces of the Social Democratic Protection League (Schutzbund) and of the rightist Home Guard (Heimwehr) were at one another's throats. Moreover, an Austrian protest against forcible Italianization of the German-speaking minority in the South Tyrol met only with a derisive tirade from Mussolini on Austrian weakness and Italian power.

In this sorry situation the importance of his German nationality loomed ever larger to Seipel. As he looked back to the days of the

32. Ibid.
33. Speech to the National Assembly, May 31, 1922, in Ignaz Seipel, *Reden in Österreich u. anderwärts,* ed. Josef Gessl (Vienna: Heros, 1926), p. 20.
34. Ignaz Seipel, *Die Geistigen Grundlagen der Minderheitenfrage* (Leipzig: Franz Deuticke, 1925), p. 8.

empire, the Austrian idea as a *Staatsidee* became identified in his
mind with a *Nationalidee,* the very thing which in 1916 he had
denied it could be. He now described the political mission of the
state as a German national mission, delegated to that branch of the
German nation living in Austria. Witness the following excerpts
from a 1928 letter:

> The old Austria did not perform its historical mission, because
> the Germans in Austria did not perform their task. . . . The
> question of whether or not anschluss ought to come at any time
> is bound up with the other question of whether or not the Aus-
> trian Germans have trifled away their historical task for all time.
> This mission might be placed before them once more, either as
> an Austrian, an eastern European, a Central European, or a pan-
> European task. . . . If we Austrians should no longer have any
> greater mission to fulfill, there still remain important tasks for us
> to do in cooperation with the rest of the Germans and for them.
> This is an argument for anschluss.[35]

By 1930 Seipel's acceptance of anschluss was complete.

Austro-Marxist Identity in the First Republic

If, during the 1920s, Christian Social leaders like Seipel displayed
a certain reluctance to see Austria disappear from the map of Europe and accepted the idea of anschluss largely for economic reasons, the leaders of Austrian socialism experienced no similar hesitation. They were for the anschluss in 1918 and remained so, even
after 1938.

Though in 1907 Otto Bauer had feared that the destruction of
Austria would serve the cause of reaction, in 1918 he saw the fact
of the empire's dissolution as a golden opportunity for an all-German Socialist revolution. In "Greater Germany" the united forces
of the working class could easily unseat the capitalist bourgeoisie.
But more than class values were involved. The unification of the
German nation was a primary value in itself, a part of the natural

35. Seipel to W. Bauer, July 30, 1928, in Paul R. Sweet, "Seipel's Views
on Anschluss in 1928: An Unpublished Exchange of Letters," *Journal of
Modern History* 19 (December, 1947): 322–23; also see Seipel to Bishop
Frind, August 16, 1928, quoted in Ward, "Ignaz Seipel," pp. 45–46.

order of things. At the Socialist party congress held in Vienna in the fall of 1918 Bauer told the assembly that they "should seek anschluss where it is to be found, where we belong by nature, and from which we have been artificially separated for decades—with the German Reich." And in *Die Österreichische Revolution*, published in 1923, we find Bauer complaining against the Allied policy of maintaining an independent Austria in the name of an oppressed Deutschtum which had been deprived of its rights by this policy. "German Austria was sacrificed in the suppression of the national revolution by the forces of imperialism. . . . The peace treaty compelled us to give the old name of Austria to the republic; Imperialism imposed on us the hated name." [36]

Bauer's views on the subject were typical of the party as a whole. The party congress of November 1919 adopted a resolution which read: "The Congress expects that all comrades will do everything in their power to bring about as soon as possible a union with the German Republic, which is a social, economic, and national necessity." The congress of 1920 reaffirmed the anschluss policy and also rejected the idea of a legal connection with Hungary or other succession states.[37] During the debate on the Geneva Protocol in the Austrian parliament in October 1922, Karl Renner said: "We shall only be able to keep alive . . . until the hour of our liberation comes, . . . until we as Germans are able to choose that state to which we belong by the nature of things." After the Christian Socialists and Pan-Germans had opted to vote for ratification of the protocol, which required a renewed renunciation of anschluss in return for Allied economic aid, Karl Seitz, who had been the first president of the Provisional National Assembly, got up to say that Social Democrats could not excuse such a "sin of high treason against our own land and people," meaning not Austria and the Austrian people, but Germany and the German people. When the vote was taken only the sixty-eight Socialists opposed ratification of the protocol, and those for "national" reasons.[38]

As a protest against the Nazi seizure of power in Germany the Social Democratic members left the executive committee of the

36. Cited in Hoor, *Österreich, 1918–1938,* pp. 44, 47.
37. Ibid., p. 47.
38. Ibid., p. 48.

German-Austrian Work Association in April 1933. Subsequently the Socialist party congress adopted a resolution abandoning the effort for anschluss, but only until a democratic order could be restored in Germany. The Socialists continued to hold this position even after the anschluss had been accomplished in 1938 under Nazi auspices. In April of that year, shortly after the anschluss had been declared, Otto Bauer wrote the following in an article that appeared in the Paris edition of *Der sozialistische Kampf,* a publication of emigré Austrian Socialists:

> Nothing would shake the faith of the working masses in the war aims of the proletarian movement more than making a war aim the independence of that Austria which for the workers is bound up with the remembrance of unemployment, suffering, aristocratic dictatorship, and the clerical restraint of conscience. . . . The watchword with which we oppose foreign rule over Austria by satraps from the Reich cannot be the reactionary watchword of the restoration of Austrian independence, but rather only the revolutionary watchword of the All-German revolution, which alone can free from the fascist tyrants the Austrian branch [*Stamm*—literally "tribe"] of the nation along with the other Germans [*mit den anderen deutschen Stämmen*].[39]

39. Ibid., p. 50. The Socialist periodical *Die Zukunft* for mid-January 1968, an issue devoted to the celebration of the fiftieth anniversary of the republic, carried a letter to the editor by Julius Braunthal, a Socialist emigré of the 1930s, entitled "Otto Bauer's Idea of an All-German Revolution: A Footnote to the Discussion about Austrian National Consciousness." In it, he discusses approvingly the Bauer thesis on Austrian independence and German union as set forth in the *Socialistischer Kampf* article quoted above. He also reports that in a recently published collection of Bauer's writings, (Otto Bauer, *Eine Auswahl aus seimem Lebenswerk* [Vienna: Verlag der Wiener Volksbuchhandlung, 1961]), which he helped edit, the last paragraph of the article in question was omitted, for reasons not understood by him. (Braunthal lives in England and for that reason was not able to supervise the Viennese publication of the book as carefully as he wished.) He added that it appeared to him to be a duty to the memory of Otto Bauer and also a demand of historical responsibility to publish the paragraph missing from the original article. The text of the paragraph runs as follows:

> Austria is finished (*ist gewesen*). Austrian clericals and monarchists may found committees abroad, who care to fantasize about the reestablishment of an Austrian state, who like to convince themselves that it is possible to organize an Austrian irredentism. But that is a child's game. Austrian socialism, which today is shattered and tomorrow will be resurrected, can-

Literary Austrianism

If leading politicians had few kind sentiments for Austria in the 1920s and early 1930s, the Viennese literati were more sympathetic. One man in particular, Jewish poet Anton Wildgans, caused at least a brief flurry of national enthusiasm in Austrian (or at least Viennese) hearts. In 1929 he prepared a "Speech about Austria" (*Rede über Österreich*) for delivery before the Swedish Court in Stockholm. Published the same year in a Swedish newspaper, in 1930 it was read by the poet over the Vienna radio. In it, Wildgans lauded the special and unique qualities of his country and painted a picture of the "Austrian man" (*Der österreichische Mensch*) and of his special role and mission in the world.[40]

Wildgans described the "Austrian man" as a person with a preeminently supranational point of view, who knows how to serve a "universal idea"; he is both European and cosmopolitan in his manner. He is a good conciliator who knows how to bring people together. He is brave, but his bravery manifests itself most perfectly in patience. The "Austrian man" is honest, upright, and hard-working, but more by nature than by education or through the influence of moral doctrine. These characteristics are related to his artistic temperament, which displays itself in ingenious improvisation and creative craftmanship rather than in discipline and mechanical invention. He is also conservative, skeptical of the promises of progress, doubtful about anything wholly new.

---

not take a reactionary stance toward the accomplished fact of the annexation of Austria by the Third Reich, but rather only a revolutionary stance. We cannot turn back the wheel of world history. Only defeat of Germany in a war could tear Austria loose from Germany once again; but such a wartime defeat of Germany would unloose the German Revolution, and from the German Revolution, Austrian socialism does not wish to tear itself loose. The future of the Austrian working class does not lie in Austrian separatism. The Austrian working class can only be free if the entire German working class is free. The future of the German-Austrian working class is the future of the German Revolution.

One can only wonder what fellow editor of Braunthal's, converted since 1945 to Austria as most Socialists have been, decided it would do the cause of the "Austrian nation" no good to have this paragraph read by impressionable young Austrian Socialists who dutifully study the writing of the great Austro-Marxist theoretician.

40. Anton Wildgans, *Rede über Österreich*, 6th ed. (Vienna: Speidel, 1930).

As an Austrian with a traditional cut of mind, Wildgans approved these qualities, which he saw as gifts of the imperial past to modern Austria. Many of them derived specifically from the role that the German-speaking "Leader and State People" (*Führer und Staatsvolk*) had played as the imperial elite. As rulers of an international empire they had learned how to adopt a supranational standpoint, to serve a grand idea (*das Dienen an einer Idee*) and to be good psychologists—in the sense of learning how to understand people of different cultures and outlooks.

Traditionalist that he was, Wildgans nevertheless found himself unable to conceptualize his Austrian national ideology in purely Austrian terms. At every point he felt compelled to describe the special Austrian way as German, as an aspect of German culture. "The 'Austrian man' is a German," he wrote "as indicated by his speech and ethnic origin, and as such he has rendered service to German culture and nationhood (*Volkheit*) in all areas of human action and creativeness." But many bloods have been mingled with the German, and he has had a special historical experience. As a consequence he is "less simple, less brittle, more conciliatory and more cosmopolitan"—presumably than the Germans of the Second Reich and the Weimar Republic. He is nevertheless, for Wildgans, still a German.[41] It was "German blood [which] beat in the heart" of the old Reich and German *Geist* which carried out the great supranational task of political and cultural mediation. The cultural

41. In the Second Republic it became evident to some Austrian nationalists that avowing a German identity weakened their argument. Making use of Wildgans's speech as a great statement of the "Austrian idea," therefore, required that it be edited somewhat. Pan-Germans have charged that Raoul Aslan put a cut version of the speech on a long-playing record made by the Amadeo-Schallplattergesellschaft and that the liberal Catholic paper, *Furche*, published an abbreviated version in the supplement to a year-end edition. The following kinds of passages allegedly were omitted: all references to Austrians as German; references to the nobility, royal house, and clergy; references to non-German peoples in the Dual Monarchy; violent and crude statements; references to the values of tradition and custom, and criticisms of those who reject tradition; sad references to the small size of republican Austria. See the introduction to a new edition of the unexpurgated speech, "Richtigstellung einer Verfälschung. Anton Wildgans' *Rede über Österreich* in der vollständigen u. der beschnittenen Fassung," Eckartschriften 4A Ergänzung zu Heft 4., Vienna, 1959.

greatness of Vienna is underscored by the statement that there "the first German national theatre was founded . . . at the end of the eighteenth century."

Wildgans's idea of an Austrian produced a certain response among the intelligentsia, especially in Vienna, and the speech went through six editions before the anschluss. Its ideas were echoed in the work of Hugo von Hofmannsthal, Robert Musil, Hermann Bahr, and other literati of the period.[42] But it would be difficult to show that these writings had any political effect during the 1930s, in terms of strengthening the will of any important segment of the Austrian public to support an independent Austrian state.

42. See Hugo von Hofmannsthal, *Österreichische Aufsätze und Reden,* ausgewählt und eingeleitet von Helmut A. Fiechtner (Vienna: Bergland, 1956); August M. Knoll, et al., *Die Österreichische Aktion* (Vienna: E. K. Winter, 1927); F. Funder, "Der Österreichische Mensch," in *Schönere Zukunft,* vol. 5/7, 1929; Oscar A. H. Schmitz, *Der Österreichische Mensch, zum Anschauungsunterricht für Europäer, insbesondere für Reichsdeutsche* (Vienna: Wiener Literar. Anstalt, 1924). The last work, in contrast with Wildgans, Hoffmannsthal, and the main line of thought in the 1920s, compares Austria to Germany in a rather sharp fashion not at all flattering to Germany. Austria produced one of the highest cultures of Europe, says Schmitz; it has been manifest in the life of the Catholic church there, the Baroque elevation of Reason, the harmonies of Haydn, Mozart, Schubert. By contrast, Weimar was only a moment and a fragment, which never penetrated the rest of Germany—only two hours distant. Germans have produced the Lutheran denial of Form, Wilhelmine *Grossprecherei,* and Ludendorff's hard-heartedness—all antitheses of civilized culture. Like those more sympathetic to the north, however, Schmitz refers to Austrian culture as "German." He does not champion the little republic of St. Germain—this *Deutschösterreich* is for him an "entirely provisional creation." It is the role of Austrians to lead in the building of a federal Europe, like that envisaged by Richard Coudenhove-Kalergi, to take the place of the lost reich, which, before the centralizing reforms of Joseph II, was a "model for the united Europe of the future." Only from a German land, he wrote, where nationalism has been markedly a problem, could come such a solution to the national problem. As was typical of many of the Austrian patriotic literati of the 1920s and later, Schmitz sees Austrian culture as identical with Viennese culture. "What are the German-Austrians without Vienna," he asks, "since Vienna is the source of the high culture that Austria can boast as her own before all the other Germans." "The German Austrian as a man of culture stands and falls with Vienna." Schmitz himself was born and raised in Frankfurt/Main, at one time a free city of the Holy Roman Empire, which he left in 1915 in disgust over the Wilhelmine mentality and from which he emigrated to Vienna.

Coup d'Etat

Between 1934 and 1938 an effort was made to rebuild the Austrian political community by negative authoritarian measures to suppress dissent and by positive efforts to inculcate an Austrian national ideal through methods of totalitarian mobilization and indoctrination. This was an experiment of the Authoritarian Christian Corporative State, inaugurated by the Christian Social leader Engelbert Dollfuss and liquidated by the Nazis.

In the German national election on March 5, 1933, the Hitler-Hugenberg group polled 52 percent of the electorate. Nazi successes in the Catholic areas of Germany must have been particularly shocking to the Austrian Christian Socialists, who could see therein the handwriting on their own wall. The local elections of 1932 had already indicated that Austrian sentiment as well as German was moving in a "Brown" direction. In Vienna the National Socialists had polled over 200,000 votes (a sharp contrast with the mere 27,000 they had received in 1930) and therewith captured fifteen seats in the Landtag, fourteen of them formerly held by Christian Socialists. In addition, Christian Social majorities in Lower Austria and Salzburg had been destroyed by the Nazis.

The identification of German nationalism with Nazi ideology, together with the soaring popularity of the combination in the face of political and economic decay, galvanized the Christian Socialists into action to preserve what was left of their power position. Taking advantage of a parliamentary crisis that had arisen accidentally on March 4, which left the National Assembly without a presiding officer, Dollfuss determined on the dissolution of the parliament *sine die*. A decision was reached at a meeting of the leaders of the Christian Social party that "now for some time the government must be carried on in an authoritarian fashion until, through negotiation with the opposition, an alteration of the constitution as well as of the rules of procedure of the parliament are secured so that the functioning of the administrative and the legislative organs of state appears assured." [43]

43. Charles A. Gulick, *Austria from Habsburg to Hitler* (Berkeley: University of California Press, 1948), 2:972, 1024; Leopold Kunschak, *Österreich 1918–1934* (Vienna: Typographische Anstalt, 1935), quoted in Gulick, *Austria,* p. 1023.

No agreement was reached with the opposition on an alteration of the constitution. Immediately following the coup against the parliament by the executive (Dollfuss had been elected chancellor by regular parliamentary process in 1932), the Christian Socialists dealt with the organized opposition forces. Following a series of Nazi terrorist acts in June, the government prohibited all activity on behalf of the National Socialist party and dissolved its paramilitary organizations. In February 1934 the Social Democratic party was disbanded and the power of its paramilitary force, the Schutzbund, which had been outlawed as early as April 1933, was broken in four days of civil war. May 1, 1934, brought the official promulgation of a new constitution creating a "Christian, German, Federal State on a corporative basis"; this was to be the instrument of government until the anschluss with Germany in March 1938[44] Ideological rigidities spawned in the prior century had begotten their final fruit.

The "Austrian Way" Versus Nazi Pan-Germanism: The Christian Corporative State

Engelbert Dollfuss was born October 3, 1892, into a Lower Austrian farm family at Texing, the illegitimate son of Josepha Dollfuss and Joseph Nenninger. For a time he believed he was called to the priesthood. Although he left the seminary at Hollabrunn without finishing the course of study, a strong religious commitment colored his political activity and thought until his death. These things, combined with a brief career as an officer of Chasseurs in the imperial army during World War I bound him to the old order of things and indicated a traditionalist content for the national ideal that he sought to create during 1933 and 1934.

One ideological effort of the corporatists in the new political game was to compete with the Nazis as the defenders of the "true Germany" and "true Germandom." This strategy had been tried before, during the last fifty years of the empire when the Habsburgs, as inheritors of the ancient tradition of the Holy Empire of the German Nation, were fighting for their lives against the upstart Hohenzollerns and their modern version of German Empire and

44. Preamble to the constitution of May 1934.

German Nation. It was, of course, an utter failure. But we find Dollfuss employing it anyway in his own losing battle.

> We want a German Austria and a free Austria. . . . At a time when the world shrinks from a certain German spirit we want to show the world that we possess a Christian German civilization.

> In our Austrian way we feel ourselves to be a true component of the German way and of German life, and to preserve this Austrian individuality, to bring it to fruition in all-German and in European life, is our national duty as well as our duty to humanity.[45]

But there is ambivalence. Dollfuss also realized that somehow a distinctively Austrian national program, not subsumed under the category *German,* might be needed to stem the Nazi tide and save his position. Despite the fact that he was long accustomed to identifying himself as a member of the German nation and as a participant in German culture, he vaguely saw that the Christian Social (and traditional Austrian) conception of German had nothing in common with that which had become authoritative in the north, and that all the values he held dear were threatened by the Nazi success in filling the idea of German with their own special ideological content to the exclusion of all else. Though anschluss had earlier been appealing to many Christian Socialists, an anschluss under Nazi auspices was a revolting concept. It implied their absolute doom. Witness the result of this realization in the rather different verbiage of other Dollfuss popular appeals. In one he speaks of the German intention to "denationalize" the Austrian people:

> That this region, once governed for centuries by the Imperial Crown, should become a province of Berlin, that our indigenous people should be *denationalized* and put under foreign rule— that is what we have sought to prevent [italics added].

> The foundation of our entire policy is the defense of our people's heritage [*Volksschatz*], of our independence, the indivisibil-

45. Speech at Dornbirn, June 30, 1933, quoted in Johannes Messner, *Dollfuss, An Austrian Patriot* (London: Burns Oates & Washbourne, 1935), p. 89; Dollfuss article in *Reichspost,* December 24, 1933, in Engelbert Dollfuss, *Dollfuss an Österreich,* ed. Edmund Weber (Vienna: Reinhold, 1935), pp. 55–56

ity of this land which has come down to us from our fathers, and the cultivation and development of the creative, cultural, political and economic powers of the Austrian people, in other words, the carrying out of the historical mission of Austria in the German and Central European lands.[46]

Despite a continued ambiguity of language, Dollfuss's strategy was to build a uniquely Austrian ideology by reviving the distinctive values, concepts, and symbols of the imperial past and adapting them to the new situation. The traditional character of the reform is revealed in small things as well as large—in the restoration, for example, of the two-headed eagle of the empire as the official seal of state, albeit the eagle's talons were empty. (The republic had shorn the eagle of one head and replaced the traditional sword and orb with a hammer and sickle clutched in the eagle's talons.)

All the major categories of the official ideology proclaimed as intellectual substance of the new constitution promulgated by Dollfuss in 1934 expressed traditional values and practices—Christian commitment, mediating mission, corporative order, and authoritarian leadership. Christian commitment meant restoration of the Catholic church to a public-law status in Austria. The first enactment of the government under the new constitution was the ratification of a new concordat with the Vatican, which was proclaimed and celebrated on the same day as, and along with, the constitution.

The mediating mission was an expression, in a new way, of the role of the old empire as a reconciler of nations, a cultural and political bridge between east and west (Slav and German) and north and south (German and Latin). In its new form the idea implied, politically, the avoidance of alignment with any single bloc of states and friendly cooperation with all—a kind of expansive neutrality, though this word was not used. Economically, mediation meant participation in a movement to free European and world trade from autarchic conceptions and to integrate Austria in as large a free-trading system as possible—again, avoiding commitment to any political bloc. The cultural dimension, though frequently discussed in abstract terms and with reference to the prec-

46. Speech at Retz, November 15, 1933, quoted in Messner, *Dollfuss*, p. 82; radio address, December 31, 1933, in Dollfuss, *Dollfuss an Österreich*, p. 207.

edent of the imperial melting pot, never achieved precise definition
in the ideology.

Corporatism (the *Ständische Idee*) also harkened back to the
tradition—to the pluralist "Franciscan" component of Austrian
political culture, embodied in the Dollfuss constitution as functional
corporatism rather than as the territorial and feudal corporatism of
the empire. Authoritarianism had always been the other side of the
coin—the "Josephinist" component. In the place of the Kaiser,
however, stood the "Millimetternich" chancellor, Engelbert Dollfuss.[47]

As the primary instrument for the inculcation of his traditionalist
ideology, Dollfuss created a Fatherland Front which was to be a
church militant of the new Austrian creed. In a letter to Mussolini
dated July 22, 1933, he described the aims of the organization:

> We are giving special attention to intensive propaganda as a
> means of arousing a kind of Austrian patriotism such as has not
> existed in the postwar period, and was scarcely possible a few
> months ago. I may here point to the activity of the Fatherland
> Front. . . . The Fatherland Front aims at non-partisan union
> of all patriotic Austrians to serve the peaceful, cultural and eco-
> nomic development of a free, independent Austrian state.[48]

The Fatherland Front was given the sole right to manipulate public
opinion in Austria. It was to be, as Kurt Schuschnigg, Dollfuss's
successor, phrased it,

> the sole association of those who participate in the creation of the
> political will. Outside the Dollfuss Front, the Fatherland Front,
> there can be no other fronts and within the Fatherland Front,
> there can be no particular Fronts.[49]

In addition to having a complicated territorial structure the front

47. See Lorenz, *AEIOU*, pp. 38–39. Lorenz argues that a continuing aspect of Austrian political culture is its characteristic combination, in always
incomplete synthesis, of decentralist and centralist attitudes, which he labels
with the names of the two leading exponents of the contradictory ideas—
Kaiser Franz II and Kaiser Joseph II.

48. Paul R. Sweet, "Mussolini and Dollfuss," appendix to Julius Braunthal, *The Tragedy of Austria* (London: Victor Gollancz Ltd., 1948), p. 190.

49. Schuschnigg's speech in Innsbruck, September 2, 1934, in Kurt
Schuschnigg, *Schuschnigg Spricht* (Graz: Styria, 1935), p. 106.

was also organized along functional lines. There were groups for public employees, for workers and employers in private firms, for members of the Bauernbund (Farm Federation) and the Gewerbebund (Crafts Federation) and for manual workers. Two youth groups were created on whose work special emphasis was placed. Their programs featured a great variety of cultural activities, including poetry readings, the exhibition of paintings, and the revival of old customs and folk music. The new generation in particular, it was hoped, would give "witness to Austria in flesh and blood," and "with idealism and enthusiasm [would] give to the 'Austrian idea' a new dimension and a new national form." [50]

The episode of the corporative state reminds us of the phenomenon of the monopoly party in non-Western emerging states that are today fighting their nation-building battles. Claude Welch describes the problem of inculcating a national ideal as it appears to African leaders in terms resembling those that Dollfuss had in mind when he seized dictatorial power and created his Fatherland Front.

> The necessary transformation of loyalties is a long-range task, one that seems, to African leaders, to require the formation of single-party dominant regimes. The creation of a "nation" within the state boundaries inherited from colonialism is the fundamental task.[51]

Or as Arnold Rivkin, citing Sekou Touré and others puts it, "For many of the African leaders one-party authoritarian systems are the

50. Guido Zernatto, *Die Wahrheit über Österreich* (New York: Longmans, 1939), p. 91. Kurt Schuschnigg succeeded to the chancellorship upon Dollfuss's assassination by a Nazi putschist in July 1934 and attempted to carry through Dollfuss's program. He resigned this office on March 11, 1938, the day before the anschluss, and was imprisoned by the Germans soon thereafter. While very loyal to the idea of Austria as it had been embodied in the empire, Schuschnigg could not escape the "magnetic pull of German loyalties," as Gordon Shepherd puts it (*The Anschluss* [London: Macmillan, 1963] p. xx) and suffered greatly from the confusion of identities so typical of his people. He resigned the chancellorship because he was unable to give the order to fire on the advancing Nazi battalions, resolved that "on no account . . . [should] German blood be spilled." His last public words also revealed the tragic tension of his loyalties: "a German word and a heartfelt wish—God protect Austria" (quoted in ibid., p. 173).

51. Welch, *Dream of Unity*, p. 345.

answer—the way to forge national unity, to build a nation-state, to create a nationality." [52] Traditional nationalism as the content of authoritarian indoctrination, however, could hardly provide a viable principle of cohesion for micro-Austria. It had nothing to say to the anticlerical sections of the middle classes or to the working class; it represented no compromise with their *Weltanschauungen* but rather totally excluded them.

Major economic policies of the Dollfuss-Schuschnigg regime also proved utopian and unworkable. Corporatism was a disaster. Josef Dobretsberger, one of Schuschnigg's ministers of social administration and during the Second Republic professor of economics at the University of Graz, has described it as the cause of the fragmentation of wage and price policy that led to overall incoherence and inconsistency in economic policy.

> When every occupational estate independently regulates wages, sets prices, carries on foreign trade, and conducts work-creation programs, the special interests have free play. Monopolies appear, clothed with the public power, which proceed to exploit the community in their own interest.[53]

Dobretsberger also attributes to corporative autonomy the failure of the government's make-work program, which may have driven many job-hungry people into Nazi arms.[54]

Finis Austriae

In the midst of a national vacuum, the political and ideological differences that separated Christian Socialists from Socialists were heightened. Neither side was capable of temporarily setting these differences aside in order to make possible the pragmatic cooperation needed to save the state. The corporatist regime at its outset systematically suppressed Socialist as well as Nazi organizations.

52. Arnold Rivkin, "The Politics of Nation-Building: Problems and Preconditions," *Journal of International Affairs* 16, no. 2 (1962): 131–43, in Harvey G. Kebschull, ed., *Politics in Transitional Societies* (New York: Appleton, Century, Crofts, 1968), p. 276.

53. Joseph Dobretsberger, *Katholische Sozialpolitik am Scheideweg,* (Graz: Ulrich Moser, 1947), p. 79.

54. Joseph Dobretsberger, "Ein missglücktes Experiment," *Civitas* 4 (1949): p. 88.

And it put down in bloody fashion the almost absent-minded Socialist uprising of February 1934. After 1935, when the Nazi danger began to loom very large, some efforts at cooperation were made, but they were never at the highest level and were always half-hearted and insincere. Under the conciliatory direction of Josef Resch as minister of social administration, the Gewerkschaftsbund, a unified trade organization created by Dollfuss, became to a degree representative of Socialist labor. "Besides the Christian workers' representatives there was a whole string of Socialists in the Gewerkschaftsbund," Julius Raab testified at the treason trial of Guido Schmidt.[55] But this did not result so much from a positive policy of the regime as from a decision of the Socialist "illegals" to play along with the Bund and to attempt to gain their ends from within it.[56] Within the Fatherland Front the Schuschnigg regime attempted a measure of conciliation by creating a Soziale Arbeitsgemeinschaft (Social Labor Community) with some 1,200 units. At the beginning of 1938 a majority of *Vertrauensleute* (representatives) in these units were former Social Democrats. But Gulick reports that, as with the Gewerkschaftsbund, the Socialists saw this cooperation as merely a tactic of "boring from within" by which they might ultimately seize control of the government.[57] And Ulrich Eichstaedt remarks that "the broad masses of the workers abjured all political activity." [58]

When a final showdown with Hitler came, Socialist functionaries in the Vienna factories sent a collective letter to Schuschnigg promising active cooperation with the government in seeking an independent Austria. They made it clear in a meeting that followed that their promise did not represent conversion to the conservative idea of Austria, but rested on the purest pragmatism. Schuschnigg met the offer with an agreement to rebuild the Soziale Arbeitsgemeinschaft as a free political organization of workers, to guarantee self-administration in the workers' cultural and sport organizations, and to return property of Socialist cultural associations which had been

55. *Hochverratsprozess gegen Dr. Guido Schmidt* (Vienna: Austrian State Printing Office, 1947), p. 117.
56. See Gulick, *Austria*, pp. 1526–27.
57. Ibid., p. 1675.
58. Ulrich Eichstädt, *Von Dollfuss zu Hitler* (Wiesbaden: Franz Steiner, 1955), p. 71.

seized. In their turn, the Socialist leadership called upon the rank and file to vote *Ja* in Schuschnigg's March 1938 plebiscite on independence. But it was too little and too late. The plebiscite never took place, and German troops crossed the border to seal the anschluss coup.

Nation building in the First Republic thus proved abortive. No "Austrian nation" achieved consensual definition either in political or cultural terms. The experience might appear to bear out the prediction of students of development like Smith who assert a necessary connection between cultural and political integration. Austrian leaders were unable to visualize Austria as a unique cultural entity, and they continued to talk about themselves as Germans. Nor were they able to separate the ideas of "political nation" and "cultural nation" from one another. The ideology of the corporative state as a unique "Austrian Idea" was a mixture of political and general cultural symbols, on which the leaders who created it could not bring themselves to bestow the legitimating concept *national*. (Schuschnigg coined the unexciting expression "Second German State.") The emotions connected with nationalism could be mobilized only for anschluss with Germany, not to support an independent Austria. Even if specialized political concepts had been detached from general cultural ones, it is unlikely that they could have been successfully propagated as the ideology of a *Staatsnation*, short of using elaborate brainwashing techniques. For the ideas of the corporative state were developed out of the world view of a particular segment and were unintelligible to other major social groups with widely different *Weltanschauungen*.

We may wonder why the separation of the "cultural" from the "political" nation was never made during the First Republic except by isolated writers.[59] And we may further ask why political

59. One polemicist during the 1930s did develop a clear conception of an Austrian political nation, using a formula like that later proposed by Etzioni. This was Ernst Karl Winter, a writer and journalist who stood at the extreme left of the Christian Social camp. He was a legitimist (he had worked as private secretary to the former emperor during the latter's years of exile), but he was also a socialist and, above all, a democrat. The categories of his political thought in general were Western rather than Central European and characteristically pragmatic and empirical rather than romantic and mystical. Perhaps the fact that his mother's family, on one side, were French Huguenot emigrants had something to do with this. That he studied with the great

ideological conflict ended in an effort to impose one view rather than in a compromise or in the "end of ideology." Would things have been different if pressure for anschluss from Germany, which was enormous, had been headed off by Western democracies mindful of threats to the balance of power? And what role did economics play? If we adopt the functionalist theory that political loyalties follow economic interest, we might argue that continued economic disorder, especially the disintegration produced by corporatism, was a major factor underlying the failure of nation building in the

---

positivist, democratic jurisprudent, and political philosopher, Hans Kelsen, was no doubt another important cause.

As early as the mid-1920s Winter had begun to write of Austria as a political nation, embracing the Western conception of the term rather than the Central European idea. Together with a little group of like-minded Christian Social ideologists and polemicists, including August Maria Knoll and Alfred Missong, he began to develop the idea in a publication entitled *Die Österreichische Aktion,* which was founded in 1927. In 1933, in a new publication, *Wiener Politische Blätter,* we find it taking on precise form:

> The meaning of Austriandom as a politically independent Germandom of a special sort, which is not merely an ethnic stem (*Stamm*) but also a separate political nation like Swissdom (*Schweizertum*) culminates in an epoch in which German thought is under heavy pressure in the area of scholarly freedom as well as otherwise [16 April 1933].

In Winter's leading work of political philosophy, *Monarchie und Arbeiterschaft* (Vienna: Gsur, 1936), in which he attempted to synthesize socialist democracy with traditional monarchy, he gives, on p. 4, the concept of an Austrian nation sharp and explicit form. This time all remaining ambiguity is removed by omitting any reference to Germany or Germandom.

> Austria, like every other state in which there are German-speaking groups, such as Belgium, Holland, Switzerland, Czechoslavakia, and others of the succession states, is the political bearer of a nationality *sui generis,* the Austrian people. Expressed in Western European terminology, there is an Austrian nation.

Winter's answer to nazism was the fusion of the forces of Christian social reform and socialism under the aegis of Austrian nationalism—a herald of the successful "Great Coalition" formula of the Second Republic. In an effort to conciliate the workers after his suppression of the February 1934 uprising, Dollfuss appointed Winter third vice-mayor of Vienna and commissioned him to carry out a "reconciliation operation" with labor—the so-called Aktion Winter. He was allowed to state his doctrines at small meetings with former Socialists, set up a network of organizers, and write in the labor press. But the operation quickly collapsed, for the Socialists refused to take it seriously; after several meetings ended in rioting, the government forbade them. See Joseph Buttinger, *In the Twilight of Socialism* (New York: Praeger, 1953), pp. 280, 291, 152.

First Republic. Nevertheless, we cannot overlook the fact that there were clear evidences of economic growth as well. Witness the impressive picture of development painted by Gordon Shepherd:

> By the middle 1930s the foundations of a stable economy were beginning to appear. . . . The Austria which Hitler seized in 1938 was not yet a flourishing state; but it at least had the marks of a going concern. The trade deficit, which was over 1,000 million schillings in 1929, had been almost wiped out. An important heavy industry was developing out of the iron and steel plants of Styria, and Austrian semi-finished and luxury goods had already become internationally competitive. The finest oil had been extracted from Zistersdorf, from whose wells a succession of foreign masters were soon to squeeze 3 million tons a year. Hydroelectric power had expanded to cover all domestic needs, and to allow for an export surplus of 341 million kilowatt hours in 1936 compared with only 20 million in 1923. Over the same period Austrian lumber exports had been raised from 8 million to over 12 million round metres a year. And . . . the Germans were glad to get their hands on the 91000 kilogrammes of gold and 36 million dollars' worth of foreign currency which had accumulated in the safes of the Austrian National Bank. . . . Within twenty years, the starving republic of 1918 had turned itself into a country 75 percent self-supporting in its food requirements.[60]

Thus, despite the traumas of political and economic reorganization, civil conflict, and authoritarian repression, and in a context of cultural disintegration (in the absence of a consensual Austrian national identity) substantial economic development was going forward. But this development was not capable of producing a level of consumer well-being that might reverse the trend to political disintegration, a trend being spurred by insistent external pressure. There was, then, no real test of the importance of economic integration and development for political integration.

The experience of the Second Republic, by contrast, shows that, given certain important situational differences, political integration and national identity as unique political identity (a "political na-

60. Gordon Shepherd, *The Austrian Odyssey* (London: Macmillan, 1957), p. 193.

tion") could be achieved in Austria in the face of continued cultural disintegration (i.e., continued disagreement on the idea of Austria as a "cultural nation" as well as ambiguity of the concept). It also shows that at a certain stage economic development can be an important integrating factor in such a situation.

2. THE POLITICS OF INTEGRATION: CONTRACT, COMPROMISE, AND RATIONAL COMMUNITY

The Austrian experience from 1918 to 1945—a mixture of political and economic collapse, civil war, and international war—approximated what Thomas Hobbes wrote of as "the state of nature," "the war of all against all." In such a condition "men live without other security, than what their own strength, and their own invention shall furnish them withall." They are in "continual fear, and danger of violent death; and the life of man, solitary, poor, nasty, brutish, and short."[1] By 1945 Austrians had had enough and were ready to "contract out" of their desperate situation. They were ready to refute Rupert Emerson's dictum that "society derives . . . not from a contract but from natural and organic growth." [2]

Anschluss

The realities of anschluss had not corresponded to Austrian expectations. The Pan-Germans of Seyss-Inquart's last Austrian government thought, as did many average citizens, that Austria would remain an identifiable unit enjoying autonomy within some sort of federal arrangement. They hoped that Austria might become a "second and more privileged Bavaria within the Reich." [3] At first some semblance of identity did remain in the use of the collective name *Ostmark* (Eastern March) for the Austrian Länder. But the authority of the Austrian government was overshadowed by that

1. Thomas Hobbes, *Leviathan* (New York: E. P. Dutton & Co., [Everyman's Library], 1950), chapter 13, p. 104.
2. Rupert Emerson, "Nationalism and Political Development," in Finkle and Gable, *Political Development,* p. 161.
3. Shepherd, *The Anschluss,* p. 180. See also Goldinger, "Der geschichtliche Ablauf," p. 273.

of Hitler's Reichskommissar, sent from Berlin to liquidate the old authority structure. A year after the anschluss the Länder were converted into seven Reichsgaue, each governed directly from Berlin, the name *Ostmark* falling thereafter into disuse.[4]

One significant point of continuity with traditional Austria did remain, however. The Länder, though relabeled, retained for the most part their historic boundaries and were not amalgamated with northern German territories.[5] Thus they could remain carriers of the provincial consciousness of the crown lands, which were as old as the empire and which would later play a major role in the rebuilding of an independent federal republic and in the patterning of its political consciousness.[6]

The blessings and curses of Nazi rule were differentially distributed among the seven Alpine and Danubian Reichsgaue, a fact which was also to have a significant effect on the structure of identity in the Second Republic. Polyglot Vienna, hated by Hitler because of its ethnically and culturally mixed character and because it had been the seat of the despised Habsburgs, suffered economic deprivation and police tyranny throughout the seven years of the anschluss. The more purely German areas of Upper Austria, Salzburg, and Tyrol actually prospered, for Hitler selected them as sites for an entire complex of new heavy industries, secure supply bases for the paraphernalia of his war machine. Especially important were the Hermann Göring Works, the new iron and steel mills established in the area of Linz, in 1938 an almost exclusively agricultural region. Also, as Allied bombing was stepped up during the war an increasing number of German factories sought refuge behind the Alps of the western Länder. Styria, in southern Austria, benefited through the modernization and mechanization of the iron mines of the Erzberg under Nazi auspices.[7] Though Russian oc-

4. *The Administrative Separation of Austria from Germany,* War Department Pamphlet no. 31–329, Civil Affairs Guide (Washington, D.C., March 1945), p. 11.

5. Burgenland, however, was dissolved and divided between Lower Austria and Styria, and the East Tyrol was incorporated into Carinthia.

6. Goldinger, "Der geschichtliche Ablauf," pp. 280–81.

7. See Friedrich Thalmann, "Die Wirtschaft in Österreich," in Benedikt, *Geschichte,* pp. 501, 502; and Vodopivec, *Die Balkanisierung Österreichs,* pp. 23–24.

cupation later brought a setback through widespread dismantlings, Hitler's plan was to make the German-speaking areas of Europe the heavy industrial centers of the Third Reich and the subject lands the producers of consumer goods. The projected dimensions of the industrial centers were great enough to have supplied all Europe.[8]

A measure of the varying degrees of psychological integration in the Third Reich produced by this differential apportionment of values in Austria may be found in a report to Hitler's headquarters by Dr. Ernst Kaltenbrunner, chief of the German Security Service, on the condition of morale in the various Austrian Gaue in mid-September 1944. Kaltenbrunner reported that defeatism was rampant in Vienna, where "Austrian tendencies" were also showing themselves and where the working class seemed ready to be influenced by "any kind of Communist propaganda." Things were somewhat better in "Lower Danube" (Lower Austria) but subject to bad influences from Vienna, which was "overcrowded with foreigners." The situation in "Upper Danube" (Upper Austria) was significantly better; Kaltenbrunner found a "fresh and still positive atmosphere there." Salzburg was in the most cheerful and loyal mood of all.[9]

"Jahr Null"

When the Third Reich fell apart in 1945 Austria found herself once again at *Jahr Null* ("Year Zero"). There would be another new beginning, but, unlike the situation in 1918, there was no clear agreement now on anschluss, independence, or any other particular arrangement.[10] Consensus on a way out of the "state of nature" was to develop only gradually after a few Austrian leaders had taken daring decisions which may even have shaped Allied policy.

8. Alfred Migsch, *Ein Volk kämpft um sein Leben* (Vienna: Verlag der Wiener Volksbuchhandlung, 1949), p. 6.
9. Quoted in Ludwig Jedlicka, *Der 20. Juli 1944 in Österreich* (Vienna: Herold, 1965), pp. 94–98.
10. Richard Hiscocks oversimplifies and anticipates much later developments when he writes: "The change that started between the Wars was completed during the German occupation. By 1945 the name 'Austria,' honoured by Hitler's disapproval, had gained a new significance. The Austrian people had acquired a will for independence." *The Rebirth of Austria* (London: Oxford University Press, 1953), p. 8.

The ruling opinion among Socialists throughout the war had been for the continued integration of Austria within a liberated Germany that the Socialist party could dominate. Nevertheless, Adolf Schärf, later to be president of the Second Republic, as early as the summer of 1943 had pronounced the anschluss dead, in response to soundings by German resistance leaders who were eager to retain the connection. In his memoirs Schärf also claims that two other top Socialist leaders, Karl Seitz and Karl Renner, had later that year come over to his position, which in the case of Seitz is confirmed by Nazi records of the 20th of July plot.[11]

Among Christian Socialists, views were also mixed. Lois Weinberger, one of the moving spirits in the resurrection of Christian Socialism as the Austrian People's party in 1945, told Carl Goerdeler, the German resistance leader, in October 1942 that he would support a putsch against Hitler but would work for Austrian independence thereafter. On the other hand Kurt Schuschnigg, a prisoner in Dachau, was reported ready in 1943 to accept the position of minister of culture in a Goerdeler government if the plot succeeded (though after the war Schuschnigg denied that he had had any contact with the Goerdeler circle). He was put forward for the job by a group of Austrian officers who later participated in the 20th of July plot of 1944. Their vision of the future polity was of a Greater Germany in which Austria would have a high degree of

11. Karl Hans Sailer, who was to serve as editor of the leading Socialist newspaper *Arbeiter–Zeitung* from 1946 to 1957, wrote in New York in 1942: There can be no doubt that Austria is German soil. Every attempt to magnify the difference between the Austrians and the other Germans to the point of talking of a separate 'Austrian nation' has proved to be a mere low grade agent's work. . . . The antagonism between South and North Germans has for long been no more than material for the comics. Nevertheless, in the present situation, it might become the source of a real hostility. To build upon it a plan for the political future, as do the Austrian reactionaries and monarchists, is a stupidity fit for reactionaries only. In September of the same year, Dr. Wilhelm Ellenbogen, another member of the Austrian Labor Committee in New York, who had been a prominent Socialist leader since 1892, declared that "in contrast to all the other countries which Hitler had subjugated, the battle of the Austrian workers against him had no national content, no national goal. Cited in Hoor, *Österreich, 1918–1938*, p. 50. See also Adolf Schärf, *Österreichs Erneuerung, 1945–1955*, 7th ed. (Vienna: Verlag der Wiener Volksbuchhandlung, 1960), pp. 23–25, Goldinger, "Der geschichtliche Ablauf," p. 282; and Jedlicka, *Der 20. Juli 1944*, p. 32.

federal autonomy. The leaders of the illegal party, however, and
the rank and file of the resistance fighters in Austria reacted nega-
tively to the plan and opted for an independent Austrian state.
Legitimists also rejected the idea of a continued anschluss, though
not all of them were ready to seek Austrian independence.[12] Some
former leaders of the corporatist period, who had once sought to
build sentiment for an independent Austria, favored the creation of
a new South German state, embracing Bavaria and Austria, which
would be cemented by the Catholic culture of the area. Still others
envisaged a Danubian federation embracing Austria, Czechoslovakia, and Hungary.[13]

As in 1919, the Allied conquerors were to play a large role in
the decision about Austria's future, though not, perhaps, as total a
one as before. The Allies had no single opinion on the subject as
the war moved into its final phase. In November 1943 they let it be
known in the Moscow Declaration that they intended to recreate
an independent Austrian state, and they made the country's treatment dependent on the contribution Austrians made to liberation.
Two years earlier, however, Churchill had considered setting up a
South German state. And by November 1944 Stalin had come to
favor this plan.[14] During the winter of 1944–45 the Allies decided
to create a separate set of four occupation zones for Austria. Yet
we can call this only a half decision.

The first concrete step toward an independent Austria was a
combined Russian and Austrian initiative. When in April 1945 the
Russians occupied Gloggnitz, a Lower Austrian town in the Alpine
foothills south of Vienna, the Socialist leader Karl Renner, who
had been a president of the First Republic, was living there. Renner
reports in a memoir of the events of this period that he decided to
go to the Russian headquarters to see whether he could use his
prestige to obtain easier treatment for the people in the locality
than would otherwise be forthcoming. On the way he realized that
it might not be impossible for him to use this meeting to do something for the whole country "and perhaps find a way out of the

12. Jedlicka, *Der 20. Juli 1944*, pp. 28, 30–31, 24–25, 27; Goldinger "Der
geschichtliche Ablauf," pp. 282–83.
13. Jedlicka, *Der 20. Juli 1944*, p. 26.
14. Goldinger, "Der geschichtliche Ablauf," p. 284.

catastrophe." He decided, therefore, to propose that he make a declaration of independence on behalf of the Austrian people and call upon them to support him.

In this declaration, as president of the last freely elected democratic government, and by virtue of the authority I had received thereby from the Austrian people itself, I wanted to call upon the country to declare its independence and to return to the democratic constitution of the republic.[15]

In the meantime a group of Socialist resistance leaders, including Adolf Schärf and Theodor Körner, both of whom would serve as presidents of the Second Republic, met in the city hall in Vienna and decided to adopt the stand that "the fascisms of both colors were to be regarded as unconstitutional and that in order to re-establish constitutional order it was necessary to go back to the relationships that existed in the year 1933."[16]

Similar decisions were being taken at this time by other Viennese resistance groups representing other major parties of the pre-anschluss period, and contacts were being established among the various party groups to consider the question of government and state form. On April 18 Socialist, Christian Social (now People's party) and Communist leaders agreed to publish a new supraparty newspaper, *Neues Österreich*. And on April 27 the three parties, constituting a provisional government, issued, with the approval of the Russian occupiers, a declaration of Austrian independence: "The anschluss is . . . null and void."[17]

The western Länder, in which democratic resistance groups had also claimed authority, at first suspected that the Renner government might be a Russian trojan horse since Vienna and Lower Austria were occupied by the Russians and since it was clear that the self-appointed regime could act only with Russian permission. The Western Allies also hesitated to accept the provisional government for the same reason. These fears among the Länder, how-

15. Karl Renner, *Denkschrift über die Geschichte der Unabhängigkeits-erklärung Österreichs* (Zurich: Europa, 1946), pp. 15, 16.
16. Adolf Schärf, *April 1945 in Wien* (Vienna: Verlag der Wiener Volks-buchhandlung, 1948), p. 58.
17. Ibid., p. 87; Heinrich Siegler, *Austria: Problems and Achievements 1945–1963* (Bonn-Vienna-Zurich: Siegler and Co., KG, 1964), pp. 6, 7.

ever, abated after conferences of the states called by Renner met in Vienna in September and October. Following the lead of Salzburg they, one by one, recognized the Renner government, and in November parliamentary elections were carried out in an orderly fashion. Before the year was out the Western Allies also decided to recognize the new central government. But it was to be ten years before all the Allies would be able to agree on a treaty granting to Austria full sovereign rights.[18]

An Integrating Context

The situation of 1945, though superficially like that of 1918, pointed in the direction of Austrian integration. Prudent leadership yielded that result. In the background was the long and fatiguing "war of all against all," which everyone wished to escape. As it turned out, the best escape was an independent and democratic Austria. Karl Renner said in April that he was declaring for Austrian independence "in order to find a way out of the catastrophe." It had never occurred to him to use language of this kind in 1918 when the Habsburg Empire rather than the Third Reich was foundering. Then, independence for the rump republic seemed itself a certain road to catastrophe. Why was it now a possible way out?

At the end of World War I, German-speaking Austrians were suddenly reduced from the status of a powerful ruling class in a Slav-Magyar empire to that of the disinherited and outcast, sent, as it were, into exile to "go it alone" in a barren wilderness. Near at hand was a still-powerful German-speaking state which offered, if union could be accomplished, a way out of the desert into a promised land of prestige and economic well-being. By contrast, in 1945 Austrians found themselves suddenly liberated from a younger brother (to some, a subject people) status in a Germany that had persecuted, not honored and protected, hundreds of thousands of their number.

In 1945 Austrians walked daily through the desolation that Hit-

18. Goldinger, "Der geschichtliche Ablauf," p. 288. See Hiscocks, *Rebirth of Austria,* pp. 23–24, 35–42; and William B. Bader, *Austria Between East and West, 1945–1955* (Stanford, Cal.: Stanford University Press, 1966), pp. 26–31, 40, for detailed discussions of the events leading to the formation and recognition of the provisional government.

ler's war had brought them. A leader of the Second Republic has summed up the sentiments of those days.

Let us think back to the spring of 1945. After seven years of war and suffering Austria stood before the burned-out legacy of an unhappy time. Ruins and rubble, demolished houses and factories, but also the ruins of souls, ravaged human lives, blood and tears: that was the sad balance of the "1,000-year Empire." [19]

Not even those who had found honor and well-being in anschluss (and there were many) could any longer see Germany as a safe haven, for the crimes of Nazi tyranny had been so great that her conquerors were determined to exact the severest penalties in retribution. Independence for Austria, and treatment as a liberated rather than a conquered country under these circumstances, appeared as a happy escape from a stern fate, not a penance as in 1918. Socialists and Christian Socialists who had spent years in Nazi concentration camps must have regarded it so. Even those Pan-Germans who had gloried in the Third Reich, despite the power of their German national feeling, must have recognized the utility of an independent Austria—at least for the time being.

Another new centripetal factor was the foreign occupation—with the Russians encamped in Lower Austria, part of Upper Austria, and the Burgenland; the British in Styria, Carinthia, and the East Tyrol; the Americans in Salzburg and Upper Austria; and the French in the Tyrol and Vorarlberg. Vienna was also carved into four zones and the old city within the Ring at the center placed under four-power administration.[20] The borders between the various zones were closely watched and, especially in the first months of the occupation, movement across them was very difficult and sometimes impossible for Austrians. (In May 1945 it took a messenger of the provisional government seventeen days to go from Vienna to the Tyrol. Among other things, he had to swim the Enns to cross the frontier of the Russian zone.)[21] The circumstances of

19. Johann Wagner, "Allzeit im Dienste der Wirtschaft," in *Österreichische Monatshefte* 21, no. 4 (April 1965): 63.
20. This was the final disposition of the occupying forces after considerable shifting around.
21. Hiscocks, *Rebirth of Austria*, p. 36.

occupation meant separation, and east-west polarization implied a continued threat of ultimate dismemberment. Negotiations for a state treaty repeatedly came to nought. Yet there remained always the hope of a united Austria because of the remarkable fact that the Allies had actually recognized a central government for all the Länder, while refusing to do so for Germany. President Schärf, in an address to a joint session of the two houses of the Austrian parliament celebrating the fifth anniversary of the finally achieved State Treaty in 1960, spoke of the maintenance of the territorial integrity of Austria after the war as "a near miracle." He noted that of all the countries occupied after World War II by both Eastern and Western powers, only Austria succeeded in achieving unification. Neither Germany nor Korea was so fortunate. Former Chancellor Josef Klaus, a leading Conservative, told the author in an interview in 1965 that the Allied decision of 1945 to treat Austria as a single political unit was an important phase in the development of Austrian national consciousness. "It was a marvel that we escaped division like Germany, despite the variety of occupation zones," he said. And Dr. Alfred Maleta, another Conservative leader, listed the felt need to make common cause against four-power occupation as one of three chief integration factors in the years after 1945.[22]

The new importance of an independent Austria for everyone's security and well-being quickly registered itself in the early appearance of national symbols, which had never been used in the First Republic. The major parties at the inauguration of the new regime in April 1945 thought it important to put the word *Austria* or *Austrian* into their names. The Conservatives called themselves The Austrian People's party (Österreichische Volkspartei—ÖVP) while the Socialists dubbed themselves The Socialist Party of Austria (Sozialistische Partei Österreichs—SPÖ). The Communists followed suit, calling themselves The Communist Party of Austria (Kommunistische Partei Österreichs—KPÖ)[23] Other institutions

22. Alfred Maleta, "Konzentration des Willens," in Ludwig Reichhold, ed., *Zwanzig Jahre Zweite Republik* (Vienna: Herder, 1965), p. 135.
23. The former Nazis, excluded from the electorate in 1945, when the franchise was returned to them in 1949 organized themselves as The Coalition of Independents (Wahlbloc der Unabhängigen—WdU). After the restoration

also had the national idea incorporated into their names. The lower house of the parliament, which in the First Republic had been known as the Federal Council (Bundestag) after 1945 was called the National Council (Nationalrat). Austria's chief public library was designated the National Library (Nationalbibliothek). And an Austrian Federation of Trade Unions (Österreichischer Gewerkschaftsbund) a nonparty labor association, something which had never before existed, was founded on the same day that the independence of Austria was proclaimed by the provisional government.

The New Leadership

Integrating factors in the circumstances of 1945 are only part of the causal complex that explains the contractarian spirit of that year. To the integrating "situation" was happily married an integrating "intention." We can discover its roots in an examination of the character and backgrounds of the political leaders who came to the fore.

The initiative in founding the Austrian People's party (Österreichische Volkspartei—ÖVP) as successor to the Christian Social party of the First Republic was taken by two men who as early as 1942 had declared themselves in favor of the reestablishment of Austrian independence. Lois Weinberger, a Viennese intellectual, had been a leader of the labor component of the earlier party, a wing which had always been democratic in outlook and close in social and economic viewpoint to the Socialists.[24] Dr. Felix Hurdes was a lawyer of Tyrolean and Moravian parentage, born in the South Tyrol, educated in Vienna, and he had practiced law in Carinthia before the anschluss. (He and Weinberger had known

of Austrian sovereignty in 1955 they reorganized as The Freedom Party of Austria (Freiheitliche Partei Österreichs—FPÖ).

24. The text from here to page 59 is based largely on the following sources: articles on the founding of the ÖVP by Felix Hurdes and Leopold Figl in *Österreichische Monatshefte* 21, no. 4 (April 1965): 11–20, 23–26 (jubilee edition for the 20th anniversary of the Austrian People's party); curricula vitae furnished me by the Federal Press Service of the Austrian government; an interview with Dr. Felix Hurdes, Vienna, February 22, 1966; Dr. Adam Wandruszka, "Österreichs Politische Struktur," in Benedikt, *Geschichte,* pp. 353–58; Shepherd, *The Austrian Odyssey,* pp. 175–76.

one another as activists in the Christian Social Student Movement, both as highschoolers and as students at the University of Vienna.) Hurdes had also been an official in the education department of the state government of Carinthia during the period of the authoritarian corporative state, and he had been a speaker for the Fatherland Front. Both Weinberger and Hurdes were among the young Christian Socialists who before 1938 had sought a rapprochement with the Socialists.

Immediately after the anschluss Hurdes was arrested by the Nazis and sent off to Dachau, probably because of his activity in the Carinthian education department. (He had transferred teachers around in an effort to diminish the Nazi impact in Carinthia and break up their organization.) Released a year later, he made contact some time thereafter with Weinberger and other Christian Social unionists. They would meet secretly in the garden of a house in Grinzing and talk about the future form of a reborn Christian Social party.

Another leading member of this illegal circle was Dr. Hans Pernter, minister of education in Schuschnigg's last cabinet, a professional bureaucrat, and a man who had wide connections among the Austrian-minded higher officialdom. A member of the Association of Catholic Academicians (Cartellverband der Katholischen Akademiker) he was in touch with the membership of a fraternity from which leading Christian Social politicians and functionaries have always been recruited.

This little nucleus of the future People's party decided early in its deliberations that the new organization ought to be as inclusive as possible in order to make the rebuilding of Austria a truly common effort. It was to be a classless party, grounded in Christian principles, though eschewing clericalism, democratic in outlook and procedures, and willing to accept support from all loyal Austrians without respect to their past political views. During the years of illegality, feelers were consequently sent out to like-minded persons in the various interest groups of Austrian society. Chief contact among farmers was Lower Austrian farm leader Leopold Figl, who had been a Heimwehr (rightist paramilitary) chief during the 1930s and director of the Farm League (Bauernbund), one of the principal constituent organizations of the Christian Social party, during the corporatist period from 1935 to the anschluss.[25] An immovable adherent of the idea of an independent Austria, he had been arrested by the Nazis in 1938 and shipped off to Dachau. Moved from one camp to another, he was finally released on May 19, 1943. Shortly thereafter Figl entered into discussions with Hurdes and Weinberger and on their behalf made contact with other leading farm figures. In the spring of 1944 the first fundamental decisions on party organization were reached by Figl, Hurdes, Weinberger, and Pernter in Figl's home in Vienna, and the name Austrian People's party was adopted for the organization-to-be.

Seeking to bring in business interests, the organizational group also made contact in the spring of 1944 with Julius Raab, a building engineer and owner of a construction company in St. Pölten, Lower Austria. Like Figl, he had been active in the Christian Social party of the First Republic and had achieved a position of eminence in the corporative state. A member of the parliament from 1927 to its dissolution in 1934, he served thereafter as founder and head of the Business and Trade Association (Gewerbebund), one of the principal organs of the corporative state. Shortly before the anschluss he held the portfolio for trade and transport in Schuschnigg's last cabinet. Although the Nazis did not imprison him they did place him under some disabilities. He felt compelled to withdraw from his family's firm in St. Pölten to prevent jeopardizing the business's existence, and when war came he was pronounced "unfit to serve in the Wehrmacht." When contacted by the illegals in the spring of 1944 Raab agreed to come into the organization as a representative of the business community. (After the inauguration of the Second Republic he founded and built up the Business Association [Wirtschaftsbund], one of the chief component organizations of the People's party.) By the spring of 1944 the corporative and confederate character of the future party had been set-

25. Participation in the Heimwehr usually implied rightist, authoritarian opinions. And as Bauernbund director under Schuschnigg, Figl implicitly supported the authoritarian, indeed Fascist, policies of the corporative state. Hurdes, nevertheless, in a *Monatsheft* article (see n. 24) speaks of him as the "right hand man of Josef Reither," the unchallenged farm leader of his time. Reither was a staunch democrat who had little use for the authoritarian course taken by his party in 1934, though he remained a political adviser to Schuschnigg until the anschluss.

tled, with a labor, a farmers', and a businessmen's association as its three chief components. The party's core group (Kernkreis—a name frequently used later to refer to the founding members and their mentality) was in being.

Two waves of arrests by the Gestapo, one following the abortive 20th of July putsch and another in October 1944, threatened to destroy the incipient party. Hurdes, Weinberger, Pernter, Figl, and other leading figures were taken into custody and slated for execution. (Participation in a secret organization "whose goal was the reestablishment of an independent Austria" was mentioned in the indictment against Hurdes.) But the Russians overran Vienna before the sentences could be carried out, and on April 6, 1945, the prisoners were all released. Since so much had been settled during the period of illegality the rudiments of organization were quickly accomplished, and the new Austrian People's party was ready to take part in the provisional government of Karl Renner, which proclaimed the Second Republic on April 27.

Signing the proclamation for the People's party was the aged Leopold Kunschak, a Christian Social labor leader who had figured politically both in the empire and in the First Republic, albeit in a peripheral way. When Dollfuss decided upon the "authoritarian course" in 1934, Kunschak was one of the few Christian Social leaders who, as a convinced democrat first, last, and always, held out against the decision to disband the parliament and outlaw the Socialists. During the illegal period Weinberger picked the old man to be the symbol and rallying point (*Fahne*—literally, "flag") of the new party. And in April 1945 he was chosen its first chairman by the preparatory group. When the presidium of the party was formally constituted in September, however, the younger and more vigorous Figl was named chairman, with Hurdes acting as secretary general. As heads of the labor and business associations, respectively (Arbeiter- und Angestellten Bund [AAB] and Wirtschaftsbund), Weinberger and Raab were named deputy chairmen. The party was ready to do business.

In summary, what were the salient characteristics of the men who founded the new People's party? Those from the left wing of the earlier Christian Social party, men like Weinberger and Kunschak, had always been democrats and during the 1930s they had constantly campaigned for an opening to the left, for cooperation with the Socialists. Those who came originally from the party's right wing, men like Figl and Raab, had been converted by their state of nature experiences to the democratic process. None had been in the first echelon of the leadership of the corporative state. Kurt Schuschnigg, the last Christian Social chancellor of the corporative state, emigrated to the United States after his liberation from German imprisonment. Austro-Fascist Heimwehr leader Richard Steidle died in a Nazi prison, and Prince Starhemberg, another of the leading Heimwehren, did not return to political life. Furthermore, the failure of the corporative state had been an absolute one, and under the Nazis these men had learned what it was to be on the "receiving end." All had been persecuted by the Nazis and most had spent time in a concentration camp. This not only brought them closer to one another; it also stimulated sympathy for the Socialists who had been their prison mates and awakened a human understanding of men who formerly had been only ideological stereotypes to them.

On the Socialist side, it was the aging officials of the right wing around Karl Renner who brought about the revival of the Socialist party in the spring of 1945. As the Russians were occupying the city, the former members of the party's executive committee who happened to be present came together in the city hall to decide on a course of action. They were joined by a number of young people representing the old revolutionary wing of the party.[26]

Adolf Schärf was chosen chairman of the resurrected party, dubbed this time the Socialist Party of Austria (Sozialistische Partei Österreichs—SPÖ). Though his origins were in the Viennese working class, Schärf (b. 1890) attended the University of Vienna where he obtained a doctor of laws degree. After military service during World War I he served as secretary to Karl Seitz, the first chief of state of the new republic, and as secretary of the Socialist parliamentary fraction. He was also a member of the party's executive committee. From 1933 to 1934 he was a member of the upper house of the Austrian parliament. After the dissolution of

26. Shell, *Transformation*, p. 29.

parliament he returned to the practice of law which the corporatist regime and the Nazis allowed him to continue, though he was arrested several times by the latter.

General Theodor Körner came from an even older generation than Schärf. Körner was born in 1873, the son of a major of artillery in the army of the Dual Monarchy, and was himself a professional soldier. During World War I he served as chief of the general staff of the army in Italy and commanded the army during the battles of the Isonzo. The general's interest in the working class dated from his days as a young officer when he used to attend meetings and lectures at the People's Home (Volksheim) in Ottakring, a district of Vienna. His first work as a Socialist came much later, in 1918, when Julius Deutsch, state secretary for military affairs in the first republican government, called on Körner to create a republican army. When the Socialists left the coalition in 1920 he acted as an expert for the parliamentary commission charged with overseeing the Defense Ministry. Thereafter he served until 1934 as a delegate from the city of Vienna to the upper house of the parliament. After being arrested briefly by the Dollfuss government in that year, he retired to private life and remained politically inactive until 1945. The reactivated party nominated him as mayor of Vienna, and the nomination was supported by the other parties and approved by the Russian commandant. Both Schärf and Körner were later to serve as presidents of the Second Republic.

Oskar Helmer and Johann Böhm, two other of the reactivators of the Socialist party, also contributed to the picture of aging conservativism. Böhm was born in 1886, Helmer in 1887. Both were Lower Austrians. Both had been politically active during the last years of the monarchy and had held positions of authority in the First Republic—Helmer as a member of the legislature of Lower Austria and also as lieutenant governor. Böhm had been a trade union functionary, which also implied a pragmatic and conservative outlook. Both remained in Austria during the anschluss and spent some time in Nazi prisons. In 1945 Helmer helped reorganize the state government of Lower Austria and held the interior portfolio in the Renner provisional government. Böhm founded the Austrian

Labor Union Federation (Österreichischer Gewerkschaftsbund —ÖGB) as a supraparty tent organization for sixteen unions; the institution was to play a significant role in the Second Republic. He also served as state secretary for social administration in the provisional government.

Even before the outbreak of civil war in February 1934, strong centrifugal tensions had developed between the conservative and radical wings of the Austrian Socialist party. The radicals, under the leadership of Otto Bauer, were in command of the Socialist paramilitary defense brigade (Schutzbund), and when this was outlawed they went underground. At this point a break with the right wing around Renner, who wanted to avoid armed conflict with the Christian Social government, was almost complete. After the brief but catastrophic civil war, for which the Schutzbund was unprepared and the Viennese workers had no taste, the split was complete. Otto Bauer fled to Prague, from where he attempted to direct an underground party of Revolutionary Socialists which had been organized in Austria by Oskar Pollak, Karl Hans Sailer, and others. The Renner group refused to have anything to do with the illegals.[27]

During the period of the corporate state the Revolutionary Socialists had been able to maintain an extensive and active underground organization. But the Nazis, making use of files that the government had developed on the underground Socialist cadres, soon made it impossible for them to carry on. Large numbers of leaders and activists were hauled off to concentration camps. The right-wingers, who had repudiated the Revolutionary Socialists, withdrew to private life and were little molested. The Nazis also hoped to capitalize on Renner's celebrated anschluss declaration (of many years earlier) for the purposes of the new regime.[28]

Its pragmatists and conservatives thus brought the Socialist party back to life in Austria. Bauer was dead in exile, and those of the

27. See ibid., pp. 20–28; Wandruszka, "Österreichs Politische Struktur," pp. 464, 471.

28. Wandruszka, "Österreichs Politische Struktur," p. 474; Shell, *Transformation*, p. 26. The biographical sketches of Schärf, Körner, Böhm, and Helmer are taken from curricula vitae supplied me by the Austrian Federal Press Service.

leading Revolutionary Socialists who had not been murdered in the concentration camps of the Third Reich had fled abroad to England and Sweden. Some, like Ernst Fischer, a former editor of *Arbeiter-Zeitung,* the leading Socialist newspaper, had gone over to communism and had sought refuge in Moscow. When the surviving radical leaders returned from exile the democratic and pragmatic tone of the new Socialist party had already been set. Moreover, many of the radicals had learned a new appreciation of democracy and pragmatism during their years in exile in England and Scandinavia, and the unity of the party was more easily reestablished than anyone had supposed possible.[29] As Kurt Shell sums it up, "With the destruction of the R. S. cadres by the Gestapo and the retreat from political life of the uncompromising revolutionaries who had come to lead them, the commitment to dictatorship of the proletariat was replaced by a remarkably unanimous and unequivocal enthusiasm for parliamentary democracy."[30]

We see, then, that the men who came forward to create a Second Republic either had always been moderates (Renner, Schärf, Kunschak, Weinberger) or had been converted to moderate democratic politics by the experiences of the concentration camp, war, and life in democratic England (Czernetz, Pollak, Figl, Raab). The new programs written by both major parties expressly embraced democratic decision making and the norms of individual rights.[31] Prohibition by the Catholic bishops on further political activity by priests helped allay the old clericalist fears of the Socialists, always a deeply divisive factor in Austrian political life. Most of the leaders of 1945 had held positions of authority in earlier governments and from practice had learned a certain regard for the practical, for the decision "that works." They had also suffered a common persecution under the Nazis, either in their persons or in the persons of close friends and party comrades, and this counted for a great deal in promoting mutual tolerance, respect, and even affection. When his book about the revival of Austria was published in 1955 Adolf Schärf presented a copy of it to Felix Hurdes with the

29. Wandruszka, "Österreichs Politische Struktur," pp. 473, 475; Shell, *Transformation,* pp. 27–28.

30. Shell, *Transformation,* p. 41.

31. See Klaus Berchtold, ed., *Österreichische Parteiprogramme 1868–1966* (Munich: R. Oldenbourg, 1967), pp. 268–77, 376–79.

inscription: "In memory of the hard times we went through together."

Contractarianism: A Pragmatism of Dissensus

One measure of a "sense of community" is ideological consensus, or, if this is sometimes difficult to assess, at least the "end of ideology." This condition did not yet exist in 1945. The leaders of the time, though moderates, had very different *Weltanschauungen*. The Socialists were Marxists, and the Conservatives proponents of Catholic social doctrine. In their 1947 program, for example, the first redrafting of Socialist principles since 1934, Socialists identified as a class party and as "battlers for a Socialist social order." There were the usual declarations of war against capitalism, though these statements were few and general. Lacking were words about the systematic cultivation of inherited Christian values, the guarantee of religious education for children, and the conclusion of a concordat with the Vatican, all of which figured prominently in the People's party program. A special testimony to the fundamentally ideological mentality of the ÖVP (Conservative) leaders is found in their felt need to generate a doctrine of "solidarism," elevating cooperation with the Socialists from the level of expedience to that of principle.

Ideological differences between "Black" and "Red" in 1945 also implied different conceptions of the meaning and values of Austria as a community, different conceptions of Austrian identity. The Austrianism of Weinberger, Hurdes, and Figl was rooted in a deeply emotional attachment to the values of the old empire. The new Austria for them would be an organic continuation of and development out of the old. They also thought of Austria in a total cultural sense, not only as a political community. Most of the Socialists, by contrast, had been cultural as well as political Pan-Germans. Their attachment to an independent Austria flowed from negative things—from the experiences of German domination during the anschluss, from the sufferings of war and the concentration camp. With the exception of Renner, Körner, and a few others, they had only bitter memories of the empire and had no desire to carry on elements of its tradition. For the former Revolutionary

Socialists the value of Austria was equivalent to the possibility of
realizing Socialist goals within a republican frame of reference.

These differences are clearly displayed in the two parties' first
programs. That of the People's party begins with an affirmative
reference to the past.

> The Austrian People's party accepts the heritage of those politi-
> cal groups which always stood on the ground of the Austrian
> tradition and defended Austria's independence.

A paragraph relating to cultural policy calls for the

> systematic cultivation of the Austrian spirit with sharpest em-
> phasis on the autonomous Austrian cultural system, rooted in
> the Christian-occidental ideals which we have received from our
> forefathers.

Immediately following this, there is a reference to the churches and
religious communities as "carriers of culture in a special way" and
a demand for the protection of their cultural institutions and monuments. Another clause calls for the

> continuing saturation of the education program at all levels and
> in all types of schools, including trade schools, with the tradi-
> tions of Austrian thought (*Gedankengut*) and the education of
> the youth as unconditional Austrians.

Toward the close of the paragraph a clause demands "most inten-
sive work in building up the Austrian nation and the formation of
a strong and proud Austrian political and cultural consciousness." [32]
Conservatives had finally decided to use the expression *Austrian
nation* and to give it a cultural meaning.

The Socialist program makes no reference to an Austrian nation
or to the cultivation of a uniquely Austrian culture, but speaks only
of striving to obtain for Austria "full political sovereignty after liberation from Fascist tyranny. She must be free of the occupation.
She must also be free of those clauses of the Potsdam agreements
which confine Austrian freedom of action." In the last paragraph
a clause demands an "international guarantee of Austria's neutrality

32. Ibid., pp. 376–78.

as a security for her existing borders, freedom, and independence." [33]

Fundamentally different conceptions of internal political structure—Conservative federalism and Socialist centralism—are also spelled out as ideological differences in the first party programs. The Conservatives called for

> an Austrian state with unified leadership based on full regard for the historical development and individuality of the states, the securing to them of the autonomy which is their due, and extensive self-administration not only for the states but also for the towns and occupational corporations.

In the Socialist program, by contrast, there is a clause that calls for "strengthening of the unitary republic on a foundation of democratic self-administration in state, county, and town." [34]

In view of all these differences, which continued to keep Conservatives and Socialists in separate ideological worlds, we cannot say that their willingness to cooperate in 1945 stemmed from a new common viewpoint. Nothing like cultural or basic political consensus had emerged, though the economic theory of the Christian Socialists had some affinity to that of the Socialists. Cooperation flowed largely from a mutual contractarian spirit produced by mutual experience of the "state of nature" which culminated in a readiness to suspend the ideological disagreements that all recognized as extant. Each party displayed a "pragmatism of dissensus," willingness to conclude agreements in a pragmatic manner, to reach compromises for the solution of pressing common problems, while remaining conscious of deep differences in principle, different visions of the good society (*Leitbilder*). While unable to forget entirely past battles and wounds, and unable to trust the other party fully to abide by the new rules, each nevertheless felt compelled to stay within those rules in its own behavior.

The emergence of a contractarian spirit within the political *Lager* of 1945 cannot be wholly attributed to the special experiences of the leaders we have been describing. Those experiences were a catalyst that reactivated a traditional mentality older than the ideo-

33. Ibid., pp. 268, 271, 277.
34. Ibid., pp. 376, 271

logical fervors that destroyed the empire and First Republic and gave abortive birth to "Great Germany." The extent of the Habsburg domains, the multiplicity of political interests they embraced, and the great complex of cultures and value systems they housed had since time immemorial made necessary a supply of broker talent to hold them together. The ability to facilitate compromises, to work out ad hoc solutions without reference to general principles (when there was no agreement), had always been treated as a primary virtue in so loosely structured a system. We can see this in the handling of disputes by the imperial judicial panels (the Reichsgerichtshof) of the medieval Holy Roman Empire. (Often such brokerage took the form of ignoring the conflicts—cases were left pending on the docket for twenty or thirty years, until they had lost substance.) Later the figure of the imperial court councillor (Hofrat) as broker and arranger of settlements became so authoritative that the name was even applied to the Socialist leader Viktor Adler, whose party's program challenged the entire old regime. Adler was known as the "Court Councillor of the Revolution" because of his ability to play the broker between the contending factions on right and left that constantly threatened the unity of his party.

The culmination and crowning example of the politics of compromise was, of course, the Great Compromise (*Ausgleich*) of 1867 which divided the empire into two halves, the one governed by Francis Joseph in his capacity as emperor, the other ruled by him in his capacity as king of Hungary. The system subsisted in tenuous unity for fifty years, held together by an elaborate system of bureaucratic brokerage. The conditions of 1914–38 were fundamentally disintegrative and so gave full play to the passions of ideological division. The integrating situation of 1945, however, reactivated the old tradition of bargained agreement in the face of ideological confusion. It is not strange that Austrians should have seen this tradition as a model for the pragmatic coalition of political opponents established in 1945, whose partners were promptly dubbed "the Black and Red halves of the empire" (*die Schwarze und Rote Reichshälfte*).[35]

35. Willy Lorenz, an Austrian traditionalist who is both a writer and a publisher, finds a detailed parallel between the two systems. First, the *Ausgleich*

Rational Contract

The condition of *debellatio,* with all former authority extinguished by unconditional surrender, was much like the classical state of nature, in a legal as well as in a political sense. The state had to be rebuilt in all its parts, from the ground up. The reconstitution of an independent Austrian republic necessarily entailed wiping out all the German administrative structures, so that the new state could come into being quite unencumbered by direct legal continuity with the institutions, practices, personnel, and vested interests of the preceding regime. By contrast, the First Republic had inherited both central and provincial parliaments and bureaucracies from the empire, with all the conflicts of interest and ideology that had grown up within them.[36]

The agents of the new "social contract" were primarily the two major political parties of the First Republic, which, as we have seen, had maintained a shadow life in illegality during the seven

---

of 1867 was renegotiated every ten years by committees of the two parliaments operating on an extraparliamentary basis. From 1945 to 1966 Conservatives and Socialists renegotiated the rights and duties of the coalition by concluding a new pact of coalition after every parliamentary election. Between elections, day-to-day negotiation of differences took place within the extraparliamentary and indeed extraconstitutional coalition committee, made up of leaders of the two parties. Second, he sees Hungary as playing a role similar to that of the SPÖ and the Cisleithanian half of the empire as playing a role like that of the ÖVP. Though the smaller partner, Hungary enjoyed rights equal with the greater one; she sought to lead the whole monarchy, just as the SPÖ, though weaker than the ÖVP, has also enjoyed equal rights with the Conservatives and sought to dominate the coalition (according to Lorenz). Lorenz finds structural similarities as well on both sides of the two coalitions—centrally governed Hungary and SPÖ, paired with the looser, more federal structure of Cisleithania and ÖVP. Hungary wished to nationalize nationalities; the SPÖ wishes to nationalize industries. Third, Lorenz also finds similarities in the structures of the two coalitions —just as the common (*kaiserliche und königliche*) ministries of the empire were controlled by two ministers representing the two imperial halves, so during the coalition from 1945 to 1955 was a minister of one party paired with a state secretary of the other in the chancellery and in the key ministries of Interior, Defense, and Foreign Affairs. Lorenz, *AEIOU,* pp. 33–38.

36. Hiscocks, *Rebirth of Austria,* p. 28. A problem, of course, would develop in the area of personnel. In large part the generation of politically experienced "fathers" had been Nazis, and the others were off at the wars. The "sons" were too young to assume political responsibility. And so the "grandfathers" would have to play a disproportionate role.

years of anschluss and were quickly reordered for public activity
by their old leaders at the moment of Nazi collapse.[37] Secondarily
there were the Länder, which maintained a continuous life throughout the years of the Third Reich despite changes in administrative
structure and personnel. It would therefore have to be in the context of both party and provincial life that conversion to the politics
of rational cooperation for the common interest of all Austrians
would take place.

The overarching legal order, the constitution of the Second Republic, was in the first instance a contract among the parties. The
signatories of the declaration of independence of April 27, 1945,
were the members of the executive committees of the parties, and
the declaration, after proclaiming the establishment of an independent Austrian state, promised to erect with the participation of all
anti-Fascist party directorates a provisional central government
that was to be entrusted with full legislative and executive power.
The personnel of that provisional regime were virtually identical
with the membership of the party executive organs. And it was this
provisional regime which immediately proceeded, by a means of a
transitional measure, to reactivate the federal constitutional law of

37. Arend Lijphart has described this system as "consociational democracy." See his article with that title in *World Politics* 21, no. 2 (January
1969): 207 ff. For an extended discussion of the operation of this system in
Austria, see also Rodney P. Stiefbold, "Elite-Mass opinion structures and
communication flow in a consociational democracy (Austria)," (Paper read
at the 1968 annual meeting of the American Political Science Association,
Washington, D.C.) For another analysis of contractual government see Val
Lorwin, "Segmented Pluralism," mimeographed (Stanford, Cal.: Center for
Advanced Study in the Behavioral Sciences, 1967), to be published in Stein
Rokkan, et al., *The Politics of the Smaller European Democracies* (Stanford, Cal.: Stanford University Press, forthcoming). Eric Nordlinger has
presented an excellent theoretical discussion of the role of elites in effecting
political integration through procedures of conflict management like those
adopted by the Austrian "contractarians." He cites the Austrian experience
at length. See *Conflict Regulation in Divided Societies,* Harvard University
Center for International Affairs, Occasional Papers in International Affairs,
#29, January 1972. Nordlinger writes: "There is a distinct overlap between
political integration and conflict regulation problems, so that studies of the
latter may inform those of the former. But political integration studies usually do not give this overlap sufficient attention. The revision of integration
studies should continue so that the problem of conflict regulation may
be accorded the attention it deserves (pp. 3–4)." This book represents just
such an effort to relate conflict regulation to political integration.

the First Republic as it stood on March 5, 1933, just prior to the Dollfuss coup.

Similar procedures were used by the parties to create regimes for the various Länder. And these in turn recognized the all-Austrian regime that Renner had set up in Vienna. The conferences of states which Renner convened to prepare the way for official recognition should also be seen as significant contracting bodies that were to have successors in the periodic conferences of state governors, which played a role of great importance in the evolution of the Second Republic. As one Austrian scholar has summed it up:

> The point of departure for all constitutional decisions . . . is . . . a coalition of the parties which rests on no legal basis. The parties are the creators of the legal foundations for the "people" [*Volk*] from whom, according to Article 1 of the federal constitution, the law of the Republic proceeds.[38]

The first elections to the National Assembly of the Second Republic, held November 25, 1945, produced an absolute majority for the People's party. Eighty-five of the Assembly's 165 seats were awarded to the Conservatives, 76 to the Socialists, and 4 to the Communists. Of 3,217,354 valid votes cast the Conservatives received 1,602,226—close to 50 percent of the total, and 167,329 more ballots than the Socialists. Leopold Figl, as the newly installed leader of the ÖVP, became chancellor and thereby head of government.

Despite his majority, Figl chose not to govern alone but invited the Socialists to join a coalition government. He realized not only that a majority of two is precarious, but also that, since almost a half million former Nazis had been excluded from the franchise, his Conservative majority was somewhat artificial. Moreover, a united front would constitute a stronger bulwark against pressures from the former occupying powers who were omnipresent, both militarily and politically. But also at work was the contractarian mentality of dissensus pragmatism that we have described above. One commentator, in a contribution to a twenty-year jubilee volume for the Second Republic, writes:

38. Gustav E. Kafka, "Die Verfassungsmässige und Staatsrechtliche Stellung der Parteien," in Weinzierl, *Der Österreicher,* p. 40.

> Leopold Figl's decision to eschew one-party rule . . . showed itself to be very useful. . . . It gave people the clearest demonstration that through common effort, without divisive party barriers, lay the only chance to make Austria capable of sustaining life again. He thereby prevented that dangerous gulf between the two large parties which had so often convulsed the First Republic.[39]

It would have been unsafe for the Conservatives in an ideologically divided society to have viewed their majority as concurrent, as a cross section of the whole. Parliamentary elections could not serve as consensus-building or declaring processes. They tallied instead the strength of opposing armies. If the existence of opposing armies was not to result in catastrophic conflict, if they *had* to be brought to agreement, this could only be by a procedure resembling a continuous treaty or contract negotiation, a constant conclave of their chiefs, resolving issues through compromise and unanimous decision—a "Grand Coalition."

It is an interesting question whether the Socialists, if they had won a majority, would also have favored a coalition of the two major parties. Their first program of 1947 says nothing of cooperation with the Conservatives but asserts: "If the Socialist Party of Austria obtains the majority at the next election she will carry out the following measures for the country's reconstruction and for the creation of a Socialist Austria." [40] The 1945 Conservative program, by contrast, a program unrevised until 1952, says nothing about majorities and speaks only of "honorable cooperation with all parties which accept Austria." [41] It may also be significant that it was a Conservative leader (Hurdes) who first approached a Socialist leader (Schärf) two years before the Nazi collapse to solicit Socialist cooperation in a common effort to rebuild Austria. The People's party ideology of "solidarism," for which we find no counterpart on the Socialist side, also implied that coalition would be the effectively "solidaristic" mode of government.[42]

---

39. Susanna Seltenreich, "Leopold Figl," in *Reichhold, Zwanzig Jahre Zweite Republik*, p. 111.
40. Berchtold, *Parteiprogramme*, p. 271.
41. Ibid., p. 377.
42. For an explication of the doctrine of solidarism see Dr. Alfred Kasamas, *Wir Wollen Österreich, Die Grundsätze und Ziele der Österreichischen*

The contractarian spirit of the Socialists is thus revealed passively rather than actively, in their willingness to enter a government led by a Conservative chancellor and to accept mutual responsibility for the acts of that government during a critical and difficult time rather than play the easier role of critic. However, an active Socialist desire for the coalition was to develop as its great value for Socialist interests gradually became manifest.

For the whole period from 1945 to 1966 the two great parties renewed their agreement to cooperate following each parliamentary election by signing a pact of coalition (*Koalitionspakt*) by which they divided between them the offices of state at the ministerial level and by which they established a rubric for the day-to-day conduct of policy making during the subsequent legislative period. Included in this was a unanimity rule and an agreement on a system of proportionalism (*Proporz*) for staffing government corporations and nationalized industries whereby each party received positions for its members in proportion to its strength in the electorate. In the regular government departments the party in control at the top was given the major say in appointments. An elaborate system of checks and balances was established at the top level for keeping the agents of each party honest through supervision by agents of the other.[43]

Volkspartei, Bundesparteileitung der ÖVP (Vienna: Österreichischer Verlag, 1947). Hurdes, in a foreword, wrote that "the way into the future could not lie in further cleavage, but solely in the welding together of all forces, in active solidarism" (p. 4). Kasamas then went on to discuss "solidarism" as one of the four pillars along with "democracy," "Austrian folkishness" (*Volkstum*), and "Austrian independence," on which, according to ÖVP ideology, the political system rested. He defined "solidarism" as "common feeling and common action for the achievement of common goals; the principle is intended in its execution to exclude every juxtaposition and opposition in human society" (p. 35). "With reference to the individual, one could call 'solidarism' that interior readiness of a man to place the ideal and material resources granted him, as far as possible, at the disposal of his fellow men for the achievement of their goals, and to work for himself only to prevent his fellow men from injuring him in his legitimately won rights and natural interests" (p. 43). Political parties acting in the spirit of "solidarism" were expected to develop a sense of togetherness in the achievement of common goals, such as "making the country stronger" (p. 44). It is interesting that the head of the political bureau of the ÖVP general secretariat in 1947 was an ideologist like Kasamas.

43. For an excellent brief description of the system of coalition and *Proporz* see Frederick C. Engelmann, "Austria: Pooling the Opposition,"

The electorate added still another compromise to those worked out by the party leaders. It consistently, down to 1970, returned a larger number of People's party representatives than Socialists to the National Assembly (though only once before 1966 did a Conservative majority emerge), thus guaranteeing the chancellorship each time to the People's party. Just as consistently, it chose at every presidential election a Socialist chief of state.

Government by Coalition

One of the first far-reaching measures of the coalition was to nationalize Austria's chief heavy industries and banking establishments. The action has been described by one scholar as an historical accident, since it could not have been deduced from the principles of the Conservatives. Nor were the industries affected chosen according to a rational scheme of priorities within the "grand plan" of the Socialists.[44] The object of the nationalization laws of 1946 and 1947 was to prevent the occupying powers from confiscating the vast economic plant that the Germans had created or acquired in Austria during the anschluss years. According to the Potsdam accords all of this property was subject to seizure as reparation for war losses of the Allies.

Seventy-one enterprises were nationalized. These included iron and coal mines, iron and steel works, and firms dealing in aluminum, oil, electric power, transport, machine tools, shipbuilding, electronics, nonferrous metals and organic chemicals. Also nationalized were the country's leading banks—the Creditanstalt Bankverein, the Länderbank, and the Creditinstitut. The United States, Great Britain, and France responded by handing the administration of the German firms in their respective sectors over to the Austrian government. The Russians, however, refused to follow suit and instead placed the German assets in their zone under the direct control of the newly created Soviet Mineral Oil Administra-

chapter 8 in Robert A. Dahl, ed., *Political Oppositions in Western Democracies* (New Haven: Yale University Press 1966), p. 265. See also Gerhard Lehmbruck, *Proporzdemokratie: Politisches System und Politische Kultur in der Schweiz und in Österreich* (Tübingen: Mohr, 1967.)

44. Dennison I. Russinow, "Notes Toward a Political Definition of Austria," *American Universities Field Staff Reports, S. E. Europe* 8, no. 8, part 4 (1966) : 3.

tion (SMV) and the Administration for Soviet Property in Austria (USIA). Only after the conclusion of the State Treaty (1955) were these concerns turned over to the Austrian government by the Russians in return for reparation payments of about $200,000,000.

A large portion of the new public economic empire came under Socialist control after the parliamentary election of 1949 when the People's party lost its absolute majority, which was due in part to the restoration of the franchise to the former Nazis. Their votes went heavily to the newly founded Coalition of Independents (Wahlbloc der Unabhängigen—WdU) (489,273 ballots) and gave the new party 16 seats in parliament. The ÖVP representation was reduced to 77 and the SPÖ to 67. Nevertheless, the SPÖ was in a relatively stronger position than before vis-à-vis the ÖVP and was able to demand control of the nationalized industries. Except for the banks, which were made the province of the "Black"-controlled Finance Ministry, the industries were at first placed under the supervision of the Socialist minister of transport, Karl Waldbrunner.[45]

The complex of large concerns, employing nearly 300,000 persons, was soon dubbed the "Waldbrunner Kingdom." The Socialist party had become a vested interest in the state. "In place of the dialectician of the inter-war period, such as Otto Bauer had been," writes one scholar of the Socialist metamorphosis, "the political manager, the party official and the technocrat stepped into the foreground." [46] The present Socialist leader, Bruno Kreisky, is quoted as having said of Waldbrunner that "in his view the human species begins with the engineer." [47]

As noted earlier, from 1945 the top positions in the bureaucracy were filled by a system of proportionality known as *Proporz*. Some ministries were mostly "Black" (e.g., Education) some chiefly "Red" (e.g., Justice). For the key ministries a Conservative minister was paired with a Socialist undersecretary or a Socialist minister with a Conservative undersecretary. In 1956 *Proporz* was adopted also for the nationalized industries. This sort of arrangement at the top naturally led to the development of an extensive

45. Ibid.
46. Alexander Vodopivec, *Wer Regiert in Österreich?* 2d ed. (Vienna: Verlag für Geschichte u. Politik, 1962), p. 112.
47. Ibid., p. 113.

patronage system, and the party rank and file on both sides were well taken care of.

The system of *Proporz* unquestionably had negative effects; by creating widespread dependence on a party for one's job, it appeared to perpetuate the *Lager* aspect of Austrian society. It led also to all kinds of inefficiency and corruption. The editor of the German magazine *Der Spiegel,* in an article attacking the coalition system in Austria on the eve of its adoption in Bonn, characterized "Proporzocracy" as follows:

> In Austria today . . . everyone knows what color his neighbor is. The engineer in a nationalized steel factory is generally a Red, the member of the army general staff a Black. The traffic cop is switched to Red, the country school teacher sees Black. If an Austrian lives in public housing built by the city of Vienna he almost certainly has a Red party book. If he lives in a dwelling subsidized by the Ministry of Trade he pays dues to the Blacks.[48]

The number of party members on each side of the coalition became extremely large. In 1965 there were 716,000 card-carrying Socialists and 600,000 Conservatives, figures which contrast sharply with the 690,000 Socialists and 385,000 Christian Democrats of the German Federal Republic, which has a population eight times that of Austria.[49]

On the other hand, the system of *Proporz* combined with the extensive nationalizations had important positive results for political community in Austria. By giving the Socialist working class a large stake in the socio-political order it won them over to Austria. Evidence of the change is found in the appearance during the 1950s of a Socialist literature of commitment to Austria, a literature which continued to grow during the 1960s.[50] Survey research shows, in fact, that Socialists of the Second Republic are the most Austrian-minded of all segments of the nation's population.[51]

Even a critical appraisal of *Proporz* by Günther Nenning, one of Austria's leading contemporary intellectuals, contains indirect

48. "Österreich: Grosse Koalition," *Der Spiegel,* 1 September 1965, p. 72.
49. Ibid., p. 74.
50. This literature will be discussed in chapter 5.
51. This will be discussed in chapter 8.

(and probably unintentional) mention of the positive results of the system.

> With contemptible seriousness many young people, when they are selecting a career, ponder the question of which organization within the almighty, all-nourishing, black-red state party they ought promptly to join.[52]

The interesting thing is that Nenning speaks in this passage of the two erstwhile ideological opponents as *one* "Black-Red state party." There is also the question of how truly divisive a system can be that reduces party allegiance to terms of pure material advantage.

Socialist identification with the Second Republic is by no means wholly an unconscious and unintended by-product of status, power, and well-being achieved. The word *national* is sometimes very self-consciously manipulated by Socialist leaders to defend specific values. Former Vice-Chancellor Bruno Pittermann, for example, in recent years has taken to speaking of the nationalized industries as *Nationalindustrien* rather than as *Verstaatlichte Industrien,* the original and more usual expression—and the expression employed in the nationalization laws of 1946 and 1947. In a discussion at the People's College in the working-class Viennese district of Brigittenau early in 1965, Dr. Pittermann was asked why he had switched to the new formula. He answered that the industries in question belonged to the Austrian nation and then turned the matter back on the interrogator by asking whether the latter had something against the Austrian nation.[53] A young Conservative with a strong emotional attachment to the idea of an Austrian nation interpreted Pittermann's language as a ploy to protect the industries in question from a possible privatization sometime in the future. As the respondent saw it, *Verstaatlichte Industrie* has the connotation of an industry that underwent change to public ownership at a particular time. The implication is that it could legitimately be privatized again. *Nationalindustrie* implies permanence, for it would be illegitimate to privatize a possession of the nation. (He also thought there might be a purely emotional-patriotic motive in Pittermann's usage. *Nationalindustrie* definitely means non-German industry,

---

52. Quoted in "Österreich: Grosse Koalition," p. 72.
53. Reported in *Wirtschaftshorizont,* no. 167, 1 February 1965, p. 12.

and there is much German capital in Austria).[54] It is interesting
that the discussion in Brigittenau occurred a little more than a year
before the election that produced a new Conservative majority and
brought the end of the coalition.

Nationalization, then, in the context of the coalition and "Proporzocracy," seems to have been one of the important contributions
of the twenty-year coalition to the development of political community among Austrians. Another was the demonstration that
Austria was, after all, capable of sustaining an independent economic life (*lebensfähig*) and even of becoming an affluent society
(*Wohlstandstaat*). The Austrian gross national product in 1945,
the year the Third Reich collapsed, was only 36 percent of what
it had been in 1937, the year before the anschluss. In two years it
was up to 62 percent of the 1937 figure. And then came a great
surge upward. By 1950, despite the constant drag of Russian occupation in the eastern parts of the country, the gross national product had more than doubled, rising to 132 percent of the 1937 level.
After the achievement of independence in 1955 there was another
great upswing to 230 percent of the 1957 gross national product
in 1960. In short, industrial production had trebled the 1937 figure by 1960.

Between 1950 and 1960 wages and salaries also more than
trebled, going from 23.47 to 74.42 billion schillings. Three years
later they were more than four times the amount for 1950. Total
income rose slightly less during the same period. Real income rose
72 percent between 1950 and 1960 and 7 percent more in the
succeeding two years. Private consumption trebled between 1950
and 1960, and by 1962 it somewhat less than quadrupled the figure
for 1960. Investment more than quadrupled from 1950 to 1960,
rising from 8.836 to 37.007 million schillings. By 1962 it had
almost quintupled the 1950 figure.[55]

The newly nationalized industries were among the first to prosper
after 1946. Having a priority claim on Marshall Plan money, and
with their products in exceptional demand at the time, the industries

54. Interview with Dr. Peter Diem, of the People's party secretariat,
Vienna, April 7, 1966.
55. Reichhold, *Zwanzig Jahre Zweite Republik*, tables on pp. 410–12.

grew by 179 percent between 1949 and 1961. The overall growth rate for Austria for these years was 156 percent.[56]

The final achievement of the State Treaty of 1955, which brought full sovereignty and the withdrawal of the occupation troops after ten years, was another coalition accomplishment which resulted in increased national consciousness. Former Chancellor Klaus sees the period of the treaty as a third phase in the growth of Austrian feeling. "There developed at that time" he said, "a feeling of having found our own way. We had no need to depend on any particular bloc. Though small, we were independent and self-reliant." [57]

Paired with the treaty was a declaration of neutrality, which was to be both an expression and an instrument of that independence and self-reliance.

The National Assembly has resolved:

Article I

1. For the purpose of the continual affirmation of her external independence and for the purpose of maintaining the inviolability of her territory, Austria voluntarily declares her perpetual neutrality. Austria will maintain and defend her neutrality with all means at her disposal.

2. To secure these goals for all future time Austria will join no military alliances and will permit the establishment of no military bases on her territory.

3. The Federal Government is charged with the execution of this Federal Constitutional Law.[58]

Germany and Italy were no longer political giants, capable of destroying Austria's independence of action as they had been in the 1930s. And it was substantially in the interest of the Western and Eastern superpowers to have a neutral buffer between their spheres of influence in Europe. Austria had achieved a position like that of

56. Russinow, "Notes," pp. 1, 2.
57. Interview with Chancellor Josef Klaus, Vienna, May 25, 1966.
58. Bundesverfassungsgesetz vom 26. Oktober 1955 über die Neutralität Österreichs, BGB für die Republik Österreich, Jg. 1955, 57. Stück, Ausgegeben am 4. November 1955.

Switzerland. Now the way was open for the development of national feeling on the Swiss model.

The withdrawal of the foreigners in 1955 removed from the scene an important stimulus to Austrian national feeling. But there is evidence that the stimulus of the preceding ten years had left behind a lasting response. Richard Hiscocks tells the following story:

> In February 1952 President Körner gave a dinner-party in Vienna to the Governors of all the Austrian provinces as a demonstration of Austrian unity and solidarity. The President spoke of the way in which the Austrian provinces had grown together organically during the previous six years. In his reply on behalf of the provinces, Dr. Gleissner of Upper Austria said that in the future there must be no mention of Eastern Austria and Western Austria, but only of a single unified State. "The zonal frontiers cut through the landscape," he added, "but they do not cut through our hearts." [59]

The foreign occupation had produced the beginnings of a mutual feeling that all the self-conscious arts of the Fatherland Front had been unable to create in the 1930s.

An unexpected bit of similar evidence emerged in an orientation lecture on Austrian politics by Dr. Hans Kronhuber, chief of the political bureau of the People's party to a group of Fulbright scholars in September 1965, immediately after their arrival in Vienna. Comparing the experience of the First and Second republics, Dr. Kronhuber remarked that in 1918 Austrians were "not a nation at all" but that the situation began to change after 1938. Seven years of German occupation were a "hard school in national feeling," a period which "developed a relationship between the people and the country." Following this, the ten years of occupation, and especially the Russian occupation in the eastern part of the country, greatly furthered the development of national feeling. "Soviet occupation is a hard school and you really learn a lot." Suffering such an occupation "is creating a nation, forming a nation." Dr. Kronhuber continued with mention of the fact that until 1965 Austrians had never had a national holiday. At that time one was to be created by law, the date chosen being October 26, on which in 1955

59. Hiscocks, *Rebirth of Austria*, p. 199.

Austria had proclaimed her perpetual neutrality and the last Russian occupation troops had left Austrian soil.

During the ten years after 1945, therefore, both "situation" and "intention" initially made for political integration. In a contractarian frame of mind, the leaders of ideological rival parties suspended disagreement in order to work together in a context of pragmatism. Finding their way out of a state of nature was everyone's concern. They met with eminent success in all their projects, notably the achievement of sovereign independence, through the State Treaty, and economic development and well-being. Both fed back into the political culture as a new and buoyant Austrian national political identity developed in all groups. In addition, the nationalization of industry by the postwar coalition won over to Austria the Socialist workers, who in the 1930s had stood aloof. Austrians had crossed the ideological line between right and left.

The Coalition Declines. From Contractarianism to Consensus: A New Phase of Integration

The State Treaty was the high water mark of coalition facility in effective policy making. After the achievement of this paramount success in 1955 the coalition began to decay as a workable form of government. It became ever more difficult for the partners to reach a meeting of minds. Compromises were no longer forthcoming, and unresolved problems began to pile up. Paradoxically, the coalition's achievements were to be the source of its doom. For the pressures of the foreign occupation, which had made the system work by coercing the ill-matched partners into cooperative effort, were at an end. A legacy remained, however. Personal friendships had developed across party lines, and these could turn ideological specters into mere men. Each party had also learned from the give-and-take of daily common effort to trust the other party to abide by the ground rules of the democratic game. These things, plus solid achievements in economic reconstruction and sound legislation, constituted a legacy which would provide the "seed money" during the next eleven years, from 1955 to 1965, for the quiet development of a different kind of political enterprise. A new kind of political elite and a new kind of voter would gradually emerge;

and in 1966 they would effect a peaceful revolution in Austrian politics by dumping the stagnating coalition and establishing the usual form of parliamentary government, with a single ruling party balanced by a loyal opposition. Policy-making would cease to have the form of treaty negotiations between the chiefs of hostile armies and would be based instead on an electoral mandate to a single party. In the background would be a new mentality, an ebullient political consensus, which, unlike the fearful contractarianism of dissensus, would be capable of understanding John Stuart Mill's dictum about opposition as a form of cooperation.[60]

Alfred Maleta, former Conservative president of the Austrian National Assembly, shrewdly observed that the coalition during its twenty-year life had "created out of a sheer will to cooperate a habit of democratic politics, a democratic tradition." One passage of his essay deserves quotation at length:

> The perpetuation of the coalition until now [1965] gives an indication that within its framework new spiritual forces were set free, forces which incline rather toward synthesis than toward that antithesis [of ideological conflict] by which the course of the First Republic was dominated. . . .
>
> The results of six coalition governments, to which the essential and basic social powers of the country have united themselves, have fashioned far-reaching social facts from which neither side can emancipate itself, because for the first time in the history of Austrian democracy these facts have come into being not through dictation but through agreement. That means, lastly, that we in Austria today have a social tradition that the fundamental political powers of the country all acknowledge. . . .
>
> Precisely, this tradition is decisive, for all peoples are welded together as peoples by the formation in the course of their history of common values, common ways of life, common institutions, things by which they recognize themselves to be a community. This process, because it encompasses the consciousness of broad classes, goes deeper than a merely ideological interpretation of some historical situation which is nourished only in the mind of a minority. While we in Austria are still battling about the con-

60. John Stuart Mill, *On Liberty,* chapter 2.

cept of an Austrian nation, the decisive foundations have long since been laid on which the Austrian people have grown together into an historical community. The formation of this community through a common political effort is the essential result of that concentration of popular will which has existed in Austria . . . since 1945.[61]

What Maleta did not realize, however, was that the democratic tradition that the coalition had fashioned was powerful enough to sustain a radical transformation of its structural form, as the experience of the healthy single-party government that has existed since 1966 has demonstrated. Contractarianism had produced the beginning of national feeling through pragmatic problem solving. In the end, like a worn-out tool, it superseded itself with a new consensual order. Structural political integration had occurred along with the emergence of a new psychological community, a political nation.

61. Alfred Maleta, "Konzentration des Willen," in Reichhold, *Zwanzig Jahre Zweite Republik,* pp. 134, 137–38. For a detailed statement of Maleta's political philosophy see Alfred Maleta, *Entscheidung für Morgen* (Vienna: Molden, 1968.)

3. STRUCTURAL DYNAMICS:
ECONOMIC, SOCIAL,
AND POLITICAL CHANGE

Hobbesian rationality, engendered by the traumas of 1945, can explain Austria's adoption of coalition democracy in that year. The abandonment of the coalition after twenty years and the substitution of regular parliamentary rule—with one party in control of the government and the other playing the role of loyal opposition —can be explained in part by the new trust between the parties learned from the experience of twenty years of cooperative problem solving. Fundamental secular developments in the structure of Austrian society, in part the product of that problem solving, promise to give stability to Austrian democracy, either in its current form or in a modification of the original coalition system. These changes can best be summarized by saying that in the period between 1945 and 1966 Austria passed from a transitional condition into a maturing urban industrial state. The country had undergone those demographic, economic, social, and psychological changes that make possible the stable operation of liberal democratic government on the basis of political consensus.

Demographic Change to 1951

A key index of modernity is the balance between city and country, between urban and rural factors in a society. If we measure this balance in Austria by comparing the number of persons employed in agriculture with the number employed in industry and trade, we find that the turbulent First Republic was the epitome of the transitional state, with the number in agriculture maintaining a narrow and declining lead over those in industry and crafts. The census of 1951, however—the first taken after World War II—showed that the balance had been reversed. For the first time there were more people in industry than there were in agriculture, as table 1 shows. Sometime during the wrenching years of anschluss, war, and the early occupation, Austria crossed a great divide between the tradi-

Table 1. Structure of the Economy: 1910, 1934, 1951

Year	Agriculture and forestry	Industry and crafts
1910	39.5%	35.2%
1934	37.1	36.5
1951	32.6	41.3

SOURCE: "Wirtschaftliche Aspekte der österreichischen Be-völkerungsentwicklung," *Monatsberichte des Österreichischen Institutes für Wirtschaftsforschung*, supplement no. 23 (November 1953), p. 7.

tional agricultural society and the modern industrial society. The economic history of the Second Republic has therefore consisted of completing the structure of industrialization rather than laying the groundwork for it, a phase of development more compatible with political integration than the foundation phase.

Regional balance, especially as it relates to the urban-rural distribution, is also important for modernization. We have already noted the vast difference between the sprawling Vienna of 1918, the sole large urban center at that time, and all the rest of the country, a hinterland of farms and small towns. Between 1923 and 1934, the year of the establishment of Dollfuss's dictatorship, the population balance began to change, but not to a marked degree. Vienna declined by only .1 percent, while the greatest population increase was in the Vorarlberg, which grew by 17.9 percent. Tyrol and Salzburg grew by 16 percent each, Carinthia by 12.2 percent, and Styria by 4.5 percent. Burgenland and Lower Austria increased by smaller percentages.[1]

By 1951, however, the demographic picture was quite different. Vienna had declined dramatically (by 16.5 percent), while the western provinces had grown in a similarly dramatic manner, the increases ranging from 22.8 to 24.6 percent, as table 2 shows.

1. Robert Holzman, ed. *The World Almanac and Book of Facts for 1935* (New York: World-Telegram, 1935), p. 615; *World Almanac for 1936*, p. 615.

84   BUILDING AN AUSTRIAN NATION

Table 2. Regional Population Shifts, 1934 to 1967

Population, by Land

	1934	1951	Variation	Percentage of variation
Vienna	1,935,610	1,616,125	−319,485	−16.5
Lower Austria	1,446,949	1,400,471	−46,478	−3.2
Burgenland	299,447	276,136	−23,311	−7.8
Upper Austria	902,965	1,108,720	+205,755	+22.8
Salzburg	245,801	327,232	+81,431	+33.1
Tyrol	349,098	427,465	+78,367	+22.4
Vorarlberg	155,402	193,657	+38,255	+24.6
Styria	1,015,106	1,109,335	+94,229	+9.3
Carinthia	405,129	474,764	+69,635	+17.2
Austria	6,760,233[a]	6,933,905	+173,672	+2.6

Percentage of Share in the Total Population by Regions

	1934	1951	1961	1967
Vienna & the East	54.5	47.5	46.3	44.7
West & South	45.5	52.5	53.7	55.3

[a] Includes 4,726 persons without fixed dwelling.
SOURCE: Karl Selber, "Die Regionale Bevölkerungsumschichtung innerhalb Österreichs in den letzten drei Jahrzehnten und ihre politische Auswirkungen," mimeographed (Vienna, 1968), pp. 3, 11. With permission.

Moreover, the east-west population balance had been dramatically reversed, as the table indicates. While the regional balance of population continued to shift westward during the Second Republic, the total change in either direction between 1951 and 1967 would be less than 2 percent. The major change had already been accomplished by the time the Second Republic came into existence.

The great population increases in the western and southern Länder between 1934 and 1951 were all within developing urban industrial centers—the Feldkirch-Dornbirn-Bregenz complex in Vorarlberg, the Salzburg-Hallein area of Salzburg Land, the area around Innsbruck in Tyrol, the Linz-Wels-Steyr triangle of Upper Austria, Klagenfurt and Villach in Carinthia, the area of Graz in Styria. Within each of the Länder the rural areas had lost heavily to these urban centers. The new picture was one of concentration of population in seven widely distributed centers, a sharp contrast with the single metropolis-hinterland distribution of the First Republic. Vienna remained, indeed, the largest city, with a population of 1,616,125. But Graz, Linz, Salzburg, and Innsbruck had all grown to be large cities with populations ranging from 100,000 to 226,000. Klagenfurt and Villach (adjacent cities) taken together represented a population of about 100,000 and Bregenz-Feldkirch-Dornbirn, more than 150,000. Moreover, vitality and growth were to be found primarily in the new centers rather than in Vienna.[2]

The rate as well as the direction of social change is important for political integration, as both Lerner and Lipset have shown.[3] It is significant that the most wrenching period of change, Austria's "great leap forward" demographically, occurred during the chaotic period of dictatorship, war, and foreign occupation, from 1934 to 1951. Since 1951, change has been more measured.

Economic Development to 1955

During the First Republic, industrialization proceeded amidst dislocation, depression, and poverty, and during the anschluss years it occurred under the wrenching imperatives of a wartime economy. During the final phase of maturation which it entered during the coalition years of the Second Republic, however, modern industrial Austria has experienced soaring productivity and consumer affluence. This has disproven once and for all the myth of economic nonviability, which was perhaps the chief inhibitor of national consciousness in the First Republic. Fifteen years of prosperity have contributed much to a new spirit of self-reliance in Austria—and thus to attachment to the state in which it has flowered.

The wise economic policies of the "Grand Coalition" were a primary cause of Austria's new *Lebensfähigheit* (economic viability). The leaders of the new political order that replaced the coalition from 1966 to 1970 ungrudgingly acknowledged this as the old system's great contribution to the health of the Second Republic. And the theme of economic viability has become a popular watchword. But the coalition alone and of itself, of course, could not have produced a viable economy if preconditions of economic development quite unconnected to the form of government had not been present. The foundations of viability were laid in part during the

2. *Source*: Öst. Stat. Zentralamt, *Volkszählung vom 1. Juni 1951,* Tabellenband 1 (Vienna: Österreichische Staatsdruckerei, 1953), pp. 2, 4.

3. Lerner, *Passing of Traditional Society*; Seymour Martin Lipset, *Political Man* (Garden City, N.Y.: Doubleday & Company, 1960).

years just preceding anschluss, built up further by the Germans, and completed by the European Recovery Program (ERP).

By 1936 Austrians had begun to build the heavy industry base that their economy lacked in 1918, and they had moved to a position of almost complete self-sufficiency in food production. But by then the First Republic had already been undermined. Political causes that no amount of economic change could impede were working for its destruction. During the Nazi period, by a rather marvelous dialectical irony (neither Hegelian nor Marxist), still more progress was made in the Austrian economy. Hitler's war planning called for a vast investment of German capital in the development of heavy industry in the Austrian Gaue. As we have already seen, most of this industry was in the western areas, which greatly diminished the *Wasserkopf* character of the Vienna Basin vis-à-vis the rest of Austria.

The period of Allied occupation, from 1945 to 1955, reinforced the trend toward overall industrial strength and economic decentralization. Vienna, Lower Austria, and parts of Styria suffered serious setbacks from Russian expropriation and the removal eastward of numerous industrial installations that were considered German property. But Marshall Plan aid provided a second great capital injection comparable in magnitude to the German investment of the war period. During 1948–1952 one-third of the net investment was financed by ERP counterpart funds. And the ensuing export boom that resulted from the working out of the multiplier effect of the international business cycle permitted not only a quick amortization of the capital invested in previous years but also a further expansion of the industrial plant which appeared to arise entirely out of profits. With the ending of the Soviet occupation in 1955, considerable private foreign capital flowed into the eastern provinces of the Vienna Basin, which has helped compensate for Russian plundering there.[4] The coalition encouraged domestic saving and investment through its fiscal policy. At one point, tax exemptions were granted on up to 20 percent of profits for amounts kept in reserve for capital expenditures. Other forms of tax exemption and depreciation allowances were also employed.[5]

4. Vodopivec, *Die Balkanisierung Österreichs,* pp. 24–28.
5. Siegler, *Austria: Problems and Achievements,* pp. 138–39.

The last years of the war and the first of the occupation had played havoc with the Austrian economy. By 1947 industrial production stood at 61.7 percent of that for 1937, the last year before the anschluss. Agricultural production was at about the same level. The gross national product was just under 71 percent of that of 1937. In three short years, however, industrial production was up to 147 percent of the 1937 level and agricultural production, recovering more slowly, to 94.1 percent. The gross national product was 120.6 percent, and it has been climbing steadily ever since.

Demographic and Economic Development from the 1950s to the Present

From 1951 onward, demographic change has been more measured than during the preceding period of civil conflict, anschluss, and war. From 1951 to 1961, for example, Vienna's population stabilized and actually increased by .7 percent. Lower Austria and the Burgenland declined in population by less than 2 percent. And the greatest population spurt in the growing areas was 16.9 percent, in the Vorarlberg. Elsewhere, increases were only between slightly more than 2 percent and slightly more than 8 percent.

The same measured pace has been maintained since 1961 according to available statistics. From 1961 to 1967 Vienna's population increased by .6 percent. Lower Austria and the Burgenland were virtually static, showing a decline of .2 percent and .9 percent respectively. Vorarlberg again showed the greatest growth rate— 15 percent. Increases elsewhere ranged from 3.5 percent to 10.2 percent.[6] In other words, only five years after the inception of coalition government the great change, which had put Austria definitely on the urban side of the rural-urban dichotomy and had broken the urban monopoly of Vienna by distributing population to half a dozen growing industrial centers, had come to an end. The fifteen years from 1951 to 1966 were a period of measured change during which the consensual attitudes necessary for the successful replacement of the coalition by majority-party government were able to

6. Statistisches Zentralamt, *Stat. Nachrichten,* 22 (N.F.), Heft 10 (October 1967): 629, cited in Karl Selber, "Die regionale Bevölkerungsumschichtung innerhalb Österreichs in den letzten drei Jahrzehnten und ihre politische Auswirkungen," mimeographed (Vienna, 1968), p. 7.

develop. The differential rate of population shifts between 1934 and 1951 and between 1951 and 1967 is shown clearly in table 3. (The percentage changes since 1961 given above refer to the table cited in note 6, whose base year is 1961, not to table 3, whose base year is 1934.)

Table 3. Growth of Population, 1934 to 1967
(1934 = 100)

		By State		
	1934	1951	1961	1967
Vienna	100	83.5	84.1	84.6
Lower Austria	100	96.8	95.0	94.7
Burgenland	100	92.2	90.5	89.7
Upper Austria	100	122.8	125.3	132.9
Salzburg	100	133.1	141.3	155.7
Tyrol	100	122.4	132.6	143.9
Vorarlberg	100	124.6	145.6	167.5
Styria	100	109.3	112.1	116.4
Carinthia	100	117.2	122.2	128.4
Austria	100	102.6	104.6	108.3

		By Region		
	1934	1951	1961	1967
Vienna	100	83.5	84.1	84.6
East	100	96.0	94.2	93.9
West	100	124.4	131.1	141.9
South	100	111.5	115.0	119.8
Austria	100	102.6	104.6	108.3

SOURCE: Same as for table 2; p. 9.

While demographic change slowed after 1951, industrial development spurred rapidly ahead. By 1963 industrial production was at 342 percent of the 1937 level, agricultural production at 128.5 percent and gross national product at 232.1 percent.[7] Since 1963 the expansion has been more measured but still noteworthy. Taking 1963 as the new base year, industrial production was up 17 percent in 1967 and agricultural production 4 percent. Total product in 1966 was 13 percent higher than that for 1963 and per capita

7. Figures published by the Austrian Institute for Economic Research.

product was up 12 percent. In dollars, the gross national product increased from $7,799,000,000 to $10,635,000,000 between 1963 and 1967.[8]

The most recent figures show that the same growth pattern is continuing. The monthly report of the Austrian Institute for Economic Research for September 1969 showed an unusually high rate of growth in industrial production for the first half of 1969, with the most marked expansion in capital goods. Industrial production per working day had increased at the summer's end by 13 percent over the 1968 figure, and overall industrial production had grown 5.5 percent. In 1970 Austria's gross national product increased by almost 7 percent, surpassing that of the Western European countries.[9]

The Urban-Rural Balance

The widely scattered new urban centers that compete with Vienna for population and economic power contribute to a balance in Austrian life in many ways. Their distribution throughout Austria and the network of communications that link them to one another have put the remaining rural areas of Austria under urban influence. No part of the country is now more than one and a half hours by car from an urban center. The goods and services of the city flow out through the countryside to the smallest village. The villager meets the city dweller constantly on holiday, listens to and watches the radio and television programs that emanate from the city, buys the newspapers published in the city. Note, for example, Burg Bernstein, one of a string of historic fortresses built in the line of hills now known as the Burgenland in defense against marauders coming across the Hungarian plain. The ancient countryside, the castle, and the tiny town which nestles at its feet look much like they must have looked 400 years ago during the Turkish Wars. Yet a modern road puts the place within slightly over an hour of Vienna. And

8. United Nations Statistical Office, *Statistical Yearbook 1968*, 20th ed. (New York, 1969), pp. 111, 166, 550, 554, 591.
9. Summarized in Austrian Information Service, *Austrian Information*, New York, September 1969, p. 2; March 1971, p. 2.

in the window of the town's hardware store are displayed all the modern appliances available in Europe, from deep freezes and televisions to the most modern of plumbing fixtures. Viennese tourists on holiday swarm through the village, buying souvenirs of local manufacture and refreshing themselves in the several inns and restaurants there.

The old parochial ways have begun to break down even in the most out-of-the-way places. One writer reports that the traditional rural reliance on neighbors for help in such things as house-raising, fire protection, care during illness, coping with death, and obtaining farm tools and animals is in sharp decline. Reciprocal neighborly help, which creates dependence on the local community, is giving way to the market principle and cash exchange, which is the way of the city. A study done in Germany in the early 1950s showed that between 14.3 and 33.5 percent of the sample were opposed to dependence on neighbors. The respondents painted an ideal of independence and said that they preferred to pay for help.[10] Similar attitudinal changes are occurring in Austria. Voluntary organizations and insurance companies are increasingly taking over neighbor-help functions, and this, in turn, creates an increasing dependence on modern organization and its leadership rather than on spontaneous community aid. Free-time relationships are changing, too; recreation groups that spread beyond the borders of neighborhoods and towns are developing rapidly. Sports groups are oriented to the nearest central town or city rather than to one small village. In addition, political parties and unions also make for meaningful nonparochial attitudes.[11]

Another bridge between urban and rural consists in the person of the commuting worker. In 1961 one-fifth of the nonagricultural Austrian workers were employed in an area distant from their places of residence. For the most part, these are persons who are unable to make a living tilling their unproductive small farms and so contract to be bussed daily to a neighboring urban center where

10. Gerhard Wurzbacher, et al., *Das Dorf im Spannungsfeld industrieller Entwicklung* (Stuttgart: F. Enke, 1954), cited in Reichhold, *Zwanzig Jahre Zweite Republik*, p. 243.
11. Ibid.

they can pursue an industrial occupation by day and be returned to their villages in the evening.[12]

The wide discrepancy between urban and rural incomes is not a factor in the movement toward integration. Productivity in the industrial sections is double that in the agricultural areas, with the result that there is an almost 3:1 difference in income between the richest and poorest counties. Nevertheless, the widespread population movements of the last twenty-five years have produced an equalizing tendency. The wide gap between farm and city income is beginning to narrow.[13] It is also significant that rationalization of production led to an average increase in agricultural productivity of 6 percent per year during the period 1951–61; this was greater than the increase in any other branch of the economy, including industry, for the same period.[14]

Austria remains a country with a conservative and traditionalist image of itself. A government spokesman addressing a Fulbright group in September 1965 expressed this by saying that when new products—a new toothpaste or breakfast cereal, for instance—are introduced in Western Europe it takes years before they are accepted in Austria. In the area of allegiance, this conservatism places *Heimatgefühl*—parochial attachment to one's hometown and home Land—at the top of the list of group allegiances. "We are first and foremost Tyroleans"; "Write well of our beloved Carinthia"; "We are Bayuvaren, they over the mountain are Alemannen." (More about these images and of their importance may be found in chapter 6.) But the increasing lateral mobility of the past twenty-five years is beginning to erode parochialism and open up people's horizons. The population of the urban centers is becoming a mixture of people from all over Austria. From 1951 to 1961 approximately two million Austrians, nearly one-third of the total population, moved to another city or town.[15] And the influx of persons from

12. Hans Seidel, et al., *Die regionale Dynamik der österreichischen Wirtschaft*, Öst. Institut für Wirtschaftsforschung, Studien u. Analysen, no. 1, (Vienna, 1966), p. 27.

13. Felix Butschek, "Regionalpolitik im luftleeren Raum," *Die Presse*, January 14/15, 1967, p. 5.

14. Seidel, et al., *Die Regionale Dynamik*, p. 19.

15. Butschek, "Regionalpolitik," p. 5.

abroad—especially from Greece, Yugoslavia, Turkey, Spain—to
work in the new and growing industries increases from year to year.

Social Change

Little empirical study has been done on social change in Austria.
Such evidence as we have, however, indicates emerging social patterns that are the logical correlates of the processes of political and
economic modernization that we have been describing. Austrian
society is becoming more and more middle class, in fact and in
mentality. Status rests on education and income as standards of
achievement rather than on background, family ties, or previous
position within the community, and intergenerational vertical mobility is on the increase.

A detailed study of social stratification subjectively perceived was
done in Vienna in 1967 by the Institute for Empirical Social Research (IFES).[16] The method used was a random sample survey
of 1,250 persons selected by street address. Approximately 1,022
usable interviews were produced. No weighting was required in
the evaluation of the results since the distribution of respondents
according to such characteristics as age, sex, occupation, education,
and income agreed very closely with the distribution reported in
the previous census.

When asked to rank themselves socially on a scale of six social
strata, the majority of those interviewed placed themselves either
in the middle-middle stratum or in the lower-middle stratum. The
polar extremes of upper stratum and lower stratum were equally
thinly populated. Subjective rankings were not fully identical with
objective rankings according to occupation, education, and income,
though a distinct correlation was found. Subjective ranking by income produced a noticeably lower stratification and ranking by
social performance (*Leistung*) a significantly higher stratification
than the one based on general considerations. Education and occupation played primary roles in determining social performance,
and the possession of prestige goods such as autos a secondary one.

It is interesting to note that when the respondents were asked to

16. Institut für empirische Sozialforschung, *Sozialschichtung im Vorstel-
lungsbild der Wiener Bevölkerung,* mimeographed (Vienna, 1967).

rank themselves in terms of a class model of society, the old ways of thought were found still to prevail. Forty-five percent of the sample saw themselves as members of the working class, an identification that met with total rejection in comparable American studies. (The choices in the class model were "upper bourgeoisie" [*Grossbürgertum*], "intelligentsia," "petite bourgeoisie" [*Kleinbürgertum*], and "working class.") This is no doubt a result of both the strong Socialist allegiance of the Viennese worker and his continued indoctrination in traditional concepts by the highly organized Socialist party in which he spends so much of his time. That the working-class identity is becoming a vestigial remain as an indicator of social division and political polarization, however, is attested by the clustering at the center of the "stratum" model. The new reality of growing social and political homogeneity is expressed when a new vocabulary is used. Consonant with this conclusion were the survey's findings on feelings of discontent with the status quo. While the lowest strata of the sample expressed a broad sense of injustice, this was vague, poorly articulated, and poorly focused, without specific and clear goals. Acute, specific material dissatisfaction was expressed by the upper half of the middle stratum, especially by academicians and persons with the equivalent of a junior college education. "The stable element of our society," concludes the IFES study at this point, "is the broad middle stratum with its tendencies to entertain an unduly grand image of itself and display a somewhat philistine self-satisfaction." [17]

The survey found considerable evidence of upward mobility, which fits well with other evidence of the emergence of an open, modern democratic society in Austria. Old established Viennese families were found to have no clear social advantage. New arrivals in Vienna tend to enter at the lower levels of social standing but

17. Ibid., p. 58. A Marxist analysis of social change in the Second Republic, using national data, points to evidence of increased upward mobility throughout the country and an increase in skilled in comparison with unskilled labor, involving a higher wage structure, shorter hours, longer vacations. In conjunction with this increased well-being of the worker there has been a loss of political consciousness and the development of an interest in public policy producing short-term benefits; this replaces the earlier interest in ideological utopias of the future. See Eduard März, "Die Klassenstruktur der Zweiten Republik," in *Probleme der österreichischen Politik* I (Vienna: Verlag der Wiener Volksbuchhandlung), 1968, pp. 67 ff.

rise relatively quickly to higher positions. It is interesting to note that persons from western Austria constitute an especially large element among the Viennese elite. It was after World War II, the survey found, that the old, rigid class barriers began to loosen up significantly. Women from working-class families, it was found, tend to rise more easily than men from the same class. Persisting immobility was found to derive chiefly from educational deficiencies and from lack of desire for educational opportunity.

We have no comparable data for other Austrian cities. But it seems fairly certain that if Vienna, the chief center of social discord and ideological politics in the past, is moving toward a more open and equal society, the same trend will be found in the newer and more vigorous cities of western Austria.

Political Change

The National Assembly elections of March 1966 may turn out to be a watershed in Austrian electoral politics. That year one of the two major parties won a clear majority of seats in the lower house of the Austrian parliament for the first time since 1945 (when a large segment of the potential electorate, former Nazis, were still excluded from the polls). The balance between the two parties had oscillated narrowly through the six previous elections, yielding a slim plurality of the popular vote first for the Conservatives, then for the Socialists, but never producing a parliamentary majority.[18] In 1966 the People's party won 85 seats, the Socialist party 74, and the Freedom party 6. The Conservative plurality in the popular vote was 48.35 percent, the largest won by any party to that time, except for the skewed result of 1945. Perhaps the most significant statistic of the 1966 election was the 5.8-percent difference between the two major parties in the popular vote, the greatest margin of difference between the two chief contenders in any election of the Second Republic, including that of 1945.

Statistics showing the distribution of votes around the country in the seven parliamentary elections between 1945 and 1966 reveal

18. For an extensive report on electoral behavior and electoral images of the parties for the period down to 1963, see Karl Blecha, et al., *Der durch-leuchtete Wähler* (Vienna: Europa Verlag, 1964.) The report is based on survey research carried out by the Social Science Study Society of Vienna.

a trend toward nationalization in Austrian politics which at a certain point in development would be expected to produce just such
a break with the earlier pattern of electoral performance as occurred in 1966 (see tables 4 and 5). Vienna, traditionally the major

Table 4. National Assembly Elections: Major Parties' Share
of Valid Ballots
(In percentages)

		1945	1949	1953	1956	1959	1962	1966
Vienna	ÖVP	34.5	35.2	30.7	35.9	34.4	34.5	37.9
	SPÖ	57.1	49.5	50.2	49.7	52.4	52.4	49.4
Lower Austria	ÖVP	54.5	52.5	48.5	51.8	50.6	52.0	54.1
	SPÖ	40.4	37.3	39.9	41.2	42.1	41.6	41.4
Styria	ÖVP	52.9	42.9	40.7	45.6	44.7	46.5	49.7
	SPÖ	41.7	37.4	41.1	44.0	45.3	43.2	43.8
Upper Austria	ÖVP	59.0	45.0	46.2	50.4	47.3	48.6	51.3
	SPÖ	38.4	30.8	38.4	40.3	42.0	41.3	40.3
Carinthia	ÖVP	39.8	33.7	28.9	33.7	32.7	34.2	36.9
	SPÖ	48.8	40.7	48.1	48.1	50.5	49.7	49.6
Tyrol	ÖVP	71.2	56.3	55.1	62.9	59.4	61.9	64.5
	SPÖ	26.6	23.8	29.2	29.6	31.5	30.0	28.2
Salzburg	ÖVP	56.7	43.7	42.5	47.2	44.2	46.1	48.1
	SPÖ	39.5	33.6	35.4	36.1	38.7	38.4	36.1
Burgenland	ÖVP	51.9	52.5	48.3	49.1	47.3	48.7	51.2
	SPÖ	44.8	40.5	44.7	46.0	46.5	46.3	45.4
Vorarlberg	ÖVP	70.0	56.4	55.5	60.8	56.4	55.9	61.8
	SPÖ	27.5	18.9	22.7	26.8	30.1	28.0	22.1
Austria	ÖVP	49.8	44.0	41.3	46.0	44.2	45.4	48.3
	SPÖ	44.6	38.7	42.1	43.0	44.8	44.0	42.6

NOTE: FPÖ, KPÖ, and other parties make up difference between totals shown
and 100 percent.
SOURCE: *Die Wahlen in den Bundesländern seit 1945*, 2. erweit. Aufl. (Vienna:
Verbindungsstelle der Bundesländer, 1966), p. 18.

Socialist stronghold, is becoming increasingly a two-party city, while
in the rest of Austria, where, for the most part the People's party
has held a large margin, greater equality is also developing between
the two parties. A 24-percent lead held by the Socialists over the
Conservatives in Vienna in 1945 had declined to slightly more than
13 points in 1966.[19] The appearance in the field of a large Socialist

19. The computation is based on comparison of the percentage share of
each party in the total vote cast for the *two parties*, not the total vote cast.
For the election of 1966 see Peter Gerlich, et al., *Die Nationalratswahl 1966*
(Vienna: Verlag für Jugend und Volk, 1968).

Table 5. National Assembly Elections: Valid Ballots Received by Major Parties

		1945	1949	1953	1956	1959	1962	1966
Vienna	ÖVP	310,803	401,854	362,148	406,570	383,534	391,985	427,760
	SPÖ	508,214	565,440	590,532	562,763	584,486	595,265	557,496
Lower Austria	ÖVP	384,214	464,784	438,348	461,635	445,569	461,783	478,978
	SPÖ	284,430	330,631	360,791	367,227	370,743	368,302	367,173
Styria	ÖVP	261,358	280,719	269,662	313,510	308,835	327,853	356,703
	SPÖ	205,779	244,482	272,360	302,325	312,776	304,810	313,763
Upper Austria	ÖVP	276,676	268,578	285,308	325,874	313,817	330,057	357,015
	SPÖ	179,975	184,042	236,944	260,938	278,538	280,696	280,310
Carinthia	ÖVP	71,265	83,801	73,015	89,996	88,813	94,639	106,421
	SPÖ	87,572	101,356	121,775	128,494	136,967	137,283	142,813
Tyrol	ÖVP	109,360	127,528	132,655	159,287	154,659	170,148	187,986
	SPÖ	40,857	53,820	70,473	74,865	82,038	82,461	82,073
Salzburg	ÖVP	71,631	75,215	79,128	90,517	86,875	94,666	104,552
	SPÖ	49,965	57,752	65,871	69,147	75,966	79,020	78,564
Burgenland	ÖVP	68,108	86,700	81,373	81,516	76,788	80,456	85,700
	SPÖ	58,917	66,739	75,240	76,265	75,587	76,389	76,006
Vorarlberg	ÖVP	48,812	57,402	60,140	71,081	69,153	72,914	85,994
	SPÖ	19,189	19,262	24,531	31,271	36,834	36,459	30,787
Austria	ÖVP	1,602,227	1,846,581	1,781,777	1,999,986	1,928,043	2,024,501	2,191,109
	SPÖ	1,434,898	1,623,524	1,818,517	1,873,295	1,953,935	1,960,685	1,928,985

SOURCE: Same as for table 4; pp. 20, 21.

splinter party, the Demokratische Fortschrittliche Partei (DFP), led by dissident Socialist chief Franz Olah, cannot account for the dramatic Socialist decline of 1966. Olah won 7 percent of the total vote cast in Vienna, but the percentage loss of the Socialist party in comparison with its 1962 vote did not match the Olah returns in any one of the Viennese districts. In many cases it was about half of the percentage polled by Olah, in some instances only one-third. At the same time, the Conservative share of the total Vienna vote increased in every district of the city by between 1.9 percent and 6.2 percent.

Outside Vienna, an original Conservative predominance was modified by marked Socialist gains until 1959, though subsequent Socialist losses reversed the trend in the 1962 and 1966 elections. While the parties are competing on an increasingly equal footing in the country as a whole, the voting in 1966 did not yield a more equal division of the popular vote between the two major parties than ever before but a decisive plurality for one party distributed in such a way as to yield a parliamentary majority. As the parties nationalize, the likelihood of an electoral victory for one or the other of them increases rather than declines. For nationalization results from increasing homogenization of the population, which flows from all the social and economic changes discussed above. These things together spell increased political consensus and therefore an increased likelihood that one of the two parties will be the bearer of the "general will" in any particular election. There has thus emerged a more purely two-party system than Austria had previously ever known.

The chief reason that the People's party rather than the Socialist party came to embody the "general will" in 1966 seems to be that the decisive stratum of the electorate, which gave it that victory, saw it as the kind of party that in its structure and program fit more into the picture of nationalized, consensual politics than any other in the field. While some interpretations of the electoral result attribute the victory to special aspects of the 1966 campaign (e.g., the Olah defection from Socialist ranks, a Socialist tactical error in not rejecting Communist support, inept Socialist politics in particular regions) the major voice holds that the Conservatives won because their "image" was more modern and forward looking than

that of the Socialists. Modern, changing Austria wanted a reform of
the coalition system of government, which had earned a reputation
for stalemate, inefficiency, and corruption and appeared to be a
hopelessly outdated instrument for leading Austria toward further
economic and social progress. At this crucial juncture it was ironic
that the conservative party appeared as the enthusiastic proponent
of change and the Socialists appeared as old-fashioned defenders of
the status quo.

During the summer and fall of 1965 impasse had piled upon
impasse, so that finally the coalition partners were unable to agree
on a budget for the coming year. This precipitated the call for new
elections. In this context the People's party made it clear that it
was making a bid for an absolute majority in order to break out of
the confines of the "Grand Coalition," which had proven itself unworkable. Without calling for majority-party government, the People's party promised a search for "new forms of cooperation" that
would give a majority party more freedom to act than the old system based on a "coalition pact" by which the partners renounced
all freedom of independent action. The Socialists, by contrast, simply called for a continuation of the coalition in its old form and
vowed to maintain it even if they won an absolute majority. The
election results show that the new voters in particular, of whom
there were about 400,000, went overwhelmingly into the Conservative column on this issue. Norbert Leser, a leading Socialist publicist
of the right wing, wrote in an election analysis about the "most
unsettling and most decisive aspect of the defeat for the future of
the Socialist movement: namely, the fact that the People's party
succeeded to a greater degree than our party in winning the support
of the young voters, whom in the past our party always led." The
Conservatives had managed to acquire the "image" of being "a
party more suited to youth and more modern than ours." From
conversations with numerous young voters he had concluded that
"the decisive error in the argumentation and general stance of [our]
party in this election was to cling unreservedly to the immobile old-
style coalition which had become discredited in the eyes of the
people." [20]

20. Norbert Leser in *Arbeiter–Zeitung*, Vienna, March 16, 1966.

Other Socialist analysts, trying to ferret out the root cause of their party's unexpected and disastrous defeat mentioned still other old-fashioned aspects of the Socialist campaign. Rupert Gmoser, a political sociologist, complained that "the young voters cannot be reached with the traditions, resentments, and arguments out of the history of the First Republic." He warned that the party could no longer count on strong, serried ranks of disciplined voters who could not be moved by arguments of the opposition. "The so-called class character of the parties" he claimed had "become at least partially an illusion." The People's party was plainly not a party of great capitalists and landlords, nor was the Socialist party a purely working-class party. As the parties further lost their class character there would develop an ever larger group of independent voters ready to switch back and forth among the parties from election to election. Günther Nenning, another Socialist publicist, argued in similar terms. "Socialism" he wrote "will come to power in this country only if it can learn to open up ideologically (*geistig*)." The strongly revisionist party program of 1958 had pointed in this direction but had been shelved because it had been viewed as a propaganda trick. Leser also warned against relying on the power of class consciousness and argued that ideological and organizational reform ought to take the 1958 program as its point of departure.[21]

Arthur Bekker, a non-Socialist analyst writing in the liberal Catholic journal *Die Furche,* echoed Nenning's charge of ideological irrelevance.

The last few years appeared to herald a regression to a new orthodoxy. But in a consumer society, which in many respects has been created by the Socialists themselves, one cannot act as though one were still living in a situation of exploitation like that of the nineteenth century. The party cannot be integrated by exploitation today. The more well-being they have the more the masses are inclined to follow those who promise them not old-time Socialist equality but rather the increase of consumer values for the individual.

21. Quotations from Gmoser and Nenning are from a multiauthored election analysis published in *Die Presse,* Vienna, March 12/13, 1966, p. 5.

And as for the youth, "What is something like 'February 1934' [the year of the Conservative-Socialist civil war] to the masses of today's youth?" [22]

It was not only its unattractiveness to new voters that cost the Socialist party the election, however. In Vienna, for example, even if all 19,000 of the city's new voters had gone Conservative, the other 16,692 of the 35,692 Conservative increase must have come from other segments of the population. Nor would adding in Freedom party losses have produced this number.[23]

One writer argues that a careful scrutiny of the results indicates that 100,000 former Socialist voters must have switched over to the Conservative side.[24] The Conservatives reported, presumably on the basis of their own survey research, that half of the 2.4 million Austrian workers had voted Conservative in the 1966 election.[25] Reasons like those catalogued may well have been motivating factors.

Other sins, all adding up to the same thing—old-fashionedness and irrelevance to the situation of modern Austria—were cast in the faces of the Socialist leaders by articulate critics within their own party. Rupert Gmoser, a Styrian, pointed to centralistic Viennese control of the party as a problem and called for more federalism. Policy ideas originating in the other Länder had little chance of acceptance, given the existing form of party organization.[26] Although he apparently differed with Gmoser on the need to move in a federalist direction, Leser also saw outmoded organization as a contributory cause of the 1966 defeat and called in his analysis for establishment of a commission on organizational reform to recommend reforms to the next party congress.[27] Gmoser hinted that the procedures for recruiting leaders who could offer strong competition to the opposing party had ossified over the years.[28] Non-Socialist

22. Arthur Bekker, "Analyse einer Niederlage," *Die Furche*, March 19, 1966.
23. Günther Templ, "Nicht nur Olah und das Glück," *Die Presse*, March 10, 1966.
24. Hannes Herber, "Wer hat wen gewählt?" *Die Furche*, March 12, 1966, p. 1.
25. *Die Presse*, March 16, 1966.
26. *Die Presse*, March 12/13, 1966.
27. *Arbeiter–Zeitung*, March 16, 1966.
28. *Die Presse*, March 12/13, 1966.

analysts also mentioned organizational superannuation as a root cause of the defeat. Peter Krön, secretary general of Catholic Action in Salzburg wrote:

> The Socialist party has lost contact not only with its voters, but in many cases with its own state and local party functionaries who more than once have been unhappy about decisions made in Vienna. It wasn't the Socialist party that lost the election but rather this self-glorifying, undemocratic, and centralist apparatus which sacrificed its principles to tactical maneuvering.[29]

Bekker commented that in the last years "the bond between the Socialist top leadership and the masses had been much weakened." [30]

The failure of the Socialist leadership to keep up with the changing character of Austrian life and mentality and the corresponding success of the Conservative "Reformers" in doing so to a considerable degree thus led to an electoral revolution that revealed that an extensive economic, demographic, and social revolution had long been going on under the surface of coalition politics. This latter revolution, paradoxically enough, was in part the product as well as the ultimate undoing of those politics.

The defeat of 1966 was a profound learning experience for the Socialists. Galvanized into energetic reform efforts by the shock of their loss of a twenty-year-old power position, the SPÖ, under the able leadership of Bruno Kreisky, bent its efforts during the next four years to updating the party's image among the electorate. By mounting a vigorous but responsible opposition and overhauling party decision-making machinery, the Socialists were able to turn the tables on the Conservatives in the elections of March 1, 1970.

29. *Die Presse*, election analysis, 12/13 March 1966, p. 5.
30. Bekker, "Analyse." From surveys carried out in the early 1960s the Social Science Research Society of Vienna concluded that independent voters "are not the interested, the informed, those who reflect on what they do, who with careful forethought cast their vote now on this, now on that side of the scale, and who thereby, and rightly, serve as the holders of the balance of power. Exactly the opposite is the case. The switchers are the uninformed voters, the unpolitical voters." What this might forebode for the future of Austrian politics were the independent vote to increase as the information above indicates, is difficult to say. See Blecha et al., *Der durchleuchtete Wähler*, pp. 50, 55.

That election did not produce a one-party majority, but the Socialists won a plurality of three seats in the National Assembly, their
first clear victory in twenty-four years, and upset the Conservative
absolute majority, which itself was an entirely new phenomenon in
1966. The victorious party's program was significantly entitled,
"For a Modern Austria." The pattern of rigid, immobile electorates
had been broken in two successive elections.

   In economy, society, and polity Austria had by 1966 acquired
all the salient marks of the developed, modern democratic state.
The economic, social, and political foundations of a viable nation
had been established. The careful behavior of the new one-party
government and its loyal opposition in the subsequent years were
to be both a sign and a guarantee of their stability.[31]

   31. Heinz Hans Fabris has described the role of the mass media in breed-
ing indifference to ideological aspects of politics and in increasing the identification of party images with the images of top leaders. See "Politik aus
zweiter Hand. Massenmedien und Politik in der Zweiten österreichischen
Republik," *Publizistik* 14, no. 3 (1969) :268–76.

4. THE NEW POLITY

Forming a Majority-Party Government

When the Volkspartei took full power in 1966 the head of their strategy-planning political bureau was sent to London to confer with the English Conservatives. He carried with him to the mecca of parliamentary democracy a large notebook filled with questions about how majority-party government is run. Instead of concentrating on collecting the spoils of victory, the triumphant party was most interested in playing the new game precisely according to the book. Learning and abiding by the rules of democratic politics was their first concern. There was to be no repetition of the debacle of 1934.

The behavior of the ÖVP all during the electoral campaign was characterized by a cautious and deliberate spirit of reform. Though making it clear that they were out for a majority in the new parliament, at no time did they say that they intended to exclude the Socialists from the government. Their announced intention was to modify, not abolish, the coalition. In reply to Socialist accusations that the ÖVP intended to establish one-party domination (*Alleinherrschaft*), Chancellor Klaus replied repeatedly that after the election he would invite the Socialists to participate "in new forms of cooperative government" (*zur Zusammenarbeit in neuen Formen auffordern.*)[1]

At no point did either the party or the independent press call for an end to the coalition. Typical was the formula proposed in an editorial in *Die Presse*: "It is . . . up to the Austrians to call the functionaries to order and by making known the will of the majority to bring them (by compelling them to more competition) to a genuine cooperation." [2] Both *Presse* and *Kurier,* however, called for an end to the coalition in its old form and for changes in the

1. *Die Presse,* February 14, 1966.
2. Otto Schulmeister in *Die Presse,* February 19/20, 1966.

system of cooperation that would break the pattern of stagnation in policy making. Beyond this they contented themselves with trying to figure out what the ÖVP had in mind in its talk about "new forms of cooperation."

Caution was still the keynote after March 6. Two days after the election the independent *Kurier* reported that the ÖVP would "invite the SPÖ to enter negotiations looking toward the creation of a new coalition government between these two great parties." [3] On March 12, in a radio address, Chancellor Klaus made this intention public and said further that he did not view the vote of confidence of March 6 as giving him a free hand to exclude the second strongest party from responsibility for the state. [4] On March 14 the invitation was formally extended to Bruno Pittermann, the Socialist party chief, and arrangements were made to have negotiations for the formation of a government conducted by a committee of six, one three-man team representing each party.

The first offer by the Conservatives provided that the Socialists would retain all ministries under their primary control, with the exception of Justice, which was to be politically neutralized. Beyond this there would be modifications in favor of the ÖVP in the distribution of functions and jurisdictions among the ministries. For example, all foreign trade matters and the power to conduct negotiations connected with Austrian economic integration in Western Europe were to be removed from the Socialist-controlled Foreign Ministry to the Conservative-controlled Trade Ministry. All functions influencing price formation were to be removed from the Interior Ministry (another Socialist preserve) to the Trade Ministry. The control of subsidies to sports was to be moved from the Socialist Ministry of Social Affairs to the Conservative Education Ministry. Various other similar changes, and a reorganization of the system for supervising nationalized industries, were included in the plan. In addition, the ÖVP refused to give a guarantee that the cooperative arrangement would be retained to any specific date.

The Conservative offer was refused forthwith. The Socialists objected in particular to the absence of a guarantee clause. A counteroffer was thereupon prepared by the Socialist team, and the

3. *Kurier,* March 8, 1966.
4. *Die Presse,* March 14, 1966.

negotiations continued during March and into April. Unable to make substantial headway in obtaining concessions, the Socialists decided to call a special party congress to discuss the possibility of the unprecedented step of going into opposition and to draw up still further coalition proposals which would have grassroots support. The congress was held but was unable to produce a clear agreement on the opposition question. The matter was then put back into the hands of the original negotiating team, which returned to the negotiating table for a few more days. When it was finally clear that no substantial concessions could be expected from the Conservatives, the Socialist Parliamentary Club decided on April 18, by a vote of 30 to 10 with approximately 10 abstentions, to go into opposition.[5] Thus, it was six weeks after the Conservatives had won a clear electoral majority before Austria was ready to embark on the uncharted course of majority-party government.

At this point caution continued to govern the councils of the Volkspartei. The sensitive Ministry of Justice was given to a well-known but politically neutral professor of law at the University of Innsbruck, Dr. Hans Klecatsky, instead of to a powerful party chief with an organized interest behind him. When photographs of the ministerial candidates were assembled for the evening papers on April 18, it was discovered that none was available of Dr. Klecatsky, who was not a party member. Chosen to head the Foreign Ministry, again formerly a principal Socialist preserve, was Dr. Lujo Toncic-Sorinj, another person known more for his expertise than as a feudal lord of the Conservative baronage. A member of the National Assembly from Salzburg, Toncic was a chief Conservative spokesman on foreign affairs in that body, and he had frequently served as a representative of his government to various international bodies. Fritz Bock retained his position as minister of trade and in addition was named vice-chancellor since he was the oldest member of the government. The intention of the Conservatives to appear as a party of all the people and to demonstrate goodwill to the workers, many of whom had defected from their Socialist allegiance in the March election, was evidenced in the apportionment of cabinet seats to the three federations that compose the Volkspartei. The Workers Federation (ÖAAB) received eight, the largest number.

5. *Wochenpresse,* April 20, 1966.

Five went to the Business Federation (Wirtschaftsbund) and three to the Farm Federation (Bauernbund).

The "new look" of a modern, up-to-date party which the Conservatives had so masterfully developed during the campaign was displayed in still other ways in the construction of the new government. For the first time a cabinet seat was given to a woman, Grete Rehor, who was put in charge of the Ministry of Social Affairs, a former province of the Socialists. A Viennese, Mrs. Rehor had figured in the Christian Labor movement as deputy chairman of the third largest union in Austria. The new federalist emphasis was evident in the choice of several provincials as ministry heads. Franz Hetzenauer, chosen as minister of the interior, was from Tyrol, as was Dr. Klecatsky, the nonpolitical justice minister. Dr. Ludwig Weiss, designated minister of communications, was a Carinthian, and Foreign Minister Toncic a Salzburger.

The same tone of responsible and up-to-date democratic leadership was sounded in the government's policy statement (*Regierungserklärung*) to the new parliament. It contained a prominent commitment to constitutional government and the efficient administration of justice, underlining the effort at political neutralization of this policy area by the appointment of Klecatsky. A determination to strengthen the policy-making role of parliament, for a long time a sore point with the public, was also stressed. And a renewed commitment was undertaken to carry forward programs in a variety of policy areas in which progress had been promised two years earlier but not made (allegedly because of the handicap of the coalition "veto"): promotion of economic growth, reorganization of the social security program, reorganization of the nationalized industries, progress in the home-building program.[6]

Learning the Role of Loyal Opposition

On the other side, the Socialists also exercised prudence in their new situation. *Die Presse* headlined: "SPÖ operates cautiously in its opposition role" in a discussion of the National Assembly debate on the program of the new government.[7] The Socialists announced

6. See editorial by Ernst-Werner Nussbaum, *Die Presse,* April 21, 1966.
7. *Die Presse,* April 23/24, 1966.

that they would oversee the government's activities carefully but that they were prepared to negotiate all technical and pragmatic (*sachlich*) questions. They would, announced Bruno Pittermann on the floor of the Assembly, compel the ÖVP to live up to such campaign pledges as reduction of the wage tax. They would make full use of their right of interpellation and of petition to force ministers, both in committees and in the full house, to state their positions on particular policy questions. They would pay special attention to the use of tax monies for various subventions.

Bruno Kreisky, who replaced Pittermann as SPÖ party chief in January 1967, made it clear at the beginning of his leadership that he intended to conduct constructive rather than obstructive opposition. He preached to his party friends that they ought not to demand from the Conservative government things that could not be accomplished by Socialists, were they to hold the reins of power.[8] The question of style came up at a May 1967 meeting of a Socialist district organization in Vienna at which representatives of three wings of the party presented their respective views on the course that the opposition ought to adopt. In a discussion of the concept of "class warfare" and its modern political implications, Josef Hindels, speaking for the party's left wing, remarked that opposition politics ought not to be confined to the halls of parliament. Kreisky, a centrist, commented that as long as he was party leader political strikes were out of the question, implying that this was what Hindels had in mind.[9] During the four legislative years from 1966 to 1970 the SPÖ played its opposition role precisely as Kreisky prescribed. The government's program was vigorously criticized in parliamentary debates and in the public media. The question period was extensively used, and Socialist alternatives to proposed government legislation were placed before the National Assembly. At the same time the Socialists avoided obstructive tactics both in and out of parliament, and at the close of debate they frequently voted for government measures in important policy areas.

Here are a few examples. In July 1966, the Socialists hotly contested the economic growth measures proposed by the Conserva-

8. *Die Presse,* February 23, May 2, 1967.
9. Hans Thür, "Partnerschaft an Stelle von Klassenkampf," *Die Presse,* May 9, 1967.

tives, calling them "tax gifts" to businessmen. The wage tax, they argued, should also be substantially diminished and widows' pensions increased. The Socialists on the committee that prepared the draft legislation presented a minority report to the parliament, and alternative legislative drafts were laid before the lower house by the Socialist leadership. At one point in the debate a Socialist speaker argued that it was only because of opposition pressure that there was any provision at all in the Conservative draft law for lowering the taxes of workers. In the end, all the Socialist proposals were voted down and the Conservative program adopted by the Conservative majority with the support of the FPÖ. Nevertheless, the Socialists joined the government to vote for the wage tax provisions of the law.

A few days later a government measure to revise the national defense law came before the National Assembly. In an unusual show of solidarity in an area that has been a controversial one among the parties, the house adopted the reform law unanimously, with both the FPÖ and the SPÖ joining the Conservatives to support it. A political commentator of *Die Presse* speculated that Socialist support for the measure derived from the fact that one of the proposed reforms contained substantial values for their party— the national defense council, an advisory body attached to the office of the chancellor, was to be expanded to include representatives of all the parties having representation on the steering committee of the National Assembly. This looked like a partial restoration of the proportionality (*Proporz*) system which had characterized the government of the "Great Coalition" years. The reform guaranteed the Socialists a voice in the making of defense policy and also established their co-responsibility for defense measures. The designation of a brigadier general sympathetic to the Socialists as chief of the operations group of the army command staff may also have helped produce Socialist support for the law.[10]

A week later a similar thing occurred in another policy area which in the past had been controversial. A law dealing with Austrian colleges and one affecting agricultural schools were adopted by the unanimous vote of all the parties in the house. For public consumption, however, the "pure opposition" stance continued to

10. Walther Urbanek, "Kein Zankapfel mehr," *Die Presse,* July 18, 1966.

be maintained. Summing up the work of the first parliamentary session under a majority-party government, Karl Waldbrunner, second president of the National Assembly and deputy chairman of the Socialist party, declared that the Conservatives had unscrupulously voted down the opposition Socialists on all important questions. In reality, the government's measures had taken form only after prolonged negotiations with the opposition party, throughout the session of parliament.[11] "Toward the end of the session," commented a journalist, "the most important legacy of the coalition came once more into its own—the human atmosphere which unmistakably distinguishes political antagonism from enmity."[12]

Events of August and September 1966 gave eloquent testimony to the workability of the new system of government. The end of August brought heavy rains to Austria which resulted in a wave of disastrous floods. They were a repetition of the catastrophe of a year earlier, during the last months of the old coalition. The parties at that time had been absolutely unable to come to an agreement on measures to relieve the disaster, something that scandalized the entire nation and was probably instrumental in bringing about the collapse of the coalition system. In sharp contrast, the new government brought swift aid to the distressed areas by establishing a comprehensive catastrophe fund as an independent public corporation under the general supervision of the Ministry of Works; this was to be financed by increased income taxes. Parliament was called into special session to deal with the flood problem. As in the case of the college legislation and the revision of the defense law in July, the flood-relief measure was a joint product of the two great parties, not an edict of the ruling Conservatives. But somehow, the parties were able to cooperate more effectively to meet an urgent public need within the framework of majority-party government than within the rubrics of coalition.

The same pattern of opposition-cum-cooperation was maintained by the two great parties thereafter. Much of the formal posturing, thought necessary in the early days, was dropped. An editor of *Die Presse* reported in March 1967 that this was especially noticeable in the work of the committees. Opposition speakers hardly ever

11. Hans Thür, "Derzeit: Befriedigend," *Die Presse,* July 19, 1966.
12. Ibid.

complained any longer that the Conservatives were inconsiderately railroading their proposals through the committee stage. And Conservative committee members seemed to have lost their anxiety about accepting minor Socialist changes in government drafts. The Socialists tended more and more to treat outstanding differences between government and opposition as simply differences of opinion concerning the most effective ways to resolve commonly acknowledged problems and ceased to pillory the Conservatives at every turn of the road as ill-willed lackeys of big business.[13] Altogether, the Socialists supported two-thirds of the laws passed by the parliament during the first year after the installation of the Conservative government.[14]

This is not to say that the Socialists had forgotten how to oppose or that all major differences were settled in the lobbies and committee rooms. Old quarrels still flared from time to time and produced a hardening of fronts and a chilling of the parliamentary atmosphere. A Conservative proposal to alter the Tenant Protection law in the interest of the landlord during the early summer of 1967 is a case in point. The press reported that the parliament was in an absolute tumult during the height of the debate which lasted from ten in the morning into the late evening hours. Even the next day, when tempers had cooled somewhat, one of the Socialist speakers referred to "the brutality of the ÖVP." "The right side of the house," he remarked, ought to take note that the SPÖ was not "His Majesty Chancellor Klaus's most humble and obedient opposition." Behind the government's measure to change the rent act he saw "the grimacing face of authoritarian fascism." [15] These were strong words after so long and pleasant a honeymoon. But they remained the exception rather than the rule. In day-to-day policy making much cooperation continued to take place across party lines. And in vital policy areas, opposition was often on matters of technical detail rather than at the level of principle. It is significant to note that when the Socialists unveiled the draft of a new overall economic plan in 1968, its basic tone and tendency appeared remark-

13. Detleff Harbich, in *Die Presse*, March 22, 1967.
14. *Die Presse*, May 20/21, 1967.
15. *Die Presse*, July 1/2, 1967.

ably like the plan that Conservative economist and Minister of Finance Koren had developed for the government.

Changing Leadership Styles: The ÖVP

The men who operated the new system of government were not the same as those who constructed and presided over the "Great Coalition" for the first fifteen years of its life. They differed markedly from their earlier counterparts in background, temperament, outlook, and political style. The difference was especially noticeable on the Conservative side, less so among the Socialists, in whom it appeared later.

Among the Conservatives the great line of demarcation between the old and the new leadership was drawn in 1960. In that year Alphons Gorbach replaced Julius Raab as party chairman, Alfred Maleta became first deputy chairman in place of Lois Weinberger, and Hermann Withalm replaced Felix Hurdes as secretary general. The top leadership cadre, which was to accomplish the electroal revolution of 1966, was complete when Josef Klaus replaced Gorbach as party chairman and chancellor in 1963. That the advent to power of the new leaders signaled a change was evident at the outset: most of these men were leaders of the faction which had already achieved an identity as Reformers.

The spirit of the regime instituted by these men has been aptly epitomized by Gottfried Heindl, who served as party manager of the ÖVP during the first years after the intraparty victory of the Reformers over the old Core Group, whose members and mentality were described in chapter 2. In an article entitled "What is a Reformer?" which he contributed to the March 1963 issue of the Conservative monthly journal, *Das Österreichische Monatsheft,* Heindl wrote: "The Reformer does not like to do politics with a wineglass, but rather with a sliderule in his hand." The new men prefer the efficiency of long-range calculation based on survey-research data to the intuitionist politics of their predecessors. They are, in short, rational managers, who use all the qualities such a label implies in their choice of goals and methods.

The Reformers have had no more use for the abstract tenets of "solidarism" (see page 71*n*) than for the Natural Law doctrines of their predecessors. Their pragmatism is infinitely more thorough-going and absolute than that of the Core Group founders, and their chief norm is efficiency rather than compromise—efficiency in democratic vote getting, coalition building, problem solving. This has led them (beginning with Gorbach, Klaus's immediate pred-ecessor, himself a former concentration camp inmate) to extend the open hand of reconciliation to the former Nazis and Pan-Ger-mans—who constitute a substantial portion of the middle class—in order to swell their electoral ranks to the proportions of a win-ning coalition. (The remnants of the Core Group now on the party's sidelines have viewed this as a kind of treason.)

The emotional bonds of penance and common suffering that the founding Core Group felt for the Socialists were entirely lacking in the Reformers. With the exception of Gorbach, all the reform leaders are a generation younger than the members of the Core Group and were not confined in concentration camps. They were critical of Raab for having given in, allegedly unnecessarily, to Socialist demands in his last years. Unlike the Core Group, whose Christian Social economic doctrine, in its corporative and com-munitarian emphasis, had an affinity in many points to the eco-nomics of socialism, these men are unapologetic, ardent proponents of private enterprise. In this area they are more properly seen as the intellectual descendants of the middle-class liberalism of the First Republic rather than as participants in the mainstream of Christian socialism. In defense of the values of private enterprise they were prepared to stigmatize local socialism by confounding it with communism and with the "threat from the East," a tactic very different from those of the "solidarist" Core Group. With all this, the reformers did not neglect to incorporate into their program values for the working man.

That the ÖVP should develop into a coalition of diverse interest groups whose chief aim is to gain and hold power through a pro-gram of pragmatic problem solving is the logical culmination of structural dynamics built into the organization at its inception. As a federation of three organizations representing widely diverging economic interests, the party was fated to develop a complicated decision-making system operating on the basis of intraparty com-

promise rather than according to the norms of Christian Social
ideology. The need for party unity to achieve such vital and un-
contested goals as the State Treaty, the removal of occupation
forces, and basic economic stability produced an unusual degree
of centralization through charismatic personal power during the
years of Julius Raab's chairmanship (1953–60). As a middle-class
businessman and head of the business wing of the ÖVP (Österreichischer Wirtschaftsbund) Raab also led the party during these
years away from its earlier Christian Social economics in the direction of liberalism. This was signaled by the appointment in
January 1952 of Dr. Reinhard Kamitz, the prototype of the liberal
economist, as minister of finance. (Kamitz's connection with the
ÖVP had been slight. He had never made a strong political commitment and was above all the technical expert. From 1934 to
1938 he had been a research associate at the Austrian Institute for
Market Research, and during the anschluss he worked for the
Chamber of Commerce on financial and organizational questions.
After the war he rose to the position of deputy secretary general
of the Federal Chamber of Commerce.) With the achievement of
independence, the end of the occupation, and the beginnings of the
"economic miracle," the urgent need for central direction had
ended, and upon Raab's retirement from the leadership in 1960
because of illness, the federal principle vigorously reasserted itself.[16]

Since 1960 there have been no more "lonely decisions" (*einsame
Beschlüsse*) by the man at the top. The watchword is now broker
politics, presided over until 1970 by a secretary general who understood how to play the role of wheelhorse of the system and
supported by a more highly structured central party apparatus than
the party had earlier had. As a young lawyer in the early 1930s,
Hermann Withalm held only the minor public office of notary
public in the Lower Austrian town of Poysdorf. Suspended from
his law practice by the Nazis, he spent most of the war years in
the army. Resuming his work in 1945, Withalm entered national
politics and won election from a Lower Austrian constituency to
the National Assembly in 1953. After a period as state secretary
in the Ministry of Finance, he accepted the post of secretary general of the Conservative party in 1960. Technically a member of

16. See Vodopivec, *Wer Regiert in Österreich?* p. 65.

the Businessmen's Association, he has no strong personal ties to the business interests and was therefore able to operate his office from a position of neutrality among the three federations of the party.

Despite the nickname "Iron Hermann," Withalm acted the honest broker rather than the strong party leader during his ten years as secretary general. He has described his role as one of "coordinating" the divergent elements of his party. Given the structure of the party, the only route to decision was through "ingenious resolution" (*geniale Lösung*) of which he was the catalyst. He played his balancing role by "talking, talking, talking" and by using the resources of his office. During the period of majority-party government from 1966 to 1970 his "office" actually consisted of three positions—secretary general of the Conservative party (which gave him leverage among the constituent federations), vice-chancellor (which gave him leverage in the administration), and Parliamentary Club chairman (which gave him leverage in the National Assembly). His job was to find ways of fitting the various interests together to further the development of party policy.[17]

When asked shortly after the ÖVP had established itself in power what the basis of its success was, Dr. Withalm replied that the party's good fortune followed from the *Ausgleichung* of Austrian society. This term literally means "equalization," "accommodation," and "settlement" and is probably best rendered as "the development of a democratic and consensual Austria." While there remain problems of regional poverty, he said, especially in eastern Austria, where the Russian occupation took a heavy economic toll, there are no longer the very rich and the very poor. Fundamental structural changes have occurred in the class system, as he sees it, and these have led to the emergence of the social prerequisites of democratic consensus. Interestingly, he sees these changes as a result of governmental policies enacted by the coalition. Only the two major parties working together could have accomplished such social reform. But the very success of these policies in producing a consensual society, as Withalm sees it, superannuated the coalition system.[18]

17. Interview with Hermann Withalm, Vienna, June 12, 1968.
18. Ibid., June 1, 1966.

Dr. Josef Klaus, the fourth chancellor of Austria (1963–70), is a rather different kind of person from the first two chancellors of the Second Republic. Born in Carinthia and educated in Vienna, he became a lawyer in Salzburg and served as governor of that province from 1949 to 1961. His ascent to office symbolizes the equalization of power between Vienna and the other Länder and therewith a step toward political homogenization. The first two chancellors, Figl and Raab, were both Lower Austrians and spent their careers there and in Vienna, extending the Vienna-centered pattern of the First Republic.

Though he was politically active in the 1930s as a Christian Social trade union leader, Klaus held only a minor position in the corporate state, while Figl and Raab were active at the second level of power in the Dollfuss-Schuschnigg period. When war came Klaus served in the German army until 1945, and so he cannot be ranked, like his predecessors, with the "concentration camp generation" whom the Nazis persecuted.

In speaking of his own approach to policy making, Klaus emphasized the importance of employing what he called a *Stil der Sachlichkeit*—an objective, realistic, impartial, and practical style. He equated this with "doing politics in the modern way" (*der moderne Stil der Politik*), an expression that the People's party employed extensively during the 1966 campaign.

The former chancellor sees "modern" or "practical" policy making as involving four things (1) a self-conscious repudiation of ideological presuppositions; (2) "dynamic" policy making; (3) long-term policy planning in place of short-run opportunism and *Durchwursteln* (muddling through), combined with a willingness to take a decision and risk unpopularity; and (4) being able to put oneself in the place of the opposition and see things through its eyes.

Speaking about the importance of having the courage to be decisive and to do unpopular things, Klaus added that the end result of such a course is greater popularity—a statement that indicated that he saw the context in which he operated as a consensual one, an assumption the Core Group never dared to make. Decisiveness in an ideologically divided society leads to civil conflict and this in turn to victory, defeat, or a standoff of an absolute sort. But one would hardly characterize the victor in such a situation as enjoying greater popularity. It is plain that Klaus was thinking of the vast array of policy problems demanding action that had piled up on the coalition's agenda following the decline of the will to cooperate after the relaxation of external pressure in 1955. Under the rules of coalition politics, which required unanimity, these problems could not be resolved, not because of ideological cleavage but because any solution would adversely affect one or more of the well-organized interests that under these rules could exercise a veto.[19]

The conversion of the ÖVP into a liberally oriented, pragmatic coalition has eliminated much of the language of Christian Social idealism from party program pronouncements—but without robbing that idealism of its influence on party policy. The old traditions are maintained, in modernized form, by a cluster of bright young intellectuals who are found for the most part in the ranks of the Austrian Workers and Clerks Federation (ÖAAB), the labor component of the Conservative party. In 1966 Dr. Josef Taus, one of the leading lights of this group and special adviser on economic policy to Dr. Alfred Maleta, head of the ÖAAB, was made head of Austria's nationalized industries and charged with their rationalization after the junking of the inefficient joint Conservative-Socialist board that ran them during the long period of proportionalism and coalition. Catholic social teaching is developed and disseminated at an Institute for Social Policy and Social Reform, which is directed by Dr. Karl Kummer, a representative of the labor wing of the ÖVP in the National Assembly. Dr. Wolfgang Schmitz, the first finance minister of the majority-party regime and subsequently president of the Austrian National Bank, gives courses in economic and social policy there. Dr. Herbert Schambeck, university lecturer, ÖAAB member, and Education Director of the Catholic Fraternity Federation (CV), from which the ÖVP draws its leaders, also teaches there. Dr. Ludwig Reichhold, editor of the party's monthly journal, *Monatsheft,* a man older than the "bright young men" but younger than the members of the Core Group, is another of the leading members of the labor wing's intelligentsia. He is sometimes called upon to ghost-write speeches for the pragmatists among the top leadership. He is the author of a book on left-wing Christian

19. Interview with Chancellor Josef Klaus, Vienna, May 25, 1966.

Social opposition to the authoritative state of 1934–38, which he has dedicated to Leopold Kunschak and Johann Staud, two leaders of that opposition.[20]

In the apparatus of the general secretariat one also finds a number of bright young men whose daily work is to maintain an efficient party organization that can win elections, but whose goals and aspirations for Austria are stated in terms of Christian Social idealism. These men and the ÖAAB intellectuals represent a rather remarkable synthesis of the basically ideological mentality of the Core Group and the pragmatic thinking Reformer. Unlike both of these, however, these intellectuals are consensualist democrats by nature, not men who have learned the politics of democratic compromise the hard way. Their Christian Social ideals are difficult to distinguish from those of a group of young Socialist intellectuals who are also practicing Catholics. More will be said about them in chapter 6.

Reform of the SPÖ

In an earlier chapter we wrote of the refounding of the Austrian Socialist party by a group of moderates who had been active in Socialist politics during the First Republic. Like their counterparts in the Core Group of the People's party, these men were able to play pragmatic roles in the context of the coalition. They remained, nevertheless, committed Marxist "true believers" and looked forward to the day when their ideology would triumph—albeit peacefully and by democratic means. Like the "contractarianism" of the Core Group, that of men like Renner, Schärf, and Helmer was one of dissensus.

In 1957 another kind of leader, the pure pragmatist, appeared on the Socialist scene in the person of Bruno Pittermann. Chosen party chairman by the party congress of that year, he replaced Adolf Schärf as vice-chancellor in the government headed by Julius Raab. Born into a Viennese working-class family in 1905, Pittermann spent his youth as a student and school teacher in Vienna. From 1929 to 1934 he served as secretary of the Chamber of La-

20. Ludwig Reichhold, *Opposition gegen den autoritären Staat* (Vienna: Europa, 1964).

bor in Klagenfurt. Suspended from this position by the Conservative dictatorship, he resumed the study of law which he had begun some years earlier and finished his degree during the period of the corporative state. During the anschluss and war years he worked in a Viennese law office. Unlike his predecessor as vice-chancellor, he was imprisoned neither by the Conservatives nor by the Nazis. Only after the war did he become active in Socialist party politics, standing for election to the National Assembly in 1945. He rose rapidly in the party councils from secretary of the Socialist Parliamentary Club to executive chairman of that group in a few years.

Alexander Vodopivec describes Pittermann as first and foremost "a tactician of power, for whom ideological battles mean little." [21] He finds a significant illustration of this mentality in Pittermann's concern with repudiating the traditional anticlerical Socialist stance and making peace between the Socialist party and the Catholic church in order to facilitate Socialist electoral inroads in those agrarian areas whose social structures were in the process of alteration because of postwar industrialization.[22]

Bruno Kreisky, Pittermann's successor as chairman, was another member of the new leadership group that took the reins of power in 1957. Then a state secretary in the Foreign Office, where he had served in various capacities since 1946, he became minister of foreign affairs in 1959. Born into a well-to-do Jewish family in Vienna in 1911, Kreisky, like Pittermann, studied law. Unlike Pittermann, however, he was active in Socialist underground politics in the mid-1930s and was among the Revolutionary Socialists of the left wing at that. Imprisoned by the Schuschnigg government, Kreisky was allowed by the regime to go into exile before the anschluss occurred. Emigrating to Sweden, he spent the war years working at the scientific secretariat of the Stockholm Consumers' Cooperative. This experience with Swedish socialism was decisive for his later ideological stance, for he came home to Austria after the war converted to a purely pragmatic, non-Marxist socialism.[23] Like Pittermann, he has worked very hard to establish good relations between his party and the Catholic church.

21. Vodopivec, *Wer Regiert in Österreich?* p. 117.
22. Ibid.
23. Ibid., p. 88.

Men of this intellectual cut were fittingly backed up by managerial and technocratic types in other branches of the Socialist leadership. The establishment of Socialist power positions in the extensive nationalized industries had brought men of this kind to the fore long before 1957. Typical of them was Karl Waldbrunner, federal minister for trade and nationalized industry from 1949 to 1956 and after that minister of trade and electrification. In the trade union movement, always a bastion of labor party socialism, even the older leadership took well to the program of pragmatic reform instituted by Pittermann and his cohorts.[24]

Unlike the Reformers of the People's party, however, the non-Marxist pragmatists of reform socialism were not able to obtain the undisputed upper hand in the years after 1959. Classical Marxism remained prominently represented among the top leaders. Christian Broda, minister of justice from 1960 to 1966 had been on the extreme left wing of the party in the "illegal" period of the 1930s and had actually joined the Communist party in Upper Austria in 1945, though he switched over to the Socialists after the November elections that year. Karl Czernetz, head of the education department of the party in the 1930s, holds the position of international secretary of the party and is a leading spokesman on foreign affairs in the National Assembly. His talent for elegant articulation of party ideology has earned him the title of the party's chief ideologist; he calls constantly for his party to return to the orthodox Austro-Marxist doctrines of an earlier day.

Down through the ranks of the Socialist party apparatus, as well as in these key leadership positions, orthodox Marxism continued to be "the true church." Seeing only one another in their daily party work and socializing exclusively in party circles, the party functionary, in contrast to the union official, lived in a closed ideological world that strongly reinforced his ideological outlook and in no way leavened it with outside influences.[25]

Illustrative of the continued importance of dogmatic Marxism for Austrian socialism after 1959 are the events of the Olah affair, which delayed the modernization of the party by several years and constituted one of the causes of the disastrous Socialist defeat in

24. Ibid., p. 119.
25. Ibid.

the 1966 elections. Franz Olah, a man of ambivalent and somewhat volatile temper but with considerable organizational talent and
great political appeal, had risen during the late 1950s to the presidency of the Austrian Labor Union Federation. An ambitious man
with an instinct for power, and unencumbered by allegiance to
Austro-Marxist ideological dogma, he had grasped the necessity
for a general overhaul and modernization of both the union movement and the Socialist party. During his tenure as vice-president
of the union federation he had worked hard to bring young academic blood into its central secretariat, and into the Chambers of
Labor in order to assure a future supply of qualified leaders for
the Socialist party. As a power in the Land organization of the
party in Lower Austria, he also had the opportunity to bring that
Land into an alliance with the western Land organizations, which
have always been pragmatic, never dogmatic, in their Marxist approach to things. As party chairman and leader of such an alliance
he could have broken the power of the Marxist-controlled Viennese organization and accomplished a thoroughgoing reform of the
party's organizational structure.[26]

The reform was not to take place, however, under Olah's auspices, for in 1962 he made the mistake of exchanging his power
position as president of the federation for the post of minister of
the interior—before he had secured the leadership of the Lower
Austrian party organization. Smelling trouble, the ideologists of the
Viennese party launched a counterattack on Olah before he could
bring his weight to bear on them. Articles appeared in the party
monthly, *Die Zukunft,* accusing him of attempting to develop a
"leadership cult." During the summer of 1964 a piece appeared in
the independent *Tiroler Tageszeitung* in which two psychiatrists
known to be of Socialist sympathies announced that they had signed
a statement to the effect that, after lengthy observation, they had
determined that Olah was not of sound mind. Shortly afterward,
charges of misappropriation of union funds during his tenure of
office as president of the union federation were filed against Olah
by his successor, Anton Benya. Law suits followed, and Olah resigned as minister of the interior, was excluded from all union

26. Vodopivec, *Die Balkanisierung Österreichs,* pp. 95–97.

federation offices and, finally, was ousted from the Socialist party.[27] In rancor, he proceeded to found a new political party, which entered the lists of the 1966 national elections and managed to deprive the Socialists of hundreds of thousands of votes because of its leader's personal following (see p. 97).

With Olah's fall accomplished, the Austro-Marxists of the Viennese party remained ensconced in power and continued to belie the "labor party" image which Pittermann, Kreisky, and others among the pure pragmatists were attempting to build. The elections of 1966, which were lost not only because of Olah's defection but also because new voters rallied overwhelmingly to the ÖVP banners, showed that an Austro-Marxist party could not win a plurality in Austria, despite the demographic effects of continuing industrialization.[28]

The results of the 1966 parliamentary elections were of such shattering proportions that the need for a thoroughgoing reform was finally clear to all. Never before had the Conservatives been able to exclude the Socialists from power. The party now found itself out in the cold after twenty years of governing the state in cooperation with the ÖVP. Reform immediately became the order of the day.

A first change was alteration of the party statutes to increase markedly the representation of the provincial party organizations in both the presidium and the executive committee of the party. This meant an automatic pragmatization of party doctrine, since Socialists in the Länder had never been dogmatic Marxists. Growing up as they had in a context of measured and enlightened industrialism, they had no experience of the Viennese class warfare that had made bitter Marxists of the party's nineteenth-century founders, who had shaped the tradition of the Viennese party.

If the Socialists were to become efficient economic problem solvers they required technical experts to advise the party's policy makers. The Conservatives, dramatically emphasizing their abandonment of "wine glass" in favor of "slide rule" politics had in 1966 fashioned their economic program, "Action 20," in collabora-

27. Ibid., p. 101.
28. See ibid., pp. 102–03.

tion with a large technical brain trust recruited from among Conservative economic experts of the academic world. Throughout the period of developing and selling the program, Conservative publicity repeatedly underlined the central role of the expert. The overwhelming victory of the ÖVP at the polls made it clear to the Socialists that they, too, were being called upon to develop a staff of technical experts.

In a symposium entitled "SPÖ—What to Do?" which appeared in *Neues Forum* for April/May 1966 three young intellectuals accused the SPÖ of being the more conservative (i.e., backward) of the two major parties and demanded that a corps of experts be brought in to advise the political decision makers, without which the Socialists could claim no right to administer the technical complexities of the modern state. In April of the following year the response came from the new leadership in the form of a monster Economic Congress of the Socialist party convened in Vienna's Auersperg Palace. It was mostly Kreisky's show. The other politicians stayed rather glumly in the background as the party leader greeted, charmed, and listened to the array of managers, mostly young technocrats of the Gewerkschaftsbund (Labor Federation) and Chambers of Labor, identifying himself and his scholarly interests with them at every point. "I am no lawyer. My sympathy is rather with national economy," he said. "Above all I was a student of economics in Sweden, where I got to know numerous famous professors, including Austrians." [29] The meeting at the Auersperg was only a beginning, he indicated. The experts were invited to organize themselves into working groups which would begin work on a new economic program for the party. Two hundred economists would take part in the discussions.

The upshot of their work was a new economic program, "For a Modern Austria," with which the SPÖ went to the electorate in 1970. Its provisions represented a clear and absolute break with the dogmas of Austro-Marxism. A socialism concerned primarily with distribution was repudiated in favor of one which gave first place to economic growth and whose chief aim was to make Austria into a modern industrial state, after the manner of Sweden. A

29. Manfred Schuhmayer, "Kreisky Mobilisiert Manager und Experten," in *Die Presse*, April 12, 1967.

carefully worked out program of investments was drawn up which included efforts to attract foreign capital. Even the legitimacy and importance of capitalist profit was recognized, and a commitment was undertaken to increase the taxes of the little man whenever necessary to protect economic growth by avoiding a too sharply progressive tax.

The outlook of the authors of the new economic program was succinctly summed up by Fritz Klenner in the January 1968 edition of *Die Zukunft:*

> Theories of class warfare and one-sided power politics will produce no economic growth nor create any jobs. We must pursue a *temperate* policy. At the end of our period in office there must be more chimneys smoking, more machines whirling, and more computers operating in the offices if economic well-being is to be increased, and, indeed, if spiritual distress is to be overcome.[30]

That such a new look in the Socialist approach to economics might well open the road for the SPÖ to gain political power was indicated as early as the spring of 1967 when an editor of the Conservative-oriented *Die Presse* commented on Kreisky's establishment of an economic brain trust.

> With a start like this, the SPÖ should finally be able to succeed in establishing good credentials in the field of economic debate, to draft usable recipes, and to compel the People's party to engage in genuine competition of expert opinion. An ÖVP monopoly in economic questions is of little use to this country. Every sort of monopoly has its disadvantages.[31]

There were to be still other innovations. The outlines of a program of general cultural and social reform were worked out, with the accents on initiative and opportunity for youth. Here again, working groups of young intellectuals were employed to develop a set of long-term perspectives under the catchy title "Horizons 80." One aspect of this program that met with very positive re-

30. Fritz Klenner, "Wir sind im Kommen—aber was kommt auf us uns zu?" *Die Zukunft,* January 1968, p. 18.
31. Schuhmayer, "Kreisky."

sponse at the polls in 1970 was a proposal for shortening the term of military service for young Austrians.

Apart from formal innovations in program, the ideological movement of Austrian socialism away from Austro-Marxism during the period since the 1966 elections has been dramatically evidenced in the party's new stance vis-à-vis the Catholic church. A considerable time before the elections a dialogue had already been opened up between groups of Socialists and churchmen who had come to believe that the fundamental values of party and church were in no way opposed to one another but, on the contrary, were entirely compatible, indeed, mutual. The way for such a dialogue had been paved by the institutional withdrawal of the church from partisan politics at the inception of the First Republic and by a continued demonstration of good will by high churchmen to erstwhile politico-ideological opponents. (The importance of the new church policy for an integrated Austrian national consciousness is discussed in detail in chapter 5.) On the Socialist side a new tolerance of the Catholic church was evidenced in the religious plank of the 1958 party program. Upon Kreisky's accession to the leadership of the Socialist party in 1967, what had formerly been a tentative probing operation became official Socialist policy, and the dialogue has been constantly expanded ever since, much to the chagrin of the small group of Austro-Marxist ideologues who retain a voice in party councils.[32]

An example of the kinds of contacts that have been made is the forum discussion which took place in Bludenz, Vorarlberg, in October 1968 between Kreisky and the Reverend Walter Riener, S.J., director of the Catholic Social Academy. Father Riener called for more Catholics in positions of leadership in the Socialist party. Dr. Kreisky, for his part, insisted that his interest in the dialogue was to spare believers within the SPÖ conflicts of conscience and declared that he did not see dialogue as simply a clever tactic to increase the number of possible Socialist votes.[33] Elsewhere,

32. See "Vorstoss der Linken in der SPÖ," *Die Presse,* January 2, 1968.
33. See "Kreisky: 'Kein Wählerfang,'" in *Die Presse,* October 14, 1968. Anton Pelinka describes the emergence of the technocrat as political leader as an aspect of ideological decline and the emergence of problem-solving politics. See "Elitenbildung in den österreichischen Grossparteien," *Wort und Wahrheit* 25 (Nov.–Dec. 1970) :534 ff.

Kreisky has gone on record as saying that he sees the Catholic church as the only institution capable of mobilizing the moral forces remaining in Austria, and therefore it is of central importance in the maintenance of a healthy and stable society. The new openness to religion may also have had an important result for the political fortunes of the Socialist party in the electoral returns of March 1970.

A last, and most important, change in the stance of the Socialist party following the debacle of March 1966 has been its vehement repudiation of Communist support. The silent acceptance of Communist endorsement in 1966 may have been the single most important factor in the Socialist downfall of that year. It certainly provided the occasion for an enormous quantity of Conservative electoral "medicine making" around the theme, "The Red People's Front Threatens." The Socialists were not going to make the same mistake again. The new stance on this question also made a logical package with the general eradication from program and ideological outlook of virtually every trace of a Marxist past.

The Political Tables Turned: The Fulfillment of Consensus Politics

As early as the fall of 1967, before the extent of the Socialist reform was clear, the electoral tide had begun to turn against the Conservatives because of what was viewed as policy failure in a number of areas. In the provincial elections in Upper Austria in October, elections in which federal issues plainly played a role, the Socialists received 5,000 more votes than the Conservatives and for the first time since 1945 showed themselves to be the strongest party in the state. The Socialists increased their vote by more than 25,000 over the national parliamentary elections of 1966, and the Conservative vote was off by more than 50,000. The phenomenon of the independent voter was manifesting itself once more, and in a different way from that of 1966. In provinical elections in the Burgenland in March 1968, the political barometer continued to show clear weather for the Socialists and storms for the Conservatives. The elections in Vienna in April 1969 showed a similar result, though voting in Lower Austria and in the Vorarlberg in November showed the two parties running neck and neck.

Another omen of an impending reversal of political fortunes at
the national level appeared in a study of party loyalty carried out
in the summer of 1969 by the Institute for Empirical Research of
Vienna. A fourth of the sample showed themselves ready in principle to vote for a different party than the one they had supported
in 1966. A third of these were either trades people, clerical personnel, or public servants. Workers and farmers were much less
prepared than these groups to make a switch. More than half of
persons who had earned high school diplomas or a higher degree
of education were ready to change their party allegiance, while the
less well educated were the staunchest in their traditional loyalty.
Examined according to party affiliation, Socialists appeared the
most loyal (81 percent), with Conservatives showing less fidelity
(76 percent) and members of the Freedom party markedly less
(only 58 percent).[34]

The great test finally came on March 1, 1970. With almost 90
percent of the eligible electorate voting, the Socialists won 48.4
percent of the total vote, Conservatives 44.7 percent and the Freedom party 5.4 percent. Communists garnered less than .5 percent.
It is significant that the greatest Socialist increases were in the
western Länder. The distribution of the vote produced a radically
new allocation of seats in the National Assembly. For the first time
in the history of the Second Republic the Socialists won a plurality
of seats—81—with the Conservatives taking second place (also for
the first time) with 79. The Freedom party lost 1 of the 6 seats it
had earlier held. Chancellor-designate Kreisky attributed the Socialist victory to the fact that his party had appeared to the voters
to be the more modern in approach and organization of the two
major parties. It seemed clear that large numbers of the 96,000
new voters, enfranchised by a law dropping the eligibility age to
19, had voted Socialist. Relevant for them were Kreisky's promises
to reduce the term of compulsory military service and improve educational opportunities for all. Post-election analysis also showed
that one-fifth of the Socialist gain could be attributed to upper-
middle-class defections from the ÖVP.[35]

34. "Der durchleuchtete Wähler," *Wochenpresse*, February 4, 1970.
35. Computer analysis by Institute for Empirical Research, cited in *Express*, March 3, 1970.

Otto Schulmeister, the editor of *Die Presse,* wrote on March 3: "This newspaper wanted an absolute majority for Klaus, and if not Klaus, then Kreisky. The electoral law wanted it otherwise. Now we must make the best of the situation." [36] After six weeks of negotiations the situation produced a new government. The coalition could not be revived, and Kreisky decided to try his luck as the head of a minority government. Austria had entered upon a new phase of consensus politics. The second of its two major parties was to have a turn at governing alone.

The reality of the new consensual pattern was to be confirmed by subsequent electoral events. A presidential election took place on April 3, 1971, with the incumbent Socialist, Franz Jonas, a former mayor of Vienna, running against Conservative candidate Kurt Waldheim (elected secretary general of the United Nations in September 1971), a politically neutral figure whose career had been largely spent as a professional diplomat. Following earlier diplomatic appointments Waldheim had served as Austrian ambassador to the United Nations from 1964 to 1968. From 1968 to 1970 he had played his only partisan political role as foreign minister, after which he returned to the UN. With a voter turnout greater than 95 percent, Jonas won reelection with a 52.79 percent majority. The Austrians had broken another rule of the contractarian period, when control of the chancellorship by one major party had always been offset by control of the presidency by the other large party. The Socialists had now, in a free election, been entrusted with both positions.

The new pattern continues to unfold according to the rules of normal parliamentary government. After a year of minority government Chancellor Kreisky decided to try in October 1971 for an absolute majority. The intervening year had seen no Socialist experiments, only efforts at technically efficient government. And just prior to the election Kreisky announced publicly that he would seek no new nationalizations in the four years ahead. The election (under a new Socialist-sponsored law) gave him a 50.22 percent popular majority—the first absolute majority ever gained by an Austrian party. The parliamentary distribution also yielded a nar-

36. *Die Presse,* March 3, 1970.

row Socialist majority. Both major parties had now experienced full majority status. Austrian democracy had reached its full maturity.[37]

37. Despite the fact that Austrian electoral behavior has created a majority-party government, survey research as late as August 1971 continued to report that coalition government remains the form preferred by a large majority of Austrians—an interesting political "lag." See *Wochenpresse*, October 13, 1971, p. 4.

5. FASHIONING A NATIONAL IDENTITY: THE INTEGRATION OF IDEALS AND SYMBOLS

Can nations, anymore than individuals, live by bread alone? The processes by which contractarian democrats, working within a context of happy historical "givens," produced the Austrian *Wohlstandstaat* have not supplied meaning and purpose as well; they have not yielded values to give focus to community life. The problem, however, is not that Austrians do not have values and purposes. Rather, they have too many of them, but they do not form an integrated whole, a single view of what the community is all about. There is a Catholic Conservative view, which draws its image of Austria from the days of the empire. There is a secularist Socialist view, which rejects the past and envisions Austria as a new reality. There is an image of Austria as a cultural nation that is non-German, even anti-German, in its emphasis, which cuts across the dividing line between Conservative and Socialist. There is an idea of Austria as a nation of purely German culture, which also crosses this line. And there are yet other combinations and modifications of these major images of what modern Austria is all about.

This chapter is about the men who preside over these various conceptions of the Austrian national idea and about the institutions through which they obtain access to the public ear. Moreover, it concerns the running ideological polemic that these intellectuals carry on in their bid for public attention. But it is also about movements toward consensus. For there are synthesizing forces at work to produce a single pattern of ideals acceptable to all. The greatest success of the synthesizers has been in the realm of values and symbols that define a political nation. They have been least successful in the broader area of general cultural values and symbols. We shall see, however, that political and cultural values are, to a great degree, separable as a logical matter, as Etzioni supposed. In chapters 6, 7, and 8 we ask whether the political elites and the rank-and-file followers, the Austrian public at large, have been able to accept this separation and reach consensus on the norms of a political nation while continuing to disagree about the existence and character of the cultural nation.

Conservative Cultural Nationalism—Old Style

" 'Heil Hitler!' said the wolf to Little Red Riding Hood." "One SS-Man and one SS-Man are two SS-Men." These sentences, from a reader and an arithmetic book respectively, are indicative of the degree to which the Nazis saturated the political culture of young Austria with the identity symbols of the Third Reich. What would the new identity symbols be, and who would fashion and teach them to the rising generation of the Second Republic?

Of all the new symbol salesmen of 1945, the Communists best understood the importance of identity words, especially in the education of the young, and their leaders came back to Austria with a well-developed identity package and a plan to take control of the school system. The facts that they had always been a small minority in Austria and that their Russian sponsors controlled only part of the country, rather than the brilliance of the plans of the other parties, prevented the Communists from succeeding. The particular position that they adopted, however, was to complicate the identity question for the next twenty years and blur the intellectual issues for great numbers of non-Communist Austrians.

In 1945 the Communists were among the first to sound the theme of the "Austrian nation" and to give that theme a central place in their propaganda. The beginnings of their tactic go back to the Seventh Congress of the Communist International in 1935, when resolutions calling for the construction of national fronts against fascism and nazism were adopted. In contrast to Communist parties in countries where genuine national feeling existed, the Communists in Austria were faced with the problem of evolving the psychological bond that was the precondition of national front politics. They proceeded therefore to discover the existence of an Austrian nation and to create a theory about it.[1]

Immediately after the Russian seizure of Vienna in April 1945, the Communist leader Ernst Fischer was flown in from Moscow, where he had taken refuge during the war. Apparently the Comintern policy of 1935 was still favored by the Russians, for Fischer immediately began to play the role of enthusiastic and vociferous Austrian patriot. In the lead article of the first issue of *Neues Österreich,* the newspaper founded by Communists, Socialists, and Conservatives at the inception of the Second Republic, Fischer wrote about the "Austrian nation," saying that "we Austrians must awaken to a true national self-consciousness. Unlike the past, we must learn to trust in our own powers. . . . What matters is the democratic and patriotic determination of the nation." [2] His method represented the purest pragmatism. Fischer needed to find an argument to refute the ethnic and linguistic arguments of the Pan-Germans who had helped make Adolph Hitler's "Great Germany." He sought it, ironically, in an adaptation of the Conservative, old-Austrian view of culture as common history. It did not occur to him to attempt to separate the idea of the political nation from that of the cultural nation. Here is a sample of the kind of argument he settled on.

> We are a people with a unique history and culture. We know that not everything in our past or in our present character is laudable, but we can still point to a contribution to world culture that is worthy of notice. We do not deny it. We are proud of Haydn and Mozart, Schubert and Bruckner, Grillparzer, Raimund, and Nestroy. We are proud of our great architects who created Saint Stephen's Cathedral, the Church of St. Charles, the Belevedere Palace. . . . We are proud of our peasant leaders

1. Josef Toch, "Enklave KPÖ" in Jacques Hannak, ed., *Bestandaufnahme Österreich, 1945–1963* (Vienna: Forum 1963), p. 66. See especially the articles of Alfred Klahr, a leading Communist ideologue of the period, in the Communist journal *Weg und Ziel* in 1937.

2. Ernst Fischer, *Neues Österreich,* no. 1, April 23, 1945, in Ernst Fischer, *Das Jahr der Befreiung, Aus Reden und Aufsätzen* (Vienna: Stern, 1946), p. 13.

. . . Fadinger, Andreas Hofer. We are proud of our Viennese [who fought the Turks], . . . we are proud of the battles and achievements of the Austrian working class.[3]

In the interparty discussions leading to the establishment of a new government for Vienna, and especially in any talks about education, Fischer pursued the Austrian nation idea vigorously. Socialist leader Adolf Schärf reports that Fischer "launched into a lengthy disquisition on the spirit of youth education in the new republic. Above all, it had to be 'Austrian' and directed to teaching Austrians that they were a nation, a self-contained people (*eigenes Volk*). The glorious Austrian past would have to be stressed." An awkward silence followed this remarkable statement. Schärf broke in with a quip that "only Kunschak [chairman of the People's party] was as 'Black-Gold' [the imperial colors] as Fischer's ideal director for the Vienna school system. Kunschak thereupon clumsily declared that he thanked him for his good opinion and that he would take the job—to Fischer's consternation. For it killed the rest of his speech, which was an attempt to demonstrate the necessity of filling the education post with a patriotic Communist!"[4] The Conservative symbols that Fischer had attempted to manipulate did not prove as flexible as he had hoped.

Fischer fared better, at least temporarily, at the federal level, where he secured for himself the top education post. But when the elections of November 1945 yielded only 174,257 Communist ballots (5.4 percent), which returned only four Communist members to the new National Assembly, Fischer was dropped from the cabinet and the post of federal minister of education went to the Conservative leader Felix Hurdes. It remained a Conservative preserve down to 1970.[5]

According to Hurdes, he not only had to battle the Socialists for control of the vacant education portfolio, but he also had to convince key people in his own party of that post's importance. They

3. Lead article in *Neues Österreich*, no. 5, April 27, 1945, ibid. pp. 172–73.
4. Schärf, *April 1945 in Wien*, pp. 78, 79.
5. The Communists had held a third of the posts in the provisional government, based on an overly high estimate of electoral strength, especially in Vienna and Lower Austria. They received no posts in the elected government.

were more intent on securing ministries concerned with the economy. Having won the latter battle, he was casting about for a professional academician to fill the post when he found that his own name had been set down by his colleagues for the job. So far as citizenship education is concerned, he must have seemed the obvious choice, for more than any of his party friends, Hurdes was an ardent adherent to the idea of an Austrian nation and believed passionately that inculcating Austrianism was a crucial task for the new government.

What aspects of Hurdes's temperament and outlook were to be significant for his conduct of the office of minister of education? For one thing, the "Austrianism" of which he wished to make his countrymen appreciative was quite divorced from any association with things German. It was actively anti-German, a radical departure from the Austrianism of the First Republic. "Austria," he declared in an interview in 1966, "had to be made a counterconcept to Nazi Germany." [6] And for Hurdes, *Nazi* and *German* had become, through his wartime experiences, absolutely equivalent terms. As minister of education Hurdes actually carried his anti-Germanism so far as to require school teachers to employ the expression "the language of instruction" rather than "the German language" in classroom teaching and administrative interchange. (Persons who thought that this was going too far lampooned Hurdes's "language of instruction" as "Hurdestani.") He was the proponent of an Austrian cultural as well as a political nation.

Hurdes had no interest in developing a school program to elicit the support of people of Pan-German sentiment. He favored exclusion of all former Nazis from political rights in 1945 and later stated that if he had had his way they would not have been readmitted to these rights in 1949.[7] "Solidarism" embraced Socialists, but Nazis and Pan-Germans were beyond the pale. A siege mentality was also very evident in his statements in 1966. Nazi persecutors were everywhere, seeking to get back at him, he thought. They had hounded him as minister and finally forced him to resign. And he believed the stories in the Socialist *Arbeiter–zeitung,* the Communist *Volksstimme,* and the left-leaning *Neues Österreich*

6. Interview in Vienna, February 22, 1966.
7. Ibid.

that his party had dropped him as a parliamentary candidate in the campaign of 1965 because of neo-Nazi machinations.[8]

Denazification of teaching personnel was one of the first tasks to which the new minister of education addressed himself, though the methods he adopted did not turn out to be foolproof. Persons who had obviously joined the Nazi party to keep or obtain jobs were allowed to remain on after the war's end, but some of these later turned out to be enthusiastic Nazis. Then there was the problem of those who had been educated during the Nazi period—for whom nazism and Pan-Germanism were simply second nature. Lastly, there was the problem of those who managed to hide their pasts and keep quiet about their Nazi sympathies for four years but who began to speak out when political disabilities were removed from former Nazis and the WdU was created as a Pan-German rallying point. It was not easy to get an Austrian idea across to the young through such people.

By 1955, however, the ministry found its task of inculcating Austrianism somewhat easier. New teachers had been educated who had not been influenced by Nazi indoctrination. Also, the State Treaty which was signed in that year gave a certain impetus to Austrianism. On the positive side the ministry launched an elaborate program of citizenship education for all elementary and secondary grades. A federal directive setting forth guidelines for school authorities throughout the country described the program's objectives as "the awakening and cultivation of an Austrian homeland consciousness (*Heimatbewusstsein*) and cultural consciousness . . . [and the] education of the youth to be faithful and valiant citizens of the Republic." [9] Again, the political nation and the cultural nation were put together.

Elementary teachers were instructed to inculcate pride in being Austrian not only by displaying to their students the monuments of

8. A young, reliable, and very Austrian-minded bureaucrat in the upper echelons of the People's party central secretariat assured me that the only reason that Hurdes's candidacy was rejected in 1965 was because of his advanced age and growing infirmity.

9. "Staatsbürgerliche Erziehung," *Sonderdruck des Erlasses vom 6. Juli 1949, A.23.575–IV/12/49, aus dem Verordnungsblatt des Bundesministerium für Unterricht*, 7.Stück, vom 1.August 1949, p. 1.

past greatness but also by pointing out the accomplishments of the Austrian present.

Repairing war damage, building new housing for the people, new bridges, factories, hydroelectric facilities, schools, churches, and other public edifices; increasing the people's standard of living; the accomplishments of workers and farmers, of the trades and commercial people, of the Austrian public administration; the successes of Austrian scholars, artists and technicians, including those abroad; the work of the various social services—all these things are not only excellent materials for patriotic instruction (*Heimatkunde Unterricht*) in the third and fourth years of the elementary school but also furnish useful themes for many of the specialized programs of the advanced classes as well.[10]

Classroom study and student activities of all kinds were brought into the program—celebrations of the accomplishments of prominent Austrians in the fields of art, science, trade, and industry and from all levels of society; student "pen pal" clubs with Austria as the theme; the cultivation of local customs; participation in conservation programs; field trips to factories to see Austrian wares manufactured; trips to places of natural beauty, to museums, to historic monuments.

To foster understanding between the rest of the country and the capital through direct contact, the Ministry of Education sponsored a program of youth and teacher exchanges. Students from the western and southern Alpine Länder were brought to Vienna to attend performances in the famous Burgtheater on the Ring and to sample the flavor of Viennese life and culture. Vorarlbergers (from the westernmost Land, which adjoins Switzerland) were brought to the easternmost province of Burgenland to view the Iron Curtain at Mörbisch, where one can see the barbed wire and watch towers stretching for miles across the countryside and dividing in two the Neusiedler See, which forms part of the international border with Hungary at this point. Mörbisch is also a Croatian community where German-speaking students from Vorarlberg could hear fellow Austrians speaking an exotic language and see

10. Ibid.

them living a different kind of farm life from that of the Alpine pastures.[11]

The educational system during the first years of the Second Republic (until 1952) was thus in the hands of Conservatives who were anti-German cultural nationalists. Germanism, still tainted with the odor of nazism, remained under a cloud, and for three years after 1945 the rank and file of the most ardent Pan-Germans, the former Nazi faithful, were excluded from the franchise. So far as the Socialists were concerned, their recent persecution by the Nazis made them uninterested in stemming the anti-German thrust of Hurdes's educational program. Moreover, they were more concerned with building Socialist positions of economic and political power in the new republic than with handling questions of national identity and political socialization. Furthermore, Hurdes's Austrian cultural nationalism, despite its Habsburg background, was married securely to the purest democratic values, which the Socialists shared. This was very different from the image of Conservative Austrian nationalism that the Socialists confronted in the time of Dollfuss. Hurdes's national ideal, therefore, despite the cultural baggage which made it potentially problematical, did open to the left politically. Thus it represented a partial ideological synthesis for two groups that had earlier been divided absolutely.

Other institutions created in 1945 by the Conservatives for the purpose of giving form to a national identity had a similar ecumenical impact. One was the Austrian Institute (Österreich Institut) which was founded by Hofrat Dr. Richard Dolberg, a political sociologist, in cooperation with Minister of Education Hurdes as a private corporation enjoying a limited public subsidy. Dr. Dolberg finds little value in an abstract polemic about the concept of *nation* and instead concentrates his efforts on cultivating and disseminating news about substantive elements of Austrian culture. This is achieved through a variety of media, including cultural congresses, expositions, research programs, and publications of all kinds.[12]

Another, entirely private, Conservative organization dedicated

11. Interview with Section Chief Anton Kolbabek, Ministry of Education, Vienna, March 24, 1966.
12. Interview with Hofrat Dolberg, Vienna, May 28, 1968.

to the formation of an Austrian national identity is the Austrian Union (Österreichische Gemeinschaft), whose origins are in the First Republic. The society was founded in 1925 for the purpose of fighting the anschluss idea. Its leaders maintained that the new Austria was a viable state and had an obligation to retain the traditions of the old Austria and prevent severance of the many cultural links with the successor states. Outlawed during the anschluss, the society sprang back into life in 1946. According to Günther Dolezal, chairman of the Vienna branch, the Austrian Union was among the first groups to realize that only the term *Austrian nation,* in the Western sense, was adequate to express the distinctive aspects of Austrian life that distinguish it from that of the Reichs-German. At the same time, the idea of the *cultural nation,* which is German in origin, had to be given up.[13] This view is not shared by all of the society's leading lights, however. And the union's support until recently came largely from older Conservatives who are practicing Catholics, who have an emotional attachment to the imperial tradition, and who are cultural nationalists of the Hurdes variety. Younger members, like Ernst F. Winter, son of Ernst Karl Winter, who pushed for the Austrian nation idea in the First Republic, form a link with the new-style republican cultural nationalism of the Austrian National Institute, which will be discussed below.

Conservative Compromise

Felix Hurdes left the Education Ministry in October 1952. The views of his successor, Ernst Kolb, on the Austrian nation presented a striking contrast with Hurdes's ideas on Austrian cultural nationalism. Kolb comes from Vorarlberg, where the federal idea takes precedence over the conception of Austria as a nation. Kolb himself is a devoted Vorarlberger, and he claims that in the *Ländle* ("statelet"—like our "little Rhody") local feeling is much stronger than Austrian national consciousness. Kolb said in 1966 that the constitution of Vorarlberg declares that "Land Vorarlberg is an autonomous state." He thought that the war had brought something

13. "Wer spinnt den Faden Rot-Weiss-Rot?" *Österreichische Hochschulzeitung,* April 15, 1968.

of an Austrian consciousness to the Vorarlberg, but he stressed the historical depth of German feeling there, albeit a German feeling that stemmed from the Germany of the Holy Roman Empire (all the cities on the Lake of Constance were imperial cities) and not from Bismarck's Germany.

By 1952 the former Nazis had been restored to the franchise, and both Conservatives and Socialists found themselves vying for the vote of this substantial bloc. Whether Kolb's appointment was intended to appeal to these people is not clear. Certainly Kolb was not a Pan-German, but as a Vorarlberger he was also not an Austrian cultural nationalist. His federalist ideology combined with a loyal political Austrianism may have seemed a good compromise. It is interesting, however, that Kolb made no substantial changes in the citizenship program Hurdes had initiated. (He has spoken with special approval of the "Youth gets to know Vienna" project, and the program that allows Viennese students to spend one school year in the countryside.) As minister he continued to purchase hostels (Landesschulheime) around the country where teachers and students from various parts of Austria could gather for special meetings and "retreats." [14]

Heinrich Drimmel, the third minister of education, took office in November 1954. The next year the Austrian State Treaty was signed. With the resulting relaxation of foreign pressures, and increasing economic prosperity, the crisis of survival, and thus the need to keep things German at arm's length, was over. The new situation seems to have been reflected in the approach of the new education minister to the question of the Austrian nation.

Drimmel told me that as minister of education his objective was to convert what he termed a purely negative (anti-Nazi) state consciousness into something positive. (He had viewed Hurdes's Austrian cultural nationalism as a reaction to the policy of the German occupiers during the years of anschluss.) As he saw it, it was impossible to rebuild Austria on the basis of so controversial a concept as *nation* because of its cultural connotations in central Europe. Drimmel wanted to neutralize this word and get it out of the debate. This amounted to trying to actively play the role of wheelhorse and mediator in order to bring together the former Nazis

14. Interview with Professor Ernst Kolb, Innsbruck, July 19, 1966.

and the rest of the Austrians by maintaining that Austria was in some sense a German state. The existence of a shared *Geisteskultur,* a shared community of culture and values between Germany and Austria, and intimate cultural exchanges with Germany he described as facts that would not change.[15]

None of this should be taken to mean that Drimmel tried to get the Education Ministry out of the business of political socialization. On the contrary, he continued to administer the program of citizenship education that Hurdes had established, and he added several new dimensions. The emphasis throughout, however, was to be political, not cultural.

On October 26, 1955, the Austrian National Assembly adopted a law declaring Austria's perpetual neutrality. On this day, too, the last occupation troops departed Austrian soil in accordance with the terms of the State Treaty. Every year from 1955 to 1965 the Education Ministry set aside October 26 as "The Day of the Austrian Flag" and sponsored local and national ceremonies to celebrate it. (The day has since become the country's only national holiday.)

The high point of each year's celebration of the "Day of the Flag" was a pageant in one of the large Vienna theaters. In 1960 the celebration was held in the great Konzerthaus, in 1961 and 1962 in the famous Burgtheater built by Emperor Francis Joseph. The event commonly took place at 10:00 A.M. and was carried over the state and school radio systems. The themes have been notably political rather than cultural, and the bulk of the pageant has typically been devoted to a recollection of Austria's past in a "death and resurrection" mood. Sometimes the recollection has begun with the collapse of the empire, sometimes with the anschluss, and the themes have been bewilderment, exile, nostalgia, physical and mental suffering, return home, hope, hard work, and accomplishment—usually in that order. In the 1960 pageant the meaning of freedom was spelled out in fivefold terms (1) life without fear of arbitrary imprisonment; (2) security from compulsory service in the armies of a foreign power (like the Janissaries of old); (3) freedom of expression; (4) freedom of occupation and residence; (5) guaranteed democratic citizenship—the right to

15. Interview with Heinrich Drimmel, Vienna, March 17, 1966.

elect and be elected in a free state. "Austria proved stronger than the Reich of the brief 1,000 years," said the speaker. From her suffering she had learned that "freedom is more powerful than compulsion, and reason more powerful than the madness of power."

Drimmel also undertook to work with other ministries in the area of political socialization. He cooperated in a variety of ways with Colonel Josef Bystricky, who in 1958 established a special citizenship program for the armed forces. When test essays written by recruits revealed an uncommitted, politically apathetic generation of young people, Drimmel made contemporary history a required course in the secondary school curriculum. And in 1963, in cooperation with the Defense Ministry, he inaugurated a program of civilian psychological defense.

An important step toward binding together the split in the historical consciousness of Austria's intellectuals was taken by Drimmel in 1960. In December of that year he sponsored a conference on the treatment of contemporary Austrian history in the formal teaching of history. Attending the conference, which was held at Reichenau, were seven leading professors of history from the major Austrian universities, a dozen chief bureaucrats of the Ministry of Education, five members of parliament who were especially interested in education questions, and about twenty other school administrators and textbook authors from various parts of the country.[16]

In a round-up session the participants agreed that the most important objective in the teaching of history was to convey to the student the realization that historical judgments are complicated and problematical. Overly simplified interpretations and clichés were to be avoided, even though this might mean a sacrifice of extensive coverage. A few important turning points ought to be examined in depth and the student left at the end of the analysis to make his own moral judgments on men and events. In this fashion the student would learn to avoid easy moralizing about history. He would see that complicated social and psychological processes rather than good and bad will are the prime movers of history.

16. For a verbatim record see *Österreichische Zeitgeschichte in Geschichtsunterricht. Bericht über die Expertentagung von 14.XII bis 16.XII 1960 in Reichenau* (Vienna: Österreichischer Bundesverlag, 1961).

The conferees also concluded that the emotional noninvolvement of the youth in the problems of the 1920s to 1940s made a shift from moralistic to descriptive history quite easy. As one discussant put it, "It's really all the same now whether in 1918 or later the Socialists or the Christian Socialists were shown to have a couple of ounces of 'anschluss fat' more or less on their bodies. The youth doesn't really care particularly how things were in 1934." [17] Involved arguments about guilt and innocence in the past tend to fatigue young people. They want to live in the present and in the future. Giving an example of the dispassionate style that they agreed to recommend to Austria's history teachers, the experts spent their last working session expanding, correcting, and fashioning into a final, mutually acceptable form a treatment of controversial events of 1927 and 1933/34 which had originally been a manuscript for a teachers' handbook on "Austria 1918–1945" that was presented to the conference as a working paper. It was agreed that this paper would later be extended to cover the period to 1955 and that a notebook for students would be drafted on the basis of the teachers' handbook.

It might appear paradoxical that the aim of the dispassionate, "value-free" historical description given by the conferees in their final report and exemplified in their editing of the handbook should be "preparation of the ground for the development of Austrian state consciousness, which it is the job of the related subject of citizenship education to execute." [18] The new patriotism would be a sober one, with both feet planted firmly on reality rather than on romance. It is interesting that the conference ended with a decision to promote "state consciousness." Once again, "political nation" triumphed over "cultural nation."

The work of the Reichenau Conference is carried forward daily in the program of the Institute for Austrian Information (Österreichkunde). Its work is in the areas of history, literature, and geography, and it specializes in the application of new research methods in these branches of scholarship. The object of the institute's programs is "to fashion a solid foundation for an image of Austria as a possession for the Austrian youth of the decades

17. Ibid., p. 176.
18. Ibid., p. 179.

ahead." [19] Publications of the institute already include a long list
of first-rate historical works dealing with a variety of periods and
problems, ranging from a study of the young Maximilian to a review of the experience of the Second Republic as a neutral state.
The institute has also conducted numerous conferences of political
historians, literary historians, social historians, and geographers,
with the participation of foreign as well as native scholars.

A continuing discussion of the meaning and mission of Austria
has for several years been carried on in the pages of a journal published by the institute, *Österreich in Geschichte und Literatur* (*Austria in History and Literature*). All shades of opinion have been
voiced in its pages. The journal has served the interest of synthesis
by providing an impartial forum for the pen barbs of the polemicists.

Theodor Piffl-Percevic, a South Tyrolean from a military family
of Meran and Austria's fourth minister of education, represented
a different mentality from that of all his predecessors. While he is
of the same generation as Drimmel (Piffl was born in 1911, Drimmel in 1912; both Hurdes and Kolb are a generation older), they
are very different kinds of people. Drimmel is an idea maker, an
ideologist, while Piffl is an administrator's administrator. Drimmel's experience, except for the war years, had been almost wholly
in the field of education. He served as an expert for college affairs
under Schuschnigg and then had the ambition of becoming a university administrator. After the war he was brought back into the
Education Ministry as director of the college section. Piffl's career,
by contrast, was in the private practice of law before the anschluss
and from 1945 until his appointment in 1964 as education minister,
in the administration of the State Chamber of Agriculture and For-
estry of Styria, where he was head of the legal division, chief of the
personnel section, and finally deputy director. He expressed himself little on the ideological questions to which both Hurdes and
Drimmel constantly addressed themselves, and in keeping with the
general tone of Reformer government under Klaus, he confined
himself to efficiency in administrative performance. At the official
level the Conservatives had ended discussion about the Austrian
nation, and the political nation had won, hands down.

19. "Wer spinnt den Faden Rot-Weiss-Rot?"

The appointment in 1969 of Alois Mock, the last Conservative education minister, meant another important generational change. Thirty-five at the time of his appointment, Mock was only a child of eleven at the founding of the Second Republic. Unlike his predecessors, he was therefore a man whose political attitudes and outlook had been almost wholly shaped by the experience of life in a thriving democracy. Mock had earlier served two years in the Education Ministry, and immediately before his elevation to the position of minister he had been executive secretary to the chancellor. His brief tenure in office brought no major policy changes in the area of citizenship education. The first Socialist minister of education, Leopold Gratz (b. 1929), also had known only the institutions of democracy and the aura of an Austrian nationality as an adult. Before becoming minister in 1970, he served as a central secretary of the Socialist party and as party spokesman on educational affairs. His successor, Fred Sinowatz, fits the same picture. He had been secretary of the Burgenland SPÖ and Landesrat for cultural questions in the Burgenland state government.

A Literary Debate with Political Overtones

Settling the question of national identity in political terms in the programs of the Ministry of Education did not settle the matter for intellectuals, however. At the very time that the Drimmel compromise began to affect educational policy, a polemic on the Austrian nation theme broke out in *Forum,* an ecumenical journal presided over by a young Socialist editor who has been playing a leading role as ideological synthesizer among Austrians. *Forum* offers its pages as an outlet for all views on matters of public interest, on the assumption that a frank airing of differences contributes to understanding, tolerance, and, ultimately, to national unity.

The debate about the Austrian nation began in 1955, and, like the changed policy of the Education Ministry, was probably sparked by the new situation of independence and the end of urgent foreign pressures. Underlying differences on the identity question could safely come to the surface again. The discussion has continued from that time to this. For the most part it interests only intellectuals in Vienna, though from time to time it arouses tempers and provokes a flood of words in the other Länder as well. One such flareup occurred during the early 1960s among the cadets at the Wiener Neustadt Military Academy when representatives of *Die Presse,* sponsored a seminar on national purposes: "In the Party Battle, where is Austria?" The discussion turned out to be too vehement to be broadcast on radio and television. In 1961 a proposal by the editor of *Arbeiter–Zeitung* that a federal commission be appointed to create a dictionary of Austrian colloquial speech raised a storm of protest in the provincial Socialist paper *Neue Zeit* of Klagenfurt, the capital of Carinthia. In 1964 the collumns *of Salzburger Nachrichten,* the leading newspaper of the western states, carried a debate on the Austrian nation theme sparked by the appearance of a Pan-German letter to the editors denying the existence of an Austrian nation. The same year a forum sponsored by a Pan-German organization on the theme "Are we Austrians Germans?" caused a near riot in Graz. When Otto Habsburg visited Innsbruck in 1968, Pan-German students there asked him brusquely to declare himself on the question of the Austrian nation. And there have been student brawls in Linz, the capital of Upper Austria, over the matter.

The debate among intellectuals began as a three-cornered discussion of the national identity question that appeared in *Forum* in December 1955.[20] The theme was "Austria's Heritage and Austria's Future." Three rather moderate statements were presented—one by Conservative Wilhelm Böhm, an Austrian cultural nationalist who had published on the theme under the auspices of the Austrian Institute and the Education Ministry during the Hurdes years; a second by the leading Socialist journalist Jacques Hannak; and a third by a Pan-German professor at the College of International Trade in Vienna, Taras Borodajkewycz. The first essay was by Borodajkewycz and was entitled "The German Connections." Identifying modern Germany with the Holy Roman Empire, he argued that Austria had come onto the stage of history as an eastern branch of the "German Empire" and that she had had significance ever since only within German history. The predominantly Slavic Empire and the Dual Monarchy of the nineteenth century were

20. There had been brief sallies immediately before this by Socialists and Conservatives on the question of how to relate the republic to both the cultural and political history of the empire.

never viable, as he saw it. Austria could simply not avoid her history, which was German. He did not use the word *nation*.

Concentrating on more recent history, Böhm argued that during the period when Central Europeans were coming to use the word *nation* as a cultural concept, there developed within the empire a *political nation* of officials, military officers, nobility, upper-middle-class persons and artists. This political nation was not a "German colony in Central Europe," as Borodajkewycz called it, but took on its own cultural form. The "foreign rule" of the anschluss period "served as the [final] nation-building factor" (*wirkte nationsbildend*) in the production of a complete political-cultural nation. "The parties won't accept the Austrian nation on tactical grounds" [desire for the former Nazi vote?] he continued, but in his view to do so would have been strategically wise. It would have clarified the relationship with Germany and given Austria more influence in the east, since the eastern states would not need to fear a new German imperialism.

Hannak insisted in his essay that the empire and its tradition, in any of their definitions, were dead and ought to be forgotten. They had no values for the working classes, either in the factory or on the farm, who now form the leading echelons of society. In his view the years of anschluss had created a new tradition of resistance and collective action among Austrians. And thereafter, for the first time in history, the two major parties had demonstrated that they could work together. The problem was not to determine *when* Austria had come into being (a reference to an earlier essay by a Conservative history professor) but rather *how* Austria could be created.[21]

The January 1956 issue of *Forum* carried two more pieces by Socialist ideologues. One by Felix Hubalek, a coeditor of the journal, simply seconded what Hannak had written in the previous December. "A new, future-oriented tradition [was] just starting to take form. . . . Austria begins today." The other by Felix Butschek, a young economist and essayist known for his nonideological, pragmatist, and revisionist economic views, represents a degree of accommodation to the tradition-based Conservative standpoint. He wrote of Austrian national consciousness as having been "deci-

21. *Forum,* December 1955, pp. 427–431.

sively strengthened" (significantly, not "created") by the "temporary extinction of our political independence." But he thought the
youth needed to be able to look back, to perceive a tradition, in
order to strengthen their patriotism. Old concepts like "the historical mission of Austria" to be a "mediator" of peoples or a "bastion
of the West" in southeastern Europe could not simply be taken over
from the "broken down traditionalism of the older generation," but
the youth could create new and viable meanings for these concepts.[22]

In an essay in the February issue of *Forum,* Adam Wandruszka,
a Conservative professor of history at the University of Vienna,
tried to find a compromise position between the opposing cultural
nationalism of Borodajkewycz and Böhm while rejecting out of
hand the Socialist "new beginning" approach of Hubalek as "rigidly
clinging to the outworn positions of the 1920s." It was true both
that Austrian history and German history were closely intertwined
and that Austria had developed in a special direction after 1866.
The solution to the problem was to understand Austria as a political
nation in the Western sense, Wandruszka wrote, and to reject the
old Central European cultural nation concept as inapplicable. This
was substantially the position taken by the Drimmel regime in the
Education Ministry and one is led to wonder whether there may
have been some ministerial initiative behind Wandruszka's article.
It certainly could not have appeared useful to the Conservative
pragmatists in power at the top of the system to have Conservatives
continue to insist that Austrians were not Germans when there were
Pan-German votes to be garnered in the 1956 elections.

A damper was not to be put on the debate, however. The next
salvo, in April, came from the pen of Roland Nitsche, an economic
consultant to the business world and a student of philosophy. His
effort was directed against the historians of the Second Republic,
most of them Conservatives, whom Nitsche accused of failing to
come adequately to terms with the question of Austrian nationality.
Heinrich Benedikt and Hugo Hantsch were singled out for particular attack. Nitsche's essay warned that "allegiance to an independent Austria is simply incompatible with an allegiance to the German
nation." Breaking away from all the stock arguments about the

22. Ibid., January 1956, pp. 19–20, 20–21.

past, Nitsche treated the matter as one of political necessity. In his view an Austrian cultural nation was simply an indispensable condition of the viability of the state. With Nitsche's article the tone of the polemic began to get sharper.[23]

A new condemnation of the historians appeared in the summer issue of *Forum,* penned this time by Ernst Hoor, a political independent and economic Liberal (in the nineteenth-century sense) and an ardent Austrian cultural nationalist. Hoor is a prominent Austrian businessman and scholar who for many years served as director general of British Petroleum, one of the largest oil companies in Austria. Developing the theme sounded earlier by Nitsche, he warned it would be dangerous to popularize expressions like those that political leaders of the 1930s had used in talking about the national question, expressions such as "one people (*Volk*) in two states," a "second German State," "the German mission." He expressed especial concern about the anomaly of the political leadership's encouraging, in the program of citizenship education, the recognition of Austrian political independence while either categorically rejecting the concept of an Austrian nation or taking a neutral position on the matter. He specifically took to task Education Minister Drimmel for refusing to promote the idea of an Austrian nation on the ground that a nation could not be created "by promulgation." The cultural uniqueness of Austria had to be stressed, he thought, or the independence of the state would be undermined.[24] Since writing this *Forum* article Hoor has been one of the most prolific polemicists for the concept of an Austrian cultural nation, and his articles have appeared in a variety of periodicals. In 1966 he published a history of the First Republic that is built around the national identity theme.

The strong language of Hoor's 1956 article brought a flurry of letters to the editor, which were published in the September *Forum.* Notable among them was a stinging reply from Borodajkewycz. The temper of the debate had now gotten very hot indeed. Borodajkewycz's letter was an excerpt from an article in the August issue of *Aktion,* which is published in Graz, a center of Pan-Germanism. It was an impassioned diatribe. (In the mid-1960s Borodajkewycz

23. Ibid., April 1956, pp. 132–36.
24. Ibid., July/August 1956, p. 260.

was to be accused of provoking violent anti-Semitic sentiments among the students in his classes at the Vienna College for International Trade.) "To the unhappiest relics of that characterless and undignified year 1945 belongs that lie about 'an Austrian nation,'" he wrote. The idea was a "swamp flower," a "bloodless literary homunculus." Hoor's essay, wrote Borodajkewycz, represented a mixture of "arrogance and ignorance." The "Austrian Nation" was a "Big Lie," "stuff and nonsense." "We German Austrians simply cannot go along with it!" [25]

The polemic thus begun has flared up and died down again several times since 1956. Most of the participants in the debate are either political outsiders or men who stand on the fringes of one or another of the political parties. Some are academicians, others are figures in the literary world. Only in a few instances has an official party spokesman taken part in the discussion. (Kreisky, then state secretary in the Foreign Office had a letter in the September 1956 *Forum* correcting a statement of Hoor's about the Socialist position on national identity in the First Republic.) The political elites who run the system usually manifest little interest in the debate and, indeed, try to ignore it when they can. They tend to treat the intellectuals closest to their party as poor relations, sometimes nuisances. A few of the younger participants in the dialogue are well integrated in the political system and enjoy places of responsibility in the party bureaucracies. Sometimes the intellectuals are associated in opinion pressure groups.

Conservative Cultural Nationalism—New Style

When for pragmatic reasons the Conservative leadership eliminated the cultural emphasis from the citizenship education program, there were isolated cries of anguish from die-hard cultural nationalists, as we have seen. When the purely pragmatic Reformers who took over the chief seats of power in 1963 began systematically to exclude from positions of authority second- and third-echelon Core Groupers, both old and young, something like an organized opposition formed both within and outside the Conservative party. It focused on the two sets of ideals the Reformers had rejected: the

25. Ibid., September 1956, p. 317.

socio-economics of Christian Social "solidarism" and the Core Group idea of Austria as a cultural nation.

A rallying point of the discomfited Core Groupers has been the Austrian National Institute, founded in 1965 by Dr. Walter Jambor, a young disciple of Felix Hurdes, who makes his living as secretary of the Book Club for Youth. *Die Republik,* a journal that the institute began to publish in that year, has become a leading voice for the ideals of Austrian cultural nationalism. The lead article in its first issue referred to the Reformer take-over as the drifting of power and responsibility into the hands of the "small manager oligarchies" and implied that this trend was a chief catalyst in the process that led to the creation of the institute.[26] The position that the journal defends represents a synthesis of Austrian cultural nationalism and an ardent republicanism like that of the Socialists, which makes it a very different thing from the cultural nationalism of Ernst Hoor, who is at heart a monarchist. The writers that Jambor has gathered around him are for the most part left-standing Conservatives, but some of them are Socialists.

Jambor views the anschluss experience and the political development of Austria as an independent and neutral democracy since 1945 as necessary conditions of Austrian national consciousness.[27] But he does not find them sufficient. In the article on the founding of the National Institute, Jambor argues that the youth receive no intellectual and spiritual nourishment for their affirmation of Austria. He asks where the will to sustain the national life would come from if an economic crisis were suddenly to occur and the material satisfactions of the *Wohlstandstaat* to be lost. The nation has no reserves, "either of gold or of the better currency of spiritual values." It was to be the task of the National Institute to deal with the problem of creating these reserves by developing a new Austrian image "which in the hour of crisis would be a genuine cover for the spiritual values of all." [28] This would have to be a combined political-cultural image, and specifically a non-German one, to be

26. "Österreichisches Nationalinstitut gegründet," *Die Republik* no. 1, 1965, p. 2.
27. Walter Jambor, "Bekenntnis zu Österreich und seinen Menschen," *Österreich in Geschichte und Literatur* 1, no. 4 (1957):47.
28. "Österreichisches Nationalinstitut gegründet," p. 2.

viable. The metaphors used by Jambor in this and later articles are reminiscent of the rhetoric of religious revival. " 'The People' " he writes, "lies obscured in total concealment behind the fried chicken and the *Heurigen* benches, behind the television programs and the automobiles." [29] They need to be called to national faith and national obligation.

Toward the end of the article on the institute's founding Jambor invokes a parallel with the non-Western developing state and implies a Smith-like solution to the problem of Austrian nation building. He asks, "How shall we manage it so that Austria gets out of the dangerous psychological neighborhood of the developing areas of Africa, all of which are already states without having first ripened to nationhood?" [30]

Though it is chiefly a rallying point for political outsiders, the Austrian National Institute has some support within the Conservative organization and has actually operated successfully as a political pressure group. Its first major legislative undertaking was to obtain an act by the National Assembly proclaiming an Austrian national holiday, something which the state had never had. (Legal holidays are for the most part feasts of the Catholic church.) The two parties of the coalition were willing to meet the institute half way and legislate a state holiday, but this, according to Dr. Jambor, would have "left all the unpleasant questions unanswered and blurred." [31] Also, the parties could not agree at the outset on a date for the holiday. At a public hearing (*Enquete*) conducted by the institute on March 11, 1965, it appeared that the Socialists favored November 12, which recalls the founding of the First Republic in 1918, while the Conservatives wanted May 15, the date of the signing of the State Treaty of 1955. Signs began to appear that the government intended to respond to the institute's initiative. On May 25, at a meeting of the Christian Teachers Association for Upper Austria in Linz, Chancellor Klaus spoke of the need to make the new generation aware of its political heritage in order to provide against the day when fair-weather democracy and prosperity might be

29. "Zwanzig Jahre Zweite Republik," *Die Republik,* April 1965, 2, pp. 49–50.
30. Österreichisches Nationalinstitut gegründet," pp. 18–19.
31. Interview with Walter Jambor, Vienna, February 21, 1966.

threatened by crisis (making use of Jambor's own formula).[32] On the Socialist side, Foreign Minister Bruno Kreisky told the Federal Youth Congress on May 14 that there was a need to construct "a new Austrian idea" and to ground it on the concept of neutrality.[33]

Two letters from the institute galvanized the government into action. Josef Klaus, the Conservative chancellor and Bruno Pittermann, the Socialist vice-chancellor agreed to make the holiday October 26, the date of Austria's neutrality proclamation and of the final withdrawal of foreign troops from Austrian soil in 1955. As the "Day of the Flag" this had earlier served as a patriotic holiday for the school children, as we have seen.[34] On July 13 Chancellor Klaus sent Jambor a letter saying that there would soon be a law to this effect.

On October 1 another hearing was held in the Lower Austrian statehouse to work out the details of a proposal for the celebration to be passed on to the federal government. The institute, wrote Jambor, did not "have to wait upon the government to hand down a preordained rite of observance from on high, but would rather from below breathe the spirit of Austria into the 26th of October." [35] Present were representatives of the chancellor's office, the Ministry of Education, the army, the Trades Union Association, the churches, the University of Vienna, the Resistance Movement (a continuing organization of the patriotic left, founded in April 1945), and the theater and radio community.

The formal presentation of the draft law to the parliament was delayed until October 25, the day before the holiday. But the order of business referred to the "Austrian national holiday," not to a "state holiday." In his address to the parliament chancellor Klaus used the expression *national holiday,* but he also spoke of the need to develop "state consciousness." He talked, however, about the unique aspects of Austrian culture and Austrian creativeness, which furnished the clearest expression of "the Austrian national character." This was a considerable concession to the position of the cul-

32. Quoted in *Die Republik,* no. 4, October 1965, p. 145.
33. Ibid., pp. 146–49.
34. Walter Jambor, "Der Österreichische Nationalfeiertag ist der Spiegel der Nation," *Die Österreichische Nation* no. 9 (September 1965) :121.
35. Ibid., p. 123.

tural nationalists[36] for a pragmatist to make in a public address. Felix Hurdes, serving his last year in parliament, also made an extensive statement on the Conservative side. A Socialist speaker quibbled about the particular date chosen for the holiday, though he was warmly in favor of having one. And two Freedom party members pursued diversionary tactics to sidetrack the debate to another subject—the decision of the government to resign after finding it impossible to agree on a budget for the following year. When it came to the vote, however, the legislative body unanimously approved the government's draft. It is interesting that, with a parliamentary election in the offing, no one thought it useful to be against a national holiday.

Allied for a number of years with the cultural nationalist position of *Die Republik* was the liberal Catholic weekly newspaper *Die Furche,* a paper popular among young Catholic intellectuals from the center to the left end of the Conservative spectrum, particularly in Vienna. Under the editorship of Kurt Skalnik, *Furche* published reams of material on the Austrian nation and took up a strong position for the adoption of the concept, especially as it represented a cultural identity. In an interview on the subject Skalnik emphasized the non-German character of the old empire—its heavily Slavic and Magyar makeup. He pointed to the many Lower Austrian towns with names of Slavic derivation—places like Krems (Kremsnitzer), Gloggnitz, Zwettl. And he repeated a current joke about the matter. Question: "What's the greatest difference between Austrians and Germans?" Answer: "Their language." [37]

Skalnik identifies strongly with Hurdes and the solidarist Core Group. And he dislikes and mistrusts the policy of the Conservative Reformers aimed at reconciliation with former Nazis and Pan-Germans. He once said that he thought that this policy had "put brakes on the development of the nation." He is not, however, of the Core Group generation but like Jambor a much younger man. Born in 1925, Skalnik was only just coming of age at the war's end. His

36. Address by Chancellor Josef Klaus to the Austrian National Assembly, October 25, 1965, *Stenographisches Protokoll, 89. Sitzung des Nationalrates der Republik Österreich, X. Gesetzgebungsperiode,* Montag. 25. October 1965.

37. Interview in Vienna, February 10, 1966.

FASHIONING A NATIONAL IDENTITY

only prewar political involvement had been as a member of Austrian Young Folk (Österreichisches Jungvolk), a Christian Social youth group, which he joined in 1937 at the age of twelve. His university career postdated the war; he took a Ph.D. in history at the University of Vienna in 1948. As a consequence, his political outlook is more that of the consensual idealist (whom we shall describe in some detail in the next chapter) than that of the contractarian ideologist who created and operated the coalition. In his writing Skalnik has tried to build an ideological bridge between Conservatives and Socialists, working from a common fund of democratic political norms that are natural and instinctive rather than self-conscious among the younger generation to whom *Furche* appeals. Skalnik has contributed articles to Socialist party journals such as *Die Zukunft,* and he has invited contributions to *Die Furche* by Socialist intellectuals.

In one article in *Zukunft,* lamenting the emergence of interest-group politics in each of the major parties, Skalnik called for the formation of a Republican Homeland Defense League (Republikanischer Heimatschutz), a synthesis of Socialist and Conservative symbols of the 1930s. "Or" he continued, "if it were a more pleasing expression to the readers of *Zukunft,* I would also have nothing against a Fatherland Protective Organization (Vaterländischer Schutzbund)." This time he used the Socialist symbol as the noun. This writer last met Skalnik shortly after the 1965 elections in Bruno Kreisky's outer office, where he was waiting to present the Socialist leader with an anthology of his articles that had just appeared. It was entitled *Republikanische Mitte (The Republican Center).*[38] Skalnik differs from the typical consensual idealist, however, in his strong anti-German sentiments and in his exclusion of German cultural nationalists and former Nazis from his conception of the Austrian community.

Pan-German Groups

Organized opposition to the idea of an Austrian cultural nation centers on a variety of groups that propagate the German national

38. See Kurt Skalnik, *Republikanische Mitte* (Vienna: Europa Verlag, 1966).

ideal. Of particular importance are the Burschenschaften, fraternities in the high schools and universities that have been fostering
German nationalism for a hundred years among important elite
segments of the youth. Typical is the Burschenschaft "Brixia" at
the University of Innsbruck, which was founded in 1876 by ten
South Tyrolean students from Brixen. Their statement of principles
carries a "pledge to carry out the obligation of Austria within the
German nation." It is significant that Italianization policies in the
South Tyrol, annexed by Italy in 1918, have stirred a hot flame of
German rather than Austrian nationalism in the North Tyrol.

In the population at large, sports provide an important focus for
German nationalism. Turnvereine—gymnastics societies—throughout the country are federally organized as an Österreichischer Turnerbund, a successor to the Deutscher Turnerbund of the First Republic and a chief carrier of the Pan-German ideal. Cultural and
political programs share the platform with sports events in the many
Turnhallen, or gym halls, owned by the constituent associations of
the Bund around the country. And at periodic national congresses
of the federation, which take place on such occasions as the summer and winter solstice (ancient Germanic religious festivals), the
assembled members are exhorted through oratory and dramatic
presentations to remember their German heritage and hold high its
ideals. The chief speaker at a solstice festival held in Mödling in
the late 1950s, for example, is reported to have closed his remarks
with the statement: "The fire is now extinguished. . . . It will,
however, burn again brightly when our victory is secure. We live,
indeed, in Austria, but our fatherland is Germany." [39]

The Turnerbund publishes a newspaper, the *Bundesturnzeitung,*
which also conveys the German national message along with reports of sporting events. An adherent of the Austrian nation idea,
in an article critical of the Turnerbund's German nationalism, cites
the following excerpt from an issue of the paper:

> State and folkdom are different realities! Beware, therefore, that
> the expression *German,* which indicates our folk membership
> (*Volkszugehörigkeit*), which lies beyond the borders of a single

39. Reported by Heribert Husinsky writing in *Neues Österreich,* November 29, 1959, in Walter Hacker, ed., *Warnung an Österreich* (Vienna: Europa, 1966), p. 62.

state (*überstaatlich*), does not in everyday usage receive a connotation which narrows it to the West German fragment-state. . . . An example: three Münchner, two Stuttgarter, and two Salzburger are seven Germans—if state membership is brought forward as a criterion—or perhaps five West Germans (*Bundesdeutsche*) and two Austrians, but never "five Germans and two Austrians," as the language regulations of our former occupiers have prescribed. For with such a designation it would be falsely maintained that we Austrians do not belong to the German people. It is high time that we undid the spiritual damage of the decades after 1945 in which the will of foreign conquerors was our highest law.[40]

Tied in with the Turnerbund is the Österreichische Landsmannschaft (Austrian Association of Compatriots), which describes itself as a "defense and cultural association." An advertisement for its journal says that this organization "has taken over the continuing tasks of the German school association. Its strictly supraparty work serves the preservation of folkdom and of folkish cultural values." [41] In addition to the journal, the association publishes a series of brochures devoted to German national themes. One of these in particular, a pamphlet by Dr. Günther Berka entitled "Gibt es eine Österreichische Nation?" is an express reply to the pro-Austrian-nation polemical literature that we have been discussing.

Veterans' organizations, federally organized as the Österreichischer Kameradschaftsbund, also indirectly propagate Great German nationalism. Their ostensible purposes are to provide occasions for festive cameraderie among old soldiers and to assist at memorial services for those who have died in Austria's many wars. Frequently, however, these occasions also present opportunities for nostalgic reminiscenses about the battles of World War II, and thus for the reawakening or strengthening of a Great German identity. The pro-Austrian polemicists find the activities of the veterans' groups a special threat to their own cause, and they take every opportunity to point out and denounce as neo-Nazi machinations

40. Quoted by Josef Hindels in *Arbeiter-Zeitung*, November 1, 1961, in ibid., p. 70.
41. Advertisement for the *Eckartbote* on back cover of *Österreichs Deutsches Bekenntnis*, Eckartschriften, Heft 7, Vienna, November 1961.

the conduct by the Kameradschaften of memorial services and other pageantry in which the days of the "Thousand Year Empire" are favorably recalled.

Last but not least among the organizations that propagate the German national ideal in Austria is the Freedom party, which between the elections of March 1970 and October 1971 held the balance of power in the National Assembly. It is the only one of the three major parties whose leaders enjoy talking about the "Austrian nation" and who have taken a clear and unequivocal stand on the matter. They are against it.

The nationality question receives considerable attention in the party's paper, *Neue Front*. A brief article by Dr. Gerulf Stix in the issue for August 7, 1965, indicates that some of the Pan-Germans find themselves fighting a losing battle against a growing Austrianism. Entitled "The Changing Meaning of 'National,' " the burden of the essay is that in Austrian usage the word *national* is coming more and more to refer to the political nation. The members of the Freedom party, Stix argues, will have to find another word for the cultural values they cherish and defend. Perhaps *folk conscious* (*volksbewusst*) would serve, he suggests, for the Freedom party is guardian of an "hereditary folkdom."

The Press and the Political Nation

On January 31, 1967, not quite twenty-two years after the appearance of its first issue, the newspaper *Neues Österreich* closed down. It had survived the coalition which begot it by less than a year. In April 1945, as the Russians were sweeping the Nazi armies out of Vienna and Lower Austria, Conservatives, Socialists and Communists founded *Neues Österreich* as an "organ of the democratic union" by which they hoped to rebuild Austria out of the ruins of Hitler's Ostmark. It was the first paper to be established in the Second Republic. The Communists pulled out of the editorship shortly after quitting the government (though they terminated their share in the ownership much later), leaving the paper as the voice of the Conservative-Socialist coalition.

From the outset *Neues Österreich* gave more editorial room to the "Austrian nation" theme than the daily party and independent press have done. And it was the only one of the Viennese dailies to give extended coverage to the proceedings of the public inquiry on the national holiday held by Walter Jambor's Austrian National Institute.

Barbara Coudenhove-Kalergi, one of *Neues Österreich*'s star reporters, told me that her paper always represented the point of view of the "1945er." This is the man for whom persistent unhappy memories of the anschluss constantly renew fear and hatred of the Germans. He is anticapitalist, or at least believes in severe limitations on capitalist endeavor. He is a passionate democrat. And he is an emotional adherent to the idea of an Austrian nation, both in its cultural and in its political dimensions, and a proselytizer for its cause.

On particular policy questions *Neues Österreich* always defended the coalition and never took a partisan position. During the years when the necessities produced by foreign occupation seemed to rule out partisan democracy as a dangerous luxury, sales of *Neues Österreich* and advertising contracts soared. But as the processes of the coalition began to stagnate after the conclusion of the 1955 State Treaty and as an increasingly partisan attitude appeared among the leadership of the two major parties, both readers and advertisers began to lose interest in the paper. The years of the paper's decline paralleled the compromise in government circles on a purely political nation.

In Vienna each of the two leading parties publishes a daily tabloid; the Conservatives put out *Volksblatt* and the Socialists *Arbeiter–Zeitung*. Each presents in a rather flat style a distillate of the salient news stories of the moment from the party's special standpoint, together with an editorial column on the major issues of the day. Much space is also devoted to human interest material and sensationalist items. Practically no space is devoted to the Austrian nation theme, which is quite in line with the view of the major parties' leadership that the less agitation on this issue the better.

The leading independent daily newspaper in Austria is *Die Presse*, which is published in Vienna and read by the better-educated middle and upper middle classes. Since the advent of the Reformers the paper has defended an economic position very close to that of the Conservative party. But especially since Bruno Kreisky's assumption of the Socialist leadership, it has given generous and sympathetic coverage to the Socialist party as well. A revival of the *Neue Freie Presse,* the great Liberal journal of the monarchy and First Republic, *Die Presse* was published until 1970 by Fritz Molden, son of the publisher of the predecessor paper.

Die Presse has published only a few articles on the Austrian nation debate. One of its most extensive treatments of the subject, which appeared in the issue for August 21/22, 1965, was a full-page essay commenting on the significance of the poll on national consciousness taken by the Social Science Study Society (see chapter 8). While the poll showed that a majority of the sample believed that Austria had become a nation or that Austrians were gradually beginning to think as a nation, substantial minorities rejected the concept, and there was little agreement on *when* the development of national consciousness began. The member of the *Presse* editorial staff who wrote the article argued that there was overwhelming evidence that a strong Austrian self-consciousness had developed in the years since 1938, but that to discuss it in terms of acceptance or rejection of the concept *nation,* understood as *cultural community,* was not only irrelevant to an understanding of reality, but indicative of divisions where there was no real conflict, and possibly productive of a real separation. The word *nation,* as he saw it, was an outworn concept, connected with old battles and divisions and unnecessary to deal with modern realities. This view was corroborated in a number of student discussions on the Austrian nation theme conducted by *Die Presse* in various parts of the country, discussions which yielded a variety of interpretations and no agreement, and all this in the face of the fact that young Austrians accepted and loved Austria without reservations, and with an unproblematical allegiance.

The editor also saw the nation concept as a problem for German-speaking Austrians in relation to the Croatian and Slovenian minorities who inhabit the eastern and southern provinces of Austria, and for these minorities in relation to the German-speaking inhabitants of their areas. Again, here was an area in which good feelings existed in fact (though they were of recent generation in the case of the Slovenians) but in which they would be endangered by insistence on the nation concept to embrace all Austria.

If the concept were understood simply as *political community* (*Staatsnation*), however, the editor saw no problem with the word. The existence of an allegiant citizenry was undeniable, but theirs was a patriotism that did not rest on cultural values but had to do "rather with economic efficiency and a decent and fully realized democratic order." [42]

Die Presse's editor in chief, Otto Schulmeister, has written three books on the Austrian nation theme, each time rejecting the nation concept for Austria as irrelevant to the kind of reality that Austria has been and today is.[43] In the first two, Schulmeister took traditional concepts of Austria as his points of departure and attempted to find new meanings for them to fit the circumstances of the Second Republic. The third volume, however, sounds a strongly existential note in its treatment of the identity problem. Emphasis is laid on brute contemporary facts—the facts of geography, economics, politics—rather than on ideas. The true *break* with the past and the irrelevance of past ideas about Austria's meaning and purpose are underlined, and the Austrian is enjoined to find a new meaning and purpose in the existential situation. Schulmeister highlights as an especial promise for Austria's future the possibilities implicit in the country's new neutrality for rebuilding central Europe and for bringing together East and West. In any case, "the future of Austria" would be "the sum of her efforts in the present. Today there are no more hereditary titles." [44] Austria's nationality would consist of what Austrians created in meeting imaginatively and energetically the challenges laid before them.

The evolution of Schulmeister's thought is symbolic of the evolving Austrian consensus. Here we have a leading intellectual—but, significantly, an intellectual of the pragmatic elites, rather than an intellectual's intellectual—moving from a typically Conservative

42. Felix Gamillscheg, "Österreich und 'Österreichische Nation,'" *Die Presse*, August 21/22, 1965, p. 5.
43. See Otto Schulmeister, ed., *Spectrum Austriae* (Vienna: Herder, 1957); idem, *Imago Austriae* (Vienna: Herder, 1963); idem, *Die Zukunft Österreichs* (Vienna: Molden, 1967).
44. Schulmeister, *Zukunft Österreichs*, p. 363.

viewpoint which emphasizes continuity and the importance of the past to an existentialist viewpoint which sees only the present circumstance. This writer feels that no Socialist—at least none of the modern, nonideological variety who are now running the party— could disagree with the way Schulmeister has written about Austria in his newest book.

Few of the independent provincial newspapers are proponents of the "Austrian nation." Typical of opinion in the Länder are the Tyrolean weekly *Volksbote* (*People's Messenger*), which presents a Catholic point of view, and the liberal and secular Salzburg daily, *Salzburger Nachrichten* (*Salzburg News*). As a Catholic and traditionalist sheet (though not tied in with the Conservative party) *Volksbote* is very Austria-minded and devotes considerable space to patriotic themes. Unlike Catholic *Furche,* however, her editors do not embrace the Austrian nation concept. In a special supplement celebrating the twentieth anniversary of Austria's liberation, *Volksbote*'s editor, Ignaz Zangerle, wrote about the development of an Austrian identity in much the same way as the pragmatic politicians at the top of the national political system talk of that identity. The lead editorial statement focused on a comparison of the material condition of things during the twenty years after 1918 and the twenty years after 1945. "How everything has changed!" wrote Herr Zangerle. "We now live in a secure political order, have a flourishing economy, and enjoy relatively peaceful relationships." The new material situation of Austria was the most salient thing for the editor. In the next section, "To love Austria means to deserve Austria," the "Fatherland" was defined as "the Federal State of Austria, the constitutional state of Austria, and the democratic Republic of Austria as inheritor of Austrian history and as bearer of Austria's future." Immediately following was a statement about the openness of this future to change. "To a possible Austrian feeling for the fatherland perhaps tomorrow there will be added an altered political reality, that of the European federal state (Bundesstaat) of Austria." The emphasis was on openness, on transition to a new and larger sphere of action, as in Schulmeister's *Die Presse.* Also underlined was the idea that "a practical-minded and future-oriented patriotism is the psychological and moral precondition (*gesinnungsmässige Voraussetzung*) for the maintenance of our economic position in the Europe of tomorrow." [45]

The position taken by *Salzburger Nachrichten* on Austrian identity is similar to this, with perhaps a stronger German cultural emphasis. Karl Heinz Ritschel, the editor in chief (b. 1930) said in an interview in 1966 that his personal position was to support the Austrian state without denying Austria's participation in German culture. In an article that he contributed to the periodical *Wort in der Zeit* Ritschel drew an interesting conclusion about the East German question from his formula for relating Austria to West Germany. The article called for West German recognition of the German Democratic Republic as a means of relaxing tensions along the Iron Curtain. To continuously call the Oder-Neisse line into question as a definitive border he saw as "disastrous utopian thinking." He added, "Whoever denies the existence of two German states also denies the independence of German-speaking Austria and German-speaking Switzerland." Bismarck's concept of a united German Reich, he argued, was contrary to the organic development of the German states. Presumably, it was fated that the German area would always consist of many states, for Ritschel went on to ask how anyone who took an historical atlas in hand and noted how recently Germany had been a region of multiple states (*Vielstaatenreich*) could deny the existence of *two* German states. To avoid the implication that he saw the boundaries of all German-speaking states as *merely* functions of the momentary balance of forces in Europe, Ritschel added that he was an "enthusiastic Austrian from an old Austrian family" and that he "identified himself as an Austrian, but without at the same time belying the Austrian connection with the German cultural area." He acknowledged that his formulation "had brought on him the enmity of all those Austrians who reject the idea that we Austrians are a *Volksstamm* of the German Nation." [46]

It is clear that Austria's leading newspapers—both Viennese and provincial, party organs and independent journals—have accepted

45. *Volksbote*, April 17, 1965.
46. Karl Heinz Ritschel "Wohin treibt die Bundesrepublik?" in *Wort in der Zeit* 12, no. 3 (1966) : 14.

the political nation compromise and have rejected the view that political viability demands a cultural foundation.

A Free Church in a Free State: Conciliation and Pragmatism

Austria is a Catholic country. Almost 90 percent of the Austrian people claim membership in the Catholic confession. Yet less than half of them perform their required Easter duty (which consists of going to confession and receiving communion during the Easter season), and only 34 percent regularly attend church. In Vienna the figure is less than 20 percent. For Vorarlberg, the westernmost province, it is much higher—over 55 percent.[47]

The particularly low rate of church attendance for Vienna mirrors the fact that Vienna is a Socialist city, and traditionally socialism has identified the Catholic church as an ideological supporter of the hated institutions of crown and aristocracy. It did not help this situation that Ignaz Seipel, the leading political figure of the First Republic, was at once a Catholic priest, a capitalist and an economic conservative, and a man who as chancellor was ever ready to use repressive measures against Socialist dissent. Things went from bad to worse during the pious Dollfuss's Christian corporative state. On the one hand, through a concordat with the Vatican, Dollfuss restored the Catholic church in Austria to a place of special prominence and power, and on the other hand he outlawed the Socialist party. The last act in this comedy of errors was played by Cardinal Innitzer, archbishop of Vienna and primate of Austria, who in a gesture of false pragmatism sent a message to Adolph Hitler blessing the anschluss of 1938.

Events since 1945, however, indicate that the church has learned a great deal from the mistakes of the past and is today striving self-consciously to be a force for unity and reconciliation in the life of the Second Austrian Republic. In an address at the University of Vienna in May 1963 Franz Cardinal König, the archbishop of Vienna, spoke of the need for the church to perform an "integrating function" in the modern democratic state. In a day when the old ideologies which had earlier supplied an emotional political bond were weakened, the state was left prey to the centrifugal pressures of interest groups, he said. It seemed to Cardinal König that the church was now in a better condition to provide an impetus for pluralistic unity than ever before. She was the prisoner of no ideology and no interest group. No longer did the church rule; she could now only serve.[48]

The cardinal was speaking in the spirit of the Manifesto of Mariazell. In 1952 the bishops of Austria met at this abbey to reflect on the mistakes of the past and contemplate the needs of the new situation. At the close of their deliberations they adopted the watchword, "A free church in a free society."

> A free church means that the church must rely on itself, and only on itself. . . . Today the church has no emperor and no government, no party, no class, no cannon, and no capital behind her. . . . And thus the church goes out from a dying age to meet a new epoch of social development.[49]

That the bishops chose to meet at Mariazell is symbolically important. During the anschluss years loyal Austrians had adopted the custom of wearing in their hats the emblem of Our Lady of Mariazell as a protest against the Nazi conquest of their ancient homeland. And during the years of repression an awakening of church consciousness had paralleled the awakening of an Austrian spirit. The new church of Mariazell would be an Austrian-minded church as well as a free church.

In what specific ways is the post-World War II church a new church? In the first place the bishops decided after 1945 not to revive many of the old Catholic organizations, which had been very numerous and in many cases tied in with partisan political organizations. Instead, a united Catholic Action organization was created and placed under the direct control of the church hierarchy. No primarily political tasks were assigned to the new Catholic Action, however. Only the CV (Cartellverband der katholischen Österreichischen Studentenverbindungen), the association of Catholic

48. Franz Cardinal König, speech at University of Vienna, August 5, 1963, in *Worte zur Zeit,* Kathpress Dokumentation, Heft 3, pp. 92–93.
49. Quoted in Richard Barta, "Freie Kirche in freier Gesellschaft," in *Zwanzig Jahre Zweite Republik,* p. 921.

fraternities, which in the past had served as a chief reservoir of Christian Social political talent and would do so again in the Second Republic, was revived in its old form.

In political campaigns the church has given up the practice of endorsing candidates. Nothing was said from the pulpit, for example, about the candidacy for the presidency of Adolph Schärf, a Socialist and a non-Catholic, and it is noteworthy that Cardinal König sent Mr. Schärf warm congratulations upon his victory. The other side of the coin is an ecclesiastical prohibition on officeholding by Catholic priests.

Though the Dollfuss Concordat of 1933 was reactivated in 1957, many of its illiberal features have fallen into disuse, and some of its provisions were considerably modified by a treaty between the Austrian government and the Vatican that was concluded in July 1960. Absolute freedom of conscience is guaranteed to all Austrians by law, and no religious tests exist for voting or holding public office. All religious communities are guaranteed the right to both private and public worship and to self-government, though only officially recognized religious groups enjoy legal personality. This hardly works any hardship, however, since in addition to the Roman Catholic church, official recognition has been given to the Evangelical church, the old Catholics, the Greek Orthodox church, the Methodists, the Church of Jesus Christ of Latter-Day Saints (Mormons), and to Jewish communities. Each of these groups receives a subsidy in a legally specified amount from the state, from which it pays its priests, ministers, rabbis, and other personnel. Public education is under state control, but religious groups are authorized to maintain private schools if they wish. Religious instruction is held in the public schools for the various confessions, but attendance is not compulsory. And ecclesiastical law no longer affects the legal status of marriages, which are now wholly regulated by the state. (The secularization of marriage, interestingly enough, was accomplished by the Nazis, whose laws in this area have been left standing.)[50]

This does not amount to an absolute separation of church and

50. See Kurt Ringhofer, "Der Staat und die Religionsgemeinschaften," in Bruno Pittermann, ed., *Mensch und Staat* 1 (Vienna: Danubia, 1962), p. 425 ff.

state on the American model, but it does constitute a substantial modification of past Austrian practice, in which a captive church did the bidding of the state in exchange for special privileges and for the legal execution of its acts. Cardinal König, for one, would like even further modifications to provide greater freedom for the church. "To what extent withdrawals from the church and the church tax are connected" he writes "has furnished food for thought in the past, and the question demands a thorough review in the future. That the clergy have been burdened by the church tax cannot be denied." [51] He thinks a fairer arrangement would be to have church subscriptions collected by the state, but he recognizes that some would see this as a "Josephinist" (i.e., state-church) solution.[52]

That a man like Cardinal König should today be archbishop of Vienna and primate of the Austrian church is also a sign of changed times. In more than one respect he is different from his predecessors. For one thing he is not a Viennese but a Lower Austrian "provincial," from the working-class town of St. Pölten. Just as the center of political gravity in the Second Republic has shifted away from Vienna to the other Länder, so even in the staffing of the ecclesiastical hierarchy one looks for talent beyond the precincts of the metropolis. König's biographer, Richard Barta, notes the reserve and the raised eyebrows with which the Viennese greeted the news that an "outsider" had been elevated to the See of Vienna. That the cardinal should stem from working-class origins as well as from an industrial town is also a new departure. That this has much to do with König's freedom from the many privileged-class blindspots of his predecessors in his views on democracy, the working class, youth, socialism, communism and a host of other questions of public policy seems clear. What is most striking is that the cardinal is not a captive of the proletarian viewpoint but a rather remarkably un-class-conscious man, and a Christian who for all his deep human concern about social problems refuses to lose sight of the preeminently transcendent and transhistorical message of the gospels.

Having served earlier as bishop coadjutor of St. Pölten, Franz

51. Franz Cardinal König in *Die Furche,* May 18, 1963; also printed in *Worte zur Zeit,* p. 104.
52. Ibid.

König was elevated by papal appointment to the archbishopric of Vienna in May 1956. Viewed in its political perspective, his style of action since then has reflected the same pragmatic and conciliatory values we have already noted in the *Weltanschauung* and behavior of the leading politicians of the Second Republic and which we shall discuss more fully in chapter 7.

Cardinal König's chief political objective in Austrian domestic politics has been to reconcile the various political forces whose divisions in the past have caused conflict and instability in Austrian political life. He has refused to play party politics and has said frankly that "no political party can expect a blank check from the church to underwrite its policies." [53] Probably more than any other churchman Cardinal König is responsible for the new attitude that the Socialist party has adopted toward the Catholic church. He has always been friendly to the Socialists, and his working-class background lends credence to his words. The first contacts, looking to the beginning of a dialogue between the church and socialism, date from the years when Franz Olah, a Socialist leader who is also an active Catholic layman, was minister of the interior. The initiative came from both sides. The upshot has been the complete cessation of cultural warfare between the two discussants and the inception of a new era of tolerance and mutual understanding.

To what extent does the church, in its work of reconciliation and integration stress the idea of Austria as a nation? Does it, like the ministries of Education and Defense, have a program for the direct inculcation of patriotism? I could not discover any, nor is there evidence that the subject is discussed from the pulpit. Cardinal König holds a middle-of-the-road position on the subject. Since 1945, he has indeed been an enthusiast about the Austrian idea, and he uses the expression *our nation* when talking about Austria in his public addresses. Thus, for example, he has spoken of the church "as the moral conscience of the nation," and he has referred to the unanimity of the youth in their "allegiance to Austria" (*Bekenntnis zu Österreich.*) [54] On the twentieth anniversary of the

53. Richard K. Barta, *Kardinal Franz König* (Vienna: Herder, 1965), p. 79.

54. Franz Cardinal König, New Year's Message, 1962, in *Worte zur Zeit*, pp. 28, 30.

reestablishment of the republic the Austrian bishops in a pastoral letter reminded Catholics of their responsibility to maintain freedom and democracy in the fatherland, and then they went on to predict that Catholics "would protect this freedom against every reappearance of anti-Austrian tendencies." [55] Speaking of European unification in his New Year's message of 1965, Cardinal König told the faithful that "only as good Austrians could they hope to be good Europeans! And this not as a museum of a rich cultural past, but rather as a community of mutual responsibility and mutual work and effort." [56]

Expressions like these, of course, entirely sidestep the issue of "cultural nation" versus "political nation," which is the point on which the most ardently emotional defenders of the Austrian nation, like Felix Hurdes, part company with all others. According to Barta, the church since 1945 "has consciously cultivated Austrian community" (which is not the same thing as cultivating the idea of an Austrian nation), but it has never tried to define that community in opposition to things German. Today, men like Cardinal König, like the pragmatic politicians who run the political system, do not see the question of the Austrian nation as a burning one, nor do they find any utility in conducting a national polemic about the matter. Barta refused to grant that champions of an Austrian cultural nationalism like Kurt Skalnik, former editor of *Furche,* and Walter Jambor, executive secretary of the Austrian Institute, typify the viewpoint of the modern, committed, churchgoing Catholic. In answer to a direct question he simply replied that Austrian Catholicism is "very pluralistic." [57]

Youth Organizations

Austrian youth have been an active as well as a passive factor in their own political socialization. One organization in particular is of special importance—the Austrian Federal Youth Council; its very existence is a sign of growing political community. This is an association of the fifteen principal youth organizations in the country, and it embraces Catholic and Protestant, Conservative and So-

55. Quoted in Barta, *Kardinal Franz König,* p. 70.
56. Ibid., p. 72.
57. Interview with Richard Barta, Vienna, March 29, 1966.

cialist groups. There are 400,000 individual members. The First Republic knew no such tent organization which could create communications links across ideological barriers and promote a common effort among youth groups of different ideological persuasions. According to the council's director in 1966, Rupert Gnant, 20 percent of Austria's youth up to twenty-five years of age are organized in some fashion or other, and 80 percent of these belong to member associations of the council.[58]

It was the need to solve a problem of widespread youth unemployment, a problem recognizing no ideological boundaries, that led to the formation of the Council in 1952. Following preliminary talks an organizational structure came into being in 1953. The presence of the president of the republic, the chancellor, and representatives of the parties, churches, and interest groups at the founding ceremonies showed that the country's chief power structures and most influential leaders were prepared to bless the efforts of the unprecedented new organization. By 1954 the council had detailed a plan for ending youth unemployment which served as a working draft for the Youth Unemployment Law passed by the parliament shortly afterward. Among other things the law requires the larger firms of the country to employ at least some young people.

Following this initial success the council proceeded to demonstrate its usefulness in a variety of other ways. In 1955 it announced its support of the declaration of Austrian neutrality and its willingness "to defend the spiritual, political, and economic freedom of the country." [59] When thousands of Hungarians fled into Austria after the abortive revolution of 1956, the council created a section for refugee assistance which operated for two years to relieve the distress of the uprooted people. In 1957 the republic recognized the council's contribution to Austrian life with the Dr. Karl Renner Prize, one of its highest awards. And in 1962 the parliament provided an annual subvention of fifteen million schillings for the work of the Federal Youth Council, to be paid in part from the

58. Interview with Rupert Gnant, director of the Austrian Federal Youth Council, Vienna, March 21, 1966.
59. "The Austrian Federal Youth Council and its Member Organizations," 1965, p. 2.

budget of the Education Ministry and in part from the budget of the Ministry for Social Welfare.

The objectives of the council contain an express commitment to democracy and a resolution to resist totalitarian tendencies of both the right and the left. The organization's work has also prominently featured programs which contribute to the development of a strong patriotic spirit among the youth. Materials on contemporary history, a subject that continues to subsist at a bare-facts level in the schools, have been disseminated by the council through its member organizations. In addition, the council has been helping make an exhibition of pictures on Austrian history since 1945. In 1966 the council was working on disseminating to other member groups Catholic Youth's brief history book, *Österreich, Mein Vaterland.*

The council has also dealt at least once with the controversial Austrian nation theme. At its fourteenth general assembly in November 1966 a change was adopted in the fourth paragraph of its statutes. For the expression "recognition of the Republic of Austria and of democracy" the following was substituted: "recognition of the Republic of Austria, the Austrian nation, and democracy." [60] The council seems to have no continuing program on this theme, however, such as that of the Austrian Institute. And Director Gnant told me that the council avoids getting involved in the "philosophical niceties" of the controversy.

It is significant that youth groups associated with Pan-German organizations and with organizations connected with the Nazi past are not members of the council. Nor does it embrace the tiny Communist youth movement. Neither the Council of Free Youth (which is associated with the Freedom party) nor the Free Austrian Youth (close to the Communist party) belongs to the council. Groups like these on the extreme right and left of the political spectrum have in fact been consciously excluded from the council, which employs a unanimity rule in processing applications. Once the council incurred the anger of Dr. Piffl, the minister of education, by turning down the application of a group patronized by him which the council deemed too far to the right to fit into a democratic consensus. All member groups must recognize the institutions of the republic,

60. Österreichischer Bundesjugendring Statut, Änderungen beschlossen am 26. November 1966 (XIV. Vollversammlung).

undertake a commitment to democracy as specified in the council's charter, and promise to resist totalitarianism. When the federal government voted subsidies for the council in 1962, it came in for some abuse by the groups excluded, and occasionally, according to Director Gnant, it has been attacked for its position on the Austrian nation.

While the Federal Youth Council serves youth up to twenty-five years of age, it does not include college organizations. Of these the most noteworthy on the Conservative side is the CV. Since the days of the empire this has been a most important organization, for it has served as a chief recruiting ground for public servants and as an instrument of political socialization for the young elite. Virtually every Conservative leader of importance is a member of this "club," which performs for Austria much the same function as the Oxbridge complex in Great Britain.

The CV was originally begun as a Catholic response to the ideological challenge of the Liberal (secular and Pan-German) brotherhoods (Burschenschaften) of the late nineteenth century. Its objects were, to begin with, religious, not nationalistic, and until 1933 the CV maintained a connection with a parallel organization in Germany. In that year the Austrian CV left the German group, however, in protest against the Nazi accession to power. It went underground in 1938 and was revived again after the war.

After two semesters of pledgeship, new members of the CV take an oath to uphold four principles: Catholicism, fatherland, scholarship, and lifelong friendship. And the last of these is not the least significant of the four. The "old boys" of the fraternity are as conscious of their "CVness" as the undergraduates, and they participate year after year in reunions and special events of various kinds.

Traditionally a conservative organization in more than one sense of the word, the CV in the last few years has evinced, especially among its younger members, a taste for change. At a leadership symposium in Graz in the spring of 1968 (theme—"the new CV") and again at the annual general assembly of the organization at Wiener Neustadt in May, the brothers debated opening membership of the fraternity to non-Catholic Christians. Admission of the fair sex to membership, in view of increased college attendance by women, was also discussed at Graz. There were calls for practical ecumenical experiments of a variety of kinds, critical statements about the conventional political parties, demands for special new ties with the neighboring Communist states to the east, a discussion of worldwide development aid, calls for a new college law that would modernize and democratize Austrian universities, and requests for conscientious implementation of the decisions of the Second Vatican Council.

The pages of the CV monthly journal *Academia* have also been ruffled by the winds of the progressive spirit. Outspoken interviews with Austrian opinion leaders of all persuasions appear frequently. Articles critical of the work of older brothers in the government are not infrequent. Stories on controversial aspects of Austrian foreign policy and on such embarrassing themes as the implications for the conscientious Christian of Vatican II's statements on the Jews, which raise the eyebrows of some of the "old boys," are becoming commonplace in the journal.

The 1968 assembly at Wiener Neustadt, acting in the spirit of the new openness to change, undertook a large-scale revision of the statutes of the CV, which had last been reworked in 1935. Significant for our theme were two changes bearing on the stance of the CVer toward things German. Article 4, which earlier had contained a statement of allegiance to "German folkdom" (*Volkstum*) and an acknowledgment of "the spiritual and cultural unity of the German-speaking area" was altered to read: "The ÖCV acknowledges its allegiance to the sovereign state of Austria and to its special tasks which derive from Austria's history and special position." The word *German* was eliminated altogether. Article 1 noted, as before, that "the ÖCV developed out of the association of Catholic German student fraternities" but dropped off the final clause of the sentence which had read: "and continues its traditions and tasks in the colleges of Austria."

The Austrian-minded chapters of the fraternity did not get everything they wished, however. The new formulas were a compromise. The reformers would have liked to have written in a confession of allegiance to "the Austrian republic" or to "an independent and democratic Austria," but they had to defer to the wishes of chapters with legitimist roots. They would also have liked to have inserted an acknowledgment of "the Austrian nation," but this was rejected by the German cultural nationalists. The opposition was a small minority, however (decisions must be unanimous), and the new statutes as they stand represent a vast change in the atmosphere of the CV. Even among the alumni there were no majorities against the changes.[61] Once again we find modernization and democratization moving hand in hand with the development of national consciousness.

The most important youth group on the Socialist side is Socialist Youth (Sozialistische Jugend), an independent association of young people between fourteen and twenty-one years of age, which serves as the chief educational organization of the Socialist party and as its primary recruiting ground for new party functionaries and leaders. Its programs are comprehensive, like those of the Socialist organizations for adults, embracing every aspect of life. It is at once a political and ideological educator, a purveyor and critic of culture, a sports club, and a social center. The association's monthly journal, *trotzdem,* for example, may contain articles criticizing the conduct of military maneuvers by the "Black"-controlled (during the coalition period) federal army, news from local branches about such things as table tennis matches and helping out the victims of flood damage, articles on the art of Picasso, a review of recently issued films, a selection of short-short stories, and a report on a conference of Austrian youth on aid to developing countries.

Kurt Hawlicek, then the international secretary of Socialist Youth, explained its organizational structure to this writer during an interview in Vienna in December 1965. In every *Bezirk* (comparable to an American city ward) there are three or four youth groups of between ten and forty young people each, which implement the goals of Socialist Youth. They meet about three times a week, with a typical week's program including a political meeting, a cultural meeting, and an outing. Hawlicek told me that at these meetings much time has been devoted to a discussion of the question of the national holiday. He claims that Socialists have been talking about the matter since about 1957. Not content with the decision setting Ocober 26 as the holiday, they are now working for the declaration of a second national holiday, to be celebrated on November 12, the anniversary of the founding of the First Re-

61. Interview with Peter Diem, a young CVer, Vienna, May 30, 1968.

public, which has always been a special day for Socialists. (Every year on this day the Socialist Youth proceed solemnly to the monument to the three Socialist fathers of the republic on the Ringstrasse, where wreaths are placed and inspirational talks heard.)[62]

Symbol of Synthesis: Günther Nenning

Much of this chapter has been devoted to evidence of continuing dissensus among Austrian intellectuals on the question of the nation. We have also seen, however, that alongside the continuing polemic there have been significant efforts to synthesize the competing political cultures. Drimmel's decision to focus the citizenship program of the Education Ministry on political values represents an important step in bringing all Austrians together on established common ground, as has his sponsorship of efforts at the rewriting of Austrian history on a nonideological basis. Though a marked line of cleavage still divides the Austrian cultural nationalists from all other shades of opinion on the nation question, it is significant that the cleavage tends to have only this single dimension and does not coincide with numerous others, as in the past. Cultural nationalists today are mostly liberal democrats, like all other Austrians, not monarchists or corporatists. And the Conservatives among them (the largest group) tend to have more in common on social and economic questions with Socialists than with the members of their own party who are economic liberals. Pan-Germans, though they orate much about the glories of German culture, have given up the anschluss dream and appear to have become reliable republicans and democrats.

Austria's major newspapers no longer speak for and to closed political-cultural camps, but to a variegated and yet single Austrian public. Variety is manifest in contrasting positions on pragmatic political issues, not on clashing ideological watchwords, and singleness is found in the substantial agreement on the concept of Austria as a political nation. The Catholic church, formerly a divisive factor both politically and culturally, has undertaken the work of conciliation and consensus building. The church has also decided to climb on the bandwagon of the political nation and ignore the

62. Interview with Dkfm. Kurt Hawlicek, Vienna, December 23, 1965.

unsettled questions of background culture. Austria's youth, with whom the future of the Austrian nation lies, have revealed a remarkable capacity for cooperative endeavor in their organizational life and for national consensus building.

One Austrian publicist represents in a very special way the degree of consensus that Austrians have achieved today in their national life. He is Günther Nenning, the talented editor of *Neues Forum,* whose pages serve the cause of consensus building. Nenning is technically a Socialist, but he is extremely disliked by the party's leaders and bureaucrats. He is known as an extreme maverick who thumbs his nose at the idea of party discipline. During the parliamentary election campaign of 1966 the Conservative press took delight in publishing in large headlines and lengthy stories the latest criticisms by Nenning of the fallacies of the ideology, policy, and strategy of his party, and especially of its unmodifiable attachment to the coalition and to *Proporz.* (Since then, of course, both major parties have left the coalition far behind.) With even more glee they reported in detail the embarrassed efforts of the leadership to censure and silence him, efforts which were always without effect.

Nenning might be called a professional synthesizer, an apostle of consensus—a new kind of ideologist whose work is entirely different from that of both the ideologists of the 1930s and the party "fringers" of today. His object is to state a national ideology by fusing *all* contemporary intellectual standpoints. As one Socialist politician put it, "Nenning wants to amalgamate everything with everything else." As a practicing Catholic his chief objective is to fuse Marxism with Christianity. But his idea of synthesis embraces "Brown" (in the form of its Liberal origins) as well as "Black" and "Red." He likes to speak of hope lying in the convergence of the "three great spiritual streams" of Austrian history. "With the Christian mother stream, from which they at one time branched off, only to lose themselves in the sea of *hybris,* liberalism and socialism will find themselves once more united." [63] And he is willing to argue that Austrian Nazis should be rehabilitated (as many

63. Günther Nenning, *Anschluss an die Zukunft* (Vienna: Europa, 1963), p. 188.

have been), that they were never as bad as the myths about them allege, and that everyone was much more sympathetic to them in the 1930s than he is today willing to admit.

The theme of his leading book, *Anschluss an die Zukunft,* is that the chief obstacle to national unity is the preservation of the *Lager* mentality by the retention of and subservience to party histories, which are in every sense partial views of the past. These views are all phantasms and need to be exorcised by a willingness to look frankly and coolly at Austria's past and to recognize that no part of it was either as virtuous or as evil as the various party accounts maintain. (We have seen that historians are in fact working on the problem.)

In writing about the idea of an Austrian nation, Nenning finds the Socialists unreasonable in their view that everything began in 1918 with the republic; he insists that the monarchy and traditional Austria be given their due as legitimate and necessary sources of contemporary values and ideals. He has many kind things to say about the Habsburgs, and about Otto Habsburg, who remains to this day a whipping boy of even the pragmatic, nonideological Socialist leadership. Though he leans toward the idea of Austria as a *Kulturnation,* Nenning is unwilling to go all the way with the various "fringers" discussed above and insists on retaining some values for Pan-Germans in the consensual view of Austria he wishes to propagate. In the process of her *Nationswerdung* he hopes Austria will develop an independent character without separating absolutely from German culture (*Besonderheit,* not *Absonderung*). And he looks forward to an "active growing up into Europe as a supranational, democratic federation of individual states with equal rights, and embracing, at last, both eastern and western Europe." [64] Not anschluss with Germany but anschluss with Europe is Austria's need.[65]

While Nenning's role as ideologist would imply an agreement with the "fringers" that the idea of Austria must be actively propagated, Nenning has said that he sees the continuing debate about the question among intellectuals as without political significance, a

64. Ibid., p. 111.
65. Ibid., pp. 117–19.

view typical of the pragmatic politicians in power. The foundations are securely laid, and the rest is not a matter of abstract argument but of historical development and "growth in quiet."

How does one explain an ideologist who in effect argues that ideology is bad? Perhaps by seeing Nenning not as someone whose role is to change minds and convert people, which is the role of the true ideologist, but rather as the spokesman of the formed or forming consensus, as someone who sums up what has been accomplished, not as an innovator. *Anschluss an die Zukunft* may be one of the last ideological works that Nenning—and Austria—will produce.

6. NATIONAL CONSCIOUSNESS AMONG ELITES

To this point we have been looking largely at processes of development—the integrating thrust of a twenty-year coalition, with attendant social and economic change; the coalition's transformation into the normal form of parliamentary democracy; the process of synthesizing an "Austrian idea." Now it is time to ask whether and to what extent these processes have produced national consciousness or national feeling among the people of Austria. How fully and in what form has a nation developed within the diminutive nation-state? What does empirical research reveal about the character and extent of national consciousness among Austrian leaders and their followers?

Studies of the elite and of the followers may reveal different patterns of consciousness, so we shall have to deal with them separately, though we must, of course, show how our findings on the two populations are related. To collect data on the elite we have chosen the interview as our most efficient method, and to study the followers, the methods of survey research. This chapter and the next report our findings about elite attitudes. In chapter 8 we deal with the Austrian people at large.

Interviews as a Measure of National Consciousness among the Elite

During the period from September 1965 to August 1966 and during the month of June 1968 this writer talked with approximately 100 Austrian leaders, using a semi-structured, open-ended approach. My respondents were for the most part from the upper and middle ranges of the political elite—top leaders and key functionaries of the two major parties and civil servants at both the federal and state levels. The rest were idea makers and communicators—academicians, writers, journalists, persons in radio and television. Many of the latter have already been discussed in chapter 5. The following deals primarily with the political elites.

The problem of obtaining reliable responses to my questions— what the respondents *really* thought and felt about the "Austrian nation"—was not great. Most of the people with whom I spoke have taken or are willing to take a public position on the matter. And it is public role playing, not private inclination, that is significant here—what one thinks he is required to say under given circumstances. It is his subjectively understood role, as projected in his words and his actions, that constitutes an elite's reality in the political system. That this may not correspond to what goes on in the man's heart of hearts does not alter his present political role.

An illustration will demonstrate the point. One of the top Conservative leaders interviewed seemed to be the embodiment of democratic pragmatism in all his replies. From other sources of information it appears that, as a leading Reformer, he has quite consistently taken a pragmatic stance in his daily decision-making roles in the government and in his party. However, a junior Socialist functionary who read the writeup of my interview with this Conservative insisted that I had misunderstood him or that he had misled me; the Socialist declared that the man was "really very ideological" in his cut of mind and a romantic in his conception of life and politics. That there is something to this claim was indicated by a certain stiffness in the manner and bearing of the Conservative leader, and by the known fact that the man's personal relations with leaders of the Socialist opposition have been far less cordial than those of other top Conservatives with the same people. Attitudes of this kind might well stem from the rigidities produced by ideological thinking.

The fact remains, however, that a possibly latent ideologism was acted out in minimal fashion and that the man in question made a great effort to play the practical democratic and consensualist politician, things which are of overwhelming importance in placing him in the spectrum of opinion and behavior. If we take into account latent or covert attitudes, we are dealing with *potential* politics— attitudes that would affect action were the system of democratic role-playing in some way made ineffective for the processing of political

demands. The following account emphasizes overt attitudes, statements, and actions. Of course when it is obvious that a subterranean
view has had an important effect on policy, this will be pointed out.

The Top Leadership

The men at the top of the hierarchies of the two major parties hold
very similar views of the Austrian nation. Leaders on both sides
emphasize the political aspects of nationality, and they see popular
acceptance of Austria as a political nation as complete. Such views
substantiate the evidence discussed in earlier chapters. As chief
causes of this evolution they cite the unhappy experience of the
anschluss, the happy postwar escape from partition into East Austria and West Austria, and the success of the pragmatic politicians
of the postwar coalition in refuting the myth of economic nonviability by creating an affluent society (*Wohlstandstaat*). Self-conscious public discussion of the nation concept and the direct prop-
agation of the idea of Austria as a nation, especially as a cultural nation, they see as irrelevant and uninteresting to the public
at best and at worst as dangerously divisive. (They therefore agree
with the functionalists that political allegiance rests on economic
foundations, and with Etzioni that politics and culture are separable.)

When this writer asked former Chancellor Josef Klaus (ÖVP)
whether Austrians also needed to think of their country as a cultural nation he replied that Austria constitutes a nation in everything *staatlich,* in everything pertaining to the state, but that there
is not a separate Austrian culture. To illustrate he pointed out
that Austria's parliament is called a Nationalrat and her chief library the Nationalbibliothek. He likes former Chancellor Raab's
formula for Austria's identity: "German is my mother tongue, Austria my fatherland." German oppression during the anschluss of
1938 to 1945 produced a "rebirth of national consciousness," as
Klaus sees it, and the subsequent success of "wise politicians on
both sides" in obtaining a united, free, and independent Austria
created a "feeling of having found our own way . . . independent
and self-reliant, though small." It is in indirect ways such as this,
said the chancellor, that national consciousness is cultivated. "It
cannot be decreed." The further maturation of Austrian national

feeling would flow from a *gute Politik*—a problem-solving effort. It would not come from "flowery speeches about the Austrian nation!" [1]

Former Vice-Chancellor Hermann Withalm (also secretary general of the ÖVP until 1970 and then party chairman to 1971), told me that 95 percent of the population were today "ardent Austrians" (*begeisterte Österreicher*). "They dote upon the fatherland." The creation of this national enthusiasm, and especially the political integration of the working class, had been the coalition's greatest service to the country, he said. Like Chancellor Klaus, Withalm had little use for self-conscious discussion of the nation concept. "It is better to act than to talk," he said, "especially when there's nothing behind the talk." [2]

Bruno Kreisky, the leader of the Socialist party who became chancellor in April 1970, emphasized that "Austria to the SPÖ *means* Republic." The nation is defined by its form of government. Like Klaus, he dates the beginnings of national feeling from the days of the anschluss, and like Withalm, he stresses the integration of the working class in the Second Republic, in contrast to their lack of attachment to the First. Jobs and a democratic share in decision making have made the difference in their attitude. Like both of his Conservative antagonists, Kreisky thinks that the coalition strengthened the identification of the Austrian people with the state. And again like both men, he found the public discussion of the nation idea to be "entirely peripheral" (*ganz am Rande*).[3]

When Nationalrat (member of parliament) Karl Czernetz, a leading Socialist member of parliament and chief ideologist of the SPÖ, was asked to explain his formulation of the Austrian nation idea, he replied with a brief history of the differences between the western and central European concepts of nation. Since 1945, he said, a majority of Austrians have supported Austrian political independence, which implicitly means an acceptance of the Western political nation concept. However, because the word *nation* in Austria has always had the central European, cultural nation connotation, he thinks the word *nation* of little value to symbolize the

1. Interview with Josef Klaus, Vienna, May 25, 1966.
2. Interview with Hermann Withalm, Vienna, June 1, 1966.
3. Interview with Bruno Kreisky, Vienna, May 17, 1966.

new sense of political community. Surely most people do not think enough about such abstract matters to be able to make the distinction between the two definitions of *nation,* he said. He therefore found discussion of the nation idea to be of little use—a rather remarkably nonideological stance for a chief ideologist! [4]

The idea of uniqueness is surely an essential part of the concept of nationality. Yet none of the four respondents we have discussed had much to say about the specific content of Austrianism, the things that make Austrians different, unique, a separate nation. Reflections of this kind, of course, intellectualize the nation concept, and, as we have seen, the pragmatist approaches political problems in nonintellectual terms. To him, national feeling is that unthinking acceptance of the political community and the regime that derives from satisfactions produced by the efficient processing of bread-and-butter issues. As Czernetz said, "most people don't think about what a nation is." Perhaps these four respondents also understood that when one begins to engage in reflections of this kind all sorts of latent disagreements, which for their purposes are better swept under the rug, immediately begin to appear. We have seen this in our survey of the intellectuals in chapter 5. Gut satisfactions that can be universalized are safer than partisan reflections for the politician who wants to get or stay in power in a democracy.

When pressed on the question of uniqueness, all the leaders interviewed avoided specificity as much as possible. There were, however, nuances of difference in their fragmentary replies. (I have data for only three of the four. In my interview with Withalm, we did not get to the subject.) When asked whether he thought that developing trade and communications patterns were strengthening Austrian feeling or were making for closer relations with Germany, Chancellor Klaus replied that despite an ever-increasing flood of German tourists (70 percent of the entire tourist population) no

4. Interview with Karl Czernetz, Vienna, December 30, 1965. Age does not seem to be an important variable in defining attitudes at the top of the party hierarchies. Leopold Gratz (at the time of my interview one of three secretaries general of the Socialist party and later minister of education) is a man in his late forties. The four leaders whose views we have discussed to this point are all men in their fifties or early sixties. Yet Gratz's responses to my questions about the Austrian nation fit precisely the same pattern as the older men's.

amalgamation of the Austrian to the German "way" was occurring. If anything, he felt that the German tourists had produced a stronger will on the part of Austrians "to have their own special way," to affirm their uniqueness. Austria, he thought, needed to cultivate something special, something different, for Germans to find when they came as tourists. But he did not explain what this might be—although the line of thought runs directly to the concept of the cultural nation, which the former chancellor rejects.[5]

The closest that Kreisky and this writer came to a discussion of uniqueness was in talking about the chancellor's definition of a nation as a "community of destiny," which he derives from Otto Bauer. "If Austria holds together long enough in independence it might become a 'community of destiny,' " he said. National feeling, forming around the memory of common experiences, would develop unconsciously, without any long discussions or propaganda. "One already senses the beginnings of this at soccer games, when Austria wins," he said. There was no mention of past common experiences, however, which Conservatives like to bring up but which evoke bitter memories among Socialists. The formula used by Kreisky was an inverted Burkeanism. Czernetz, too, expressly said that Austrian identity could not rest on the past but would have to develop out of new elements, and then he added a problematic note by talking about the universalization of culture as "world art, or at least Western culture"; it was to this that Austria needed to contribute rather than attempt to build a parochial identity. Our discussion turned at this point to European integration. The top leaders are content to have great ambiguities in national definition—and to ignore them as much as possible.[6]

National Party Functionaries

The officials of the central party organizations in Vienna sit at a point in the political system where parochial conceptions and attitudes from all over the country flow together for possible synthesis into a national point of view. These men control important lines of

5. Interview with Josef Klaus, Vienna, May 25, 1966.
6. Interviews with Bruno Kreisky and Karl Czernetz, Vienna, May 17, 1966, and December 30, 1965.

communication between the top leadership and the grass roots. They collect and digest ideas for party programs from every quarter, frequently feeding ideas of their own into the hopper at the same time. They define issues, synthesize programs, plan strategies. They pass on directives, admonitions, and encouragement from the leaders to the local activists and help to funnel gripes from the grass roots up to the top of the system. They organize election campaigns and keep the party operating as a national entity between the great quadrennial battles at the polls. Do they also synthesize or in some way represent a national outlook?

The central functionaries are a varied lot both in terms of the roles they perform and the age groups represented among them. The patterns of their political ideas, as a consequence, are also varied, and on the issue of national consciousness they do not display the singleness of mind that is found among the few leaders at the top. Rodney Stiefbold, who has directed an extensive survey of Austrian elites, asserts that a leading characteristic of the middle-range political elite as a whole, to which central party functionaries belong, is a highly ideological attitude, which contrasts sharply with the pragmatism of their masters.[7] These people, he asserts, are carriers of the *Lager* mentality that historically has been a major factor in keeping Austria a divided society. My own research, however, indicates that this generalization does not obtain without qualification for the subgroup of central functionaries.

For one thing, it is important to distinguish between idealism and ideologism. Interest in normative abstractions, connoted by the first word, is perfectly consistent with community and consensus. Only when those abstractions are battle cries which distinguish "us" from "them," the faithful from the infidels (or heretics), do they produce ideologism. While the interviews indicated a much higher interest in abstract value ideas among the party central functionaries than among the top leaders, many of the abstractionists appeared as consensualist idealists, not ideologists in Stiefbold's sense (see

7. See Rodney P. Stiefbold, "Elite-Mass Opinion Structure and Communication Flow in a Consociational Democracy (Austria)" (paper delivered at the 1968 convention of the American Political Science Association, Washington, D.C.), pp. 20, 21, 23; Stiefbold cites Karl W. Deutsch, *The Nerves of Government: Models of Political Communication and Control* (New York: The Free Press, 1963), pp. 154–57.

note 7). And even among the ideologists there were frequently offsetting factors at work which tended to reduce the divisive impact
of their ideas. I also found pure pragmatists like those among the
top leadership in the middle echelon.

The consensual idealists among the middle-echelon, central-office
respondents (mostly men in their early thirties) all embraced the
idea of Austria as a cultural nation, in contrast with the contractarian pragmatist leaders, who, as we have seen, preferred the nar-
rower concept of political nationality. The ideologists did not have
a common attitude toward the Austrian nation, except that they
tended to view the concept more as a political weapon in the electoral battle than as the symbol of a reality that demands recognition because it is real.

A senior functionary in the Conservative general secretariat, a
man in his fifties, exemplifies the moderate ideologist. (In no case
was an extreme ideological temperament observed in any of the
respondents.) On the subject of dialogue with the Socialists, he
rejected the idea that the blurring of ideological lines would be good
for the country. He preferred that differences between Conservatives
and Socialists be depicted in the sharpest outline, so that people
would know what they were choosing. Ideological blurring in the
past, he said (referring to the period of Core Group ascendancy),
had worked in favor of Socialist power. He expressed intense disapproval of Cardinal König, archbishop of Vienna, who is known
for his interest in Catholic-Socialist dialogue and for his social reform orientation.

Instead of shying away from the nation concept as inherently
ambiguous and fraught with political difficulties, as the topmost
leadership did, this man stated that he saw the problem of Austrian
nationality as one of definitions, which could be easily managed.
"Someday, and not too far away now, we will have a commission of
experts who will settle the matter." He denied that the present
reluctance of the party leadership to push the idea of the Austrian
nation derived from a fear of losing Pan-German votes. "We all
agree that there is nothing to lose on the Right." But he did not
explain *why* the Conservatives have refrained from espousing the
"full Austrian" position now. "In a few years it will be the time to
accept the Austrian nation," he said. "The Socialists will not be

able to play the 'Red-White-Red' game much longer. They cannot manage the concept of the Austrian nation, because it is obvious that Austria didn't start in 1918, as they claim. It is impossible to reject the past the way they do." In other words the Austrian nation, he thought, would soon be a good weapon with which to trounce the Socialist opposition. To be fair, it should be noted that in another situation this respondent has expressed genuine and spontaneous Austrian nationalism. It was only in the context of reflection on the nation concept that ideological partisanship, his work-day frame of reference, reduced the idea to a political instrument.

An official in a closely related branch of the Conservative secretariat, a man in his late forties whose competence, like that of the first respondent, includes considerations of party strategy, rejected the Austrian nation idea entirely. Very cordial and at ease at the start of our discussion, he grew more uncomfortable every moment as I unfolded the details of my project to him in the form of asking his advice on the rewording of a formal questionnaire that I had used in earlier interviews. This man was thinking of problems in the short run; he seemed to think that my study of the Austrian nation might throw a wrench into the national election campaign that was just shaping up. And it was plain that he feared that the Austrian nation issue might lose right-wing votes for the Conservatives, especially if the secretariat appeared to be involved with the concept in the context of a foreigner's research project! He did not directly say any of these things, but the obvious escalation of his anxiety as we talked made them a reasonable inference from the comments he did make. When we reached the question "Do you believe that most Austrians possess an Austrian national feeling or consciousness or not? A state consciousness?" he ceased to advise me on details of wording and began to debate substantively the meaningfulness of the Austrian national concept. It was only the pessimists, doubtful of Austria's independence of will and ability to solve her problems, who wanted to stress the so-called Austrian nation, he said. They were fearful that without such a label Austria would be unable to hold her own as she moved into an increasingly integrated Europe, and they were anxiously looking for an unnecessary immunization against the anschluss idea. In a long aside he insisted that national consciousness was identical with nationalism and that the world had had enough of it; it had always produced dangerous feelings of superiority. He wanted nothing to do with the Austrian nation concept in any form, either as a political or a cultural concept, and he exhibited a much greater distaste for it than had any of the top party leadership.

The contrast between the ideologist's regard for words and the pragmatist's stress on actions was particularly striking in these two interviews. While the first subject rejected Conservative-Socialist dialogue as likely to obfuscate differences between the two parties, subject number two rejected such discussions as politically irrelevant. Symbols for this second man are meaningful only when tied to experienced reality, not in the abstraction of academic discussion. As an example he cited the flying of Austrian flags on the Hungarian border at the time of the Hungarian revolution against the Russians to let refugees know where they could find freedom and asylum. He also commented adversely on the wording of a questionnaire item which read, "Who, in your opinion, are the most prominent exponents of the Austrian national idea?" This, he said, could only produce the response "Jambor"—a name we have met in chapter 5—a man whom he considers an ineffectual intellectual. Perhaps, my respondent suggested, I wished to ask, "Which people do you consider the best embodiment of the Austrian state?" Again we see the pragmatist's respect for actions rather than words. At another time he spoke of community emerging from common problem-solving efforts by Austrians of varying ideological commitment rather than from ideological propaganda, again an echo of ideas typically voiced by the top elites.

A younger man (thirtyish), an organization specialist in the Conservative secretariat, presents a sharp contrast with both the ideological and the pragmatist functionary. He is a passionate believer in the idea of the Austrian nation and publicly affirms the concept both in the cultural and in the political sense. His Austrianism is in no way a divisive ideology, however. Standing in the Christian Social tradition of reform and welfare rather than in the classical Liberal tradition of economics, like his senior colleagues whom we have described above, this respondent's views on economic and social order are close to the Socialist position. His deep attachment to the Austrian idea and his reformist social theory are derived from the Core Group ideology that we discussed in chapter 2. Yet his total position is very different from that of the Core Group. He does not feel guilty about any past sins his party may have committed against the Socialists; such feelings can only eventuate in a sentimental wish to make amends by giving away political values. He fights the Socialists as Democrats fight Republicans in the United States and he plays an important role in a Reformer-controlled secretariat—he conducts basic political research and helps develop campaign materials. He frankly despises the impressionistic "politics-with-a-wine-glass" approach of the Core Group—the politics of intuition, improvization, and impulse. He both admires and practices the calculating and dispassionate computer politics of the pragmatic Reformers, which has met with great success. In short, he is a consensual idealist cum pragmatist, although this may seem a contradiction in terms. His heart is on the old Christian Social left, but his mind and methods are with the Reformers.

While my young respondent enthusiastically affirms the idea of Austria as a cultural nation—he agrees with writers like Jambor that political nationality without cultural roots is not ultimately viable—he is not anti-German in the manner of the older cultural nationalists like Hurdes or the party fringers who write so voluminously about the Austrian nation today. While as a Conservative he thinks of the Austrian nation as an outgrowth of the imperial past, he does not, like the older people, insist on specific symbols of that past that offend the Socialists. In fact, he readily accepts some of the symbols that the Socialists introduced. For example, he will passionately defend the hammer and sickle in the official state seal. He does not see them as specifically Marxist (either Communist or Socialist) but simply as emblems of the laboring man as factory worker and farmer. And, as a conscientious believer in the equalitarian doctrines of Christian Social reform, he cherishes such working-class symbols. He wishes to develop a specifically Austrian culture largely out of contemporary materials, not by slavishly harking back to the past, which is largely a museum for him. The chief source of that culture is a dynamic liberal Catholicism which, rooted in the past, strives valiantly to be contemporary. In the purely secular realm he sees the idea of neutrality, rooted in the political realities of the Declaration of 1955, as a fruitful source of the new Austrian culture and at the same time a continuation of the historical Austrian ideal of bridge-builder among the peoples and mediator of contrasting cultures.

In every respect, then, the Austrian nationalism of this young Conservative organization specialist is a consensualist one which is not so much a self-conscious synthesis of "Black" and "Red" cultures (such as Nenning would effect) as a new reality that ignores the boundaries of the old *Lager*. It has grown up spontaneously in the political peace and quiet purchased for twenty years by the wise contractarians who in 1945 suspended warfare between the *Lager* and forced themselves to work with one another.

This consensualist Austrianism is not a chance phenomenon, a unique "sport" represented only in the person of the organization specialist. There are many other up-and-coming young officials in the Conservative party who share the consensualist mentality and who hybridize idealism with pragmatism in their world view. In the highest echelons these include Wolfgang Schmitz, the able former finance minister, and Joseph Taus, a teacher of economics and chief political-economic adviser to the head of the Austrian Workers and Clerks Federation who was recently put in charge of Austria's nationalized industries and made responsible for their rationalization after the junking of the old, inefficient Conservative-Socialist board that ran the nationalized industries during the long period of proportionalism and coalition. Others are Erhard Busek, secretary to the Conservative parliamentary delegation; Robert Prantner, executive secretary of Alfred Maleta, the wily head of the Workers and Clerks Confederation of the Volkspartei; and a dozen others in similar positions. All these men, as can be seen from their titles, hold key jobs through which they can exercise profound control over the future of the Austrian nation.

There are similar types to be found on the Socialist side, though I found their emotional attachment to Austria less strong than that among the consensualist Conservatives. One is a quiet and efficient young (early thirties) administrative aide to the Socialist parliamentary delegation. When asked what he thought about the idea of an Austrian nation, and whether he believed there was one and in what sense, he answered that Austria was already a political nation and that since 1945, when she ceased to "feel" German, "she has gradually been developing into a cultural nation." As evidence he cited the proclamation in October 1965 of the first national holiday, which at the outset was to be called a "state holiday." Yet when I asked him which concept, in his opinion, was most meaningful to an Austrian—that of nation, state, or homeland (*Heimat*)—he said that the state concept was the most important and went on to discuss the importance of the republican state form in the Socialist version of what Austria means and stands for. Pressed further to say whether he thought most Austrians now had a "state consciousness," he said that he thought the majority had a "national consciousness" but that this was all a matter of development. In short, while he apparently thinks of Austria primarily in terms of political and constitutional community, these concepts do not have for him a purely rational character but are full of emotional overtones. How one might convert them into the substance of a "cultural nation," however, is not clear. Thus we are left with the idea that, anyway, Austrians are not German.[8] Like the contractarian pragmatist, the parliamentary aide rejects the idea of a rational scheme or a master plan for the development of national consciousness, and he sees the deepening of national consciousness as something that gradually emerges from the entire experience of Austrians.

Another representative of the young consensualist mentality in the SPÖ is a party organizer and troubleshooter in the Vienna Socialist organization and a former leader of the Socialist Youth Association. When we were talking about the applicability of the cultural nation concept to Austria he said flatly that a single language does not make a united culture. Goethe was his heritage, indeed, but so was Dante. Mozart and Grillparzer were certainly Austrians, not Germans, and Beethoven, he said, though born in Bonn, lived by choice in Vienna and was more Austrian than German. Here was a Socialist functionary, from the middle, ideological range of elites, spontaneously selecting illustrations of Austrian culture from the days of the despised Habsburgs. When I suggested the importance of extending the area of national consensus, he was

8. Another young Socialist patriot in the communications field, when asked what he thought about Austria as a cultural nation, actually said that all he was sure about was that it was not German.

happy to entertain the idea of ideological dialogue with the Conservatives, and he reflected at length on the death of the old conflicts. In his work with the Socialist youth it had struck him how uninterested they were in the battles of the 1930s and the persecution and martyrdom of that generation of Socialists at Conservative hands. That was simply beyond their experience, and what was the point of rehashing it all? He liked Conservative former Chancellor Gorbach's statement of 1964 comparing the politics of that year with the politics of 1934—the patriots of the 1930s had in the meantime become democrats, and the democrats of that era had since then become patriots.

Like the Conservative consensualists, this man ties his ideals together with pragmatic practice. This is evident from an article that he contributed to the Socialist monthly journal *Die Zukunft* when the Socialists were in the process of updating their party platform. Commenting on the youth planks, he wrote that the authors of this part of the program had not hauled out the old slogans to accomplish their task but instead had made use of the resources of modern social science to find out what Austrian youth wanted and needed. They had found the youth down-to-earth (*nüchtern*) and sceptical in their outlook and had accepted them as such. The youth plank proposed for the new program reflected this finding. It was realistic in its tone and dealt with specific problems in the daily lives of the young—housing, military service, access to college, popular culture. In the paragraph on military service, he noted, there were calls for shorter terms of service and for the playing down of what he called *Hurra Patriotismus*. "Just because this young generation will have its lack of idealism thrown up to it by zealots in the army," he wrote, "it should be pointed out that this is the first generation of Austrians who can be treated as the bearers of a genuine Austrian-republican state consciousness. This is an essential fact and might perhaps play a weighty role in the event that another system than the existing one of the great coalition had to be found in order to form a government." Here was a consensualist who had a theoretical grasp of what consensual politics are made of, and he was a prophet as well!

Among the younger members of the Socialist middle-range elite, even the most passionately ideological in a partisan Socialist sense cannot be said to reinforce the old *Lager* mentality in a significant way. When some of these young people scornfully criticize their leaders for betraying Marxism in their eagerness to reach practical compromises with the Conservatives, they are not calling for a return to the old ideological politics but for a recognition of the importance of ideals in political life; they are confessing that democracy does not consist solely of effective game playing. An example of the fiery young Socialist ideologue is a leader in the Socialist Youth Association. He complained of the pragmatic stance of his party's chiefs and made it clear that he rejected ideological bridge building. It was an insult to suggest that dialogue take place, for, after all, youth leaders on both sides were educated men with well-formed world views. He had no use for professional synthesizers in the Socialist ranks like Nenning. Yet in speaking of the bones of contention between Socialists and Conservatives he argued entirely in terms of specific policy issues capable of being processed by normal democratic procedures, such as inequities in the penal law and inadequate access for working-class youth to the system of higher education. He never resorted to abstractions like "class warfare" or "capitalist exploitation." He also spoke at length about the many occasions on which he had worked with Conservative youth leaders toward the realization of specific goals that they had in common, such as a program of Austrian aid to the developing countries and the four-week vacation. Both of these cooperative efforts had been in the context of the Federal Youth Council. It is hard to see how partisan ideological ardor like this man's can be deeply divisive in the institutional setting of the Second Republic.

Our young Socialist ideologist would not accept the cultural nation concept because of the language tie with Germany. He also saw German and Austrian literature as one. He seemed to accept the political nation formula, but, like the older ideologist in the Conservative secretariat, he tended to reduce it to a political instrument. The proclamation of a national holiday, he told me, had been much discussed by Socialist youth, and he had taken part in the discussions. Though October 26 had been agreed on by the parliament and the first national holiday had been already celebrated on that day, Socialist youth were unhappy with the arrangement. They want a second national holiday proclaimed for November 12, the anniversary of the proclamation of the republic in 1918, a major holiday in the Socialist calendar and a sore point for many Conservatives with attachments to the old regime. Like his older counterpart among the Conservatives, this young ideologist wants to use the nation to triumph over his political opponents, not to express areas of consensus with them.

Local Political Elites

In the various Länder which make up the federal republic of Austria I interviewed both top and middle-range politicians. I spoke with governors, lieutenant-governors, cultural officers, press officers, members of the national parliament, state legislators, and secretaries of the state party organizations. My conversations revealed some similarities but also marked differences, especially in overall pattern, between the thoughts of these people on the Austrian nation and the ideas of national leaders and central party officials with whom I spoke in Vienna.[9]

Few of the provincial respondents were ready to apply the nation concept to Austria in any way. They (with notable exceptions, such as Styrian Governor Krainer, who was, however, high in the national councils of the ÖVP) obviously had not assimilated the limited Western European idea of the political nation as many of the pragmatist national leaders have. Nor did they seem familiar with the political nation-cultural nation distinction. Like my Viennese respondents, however, nearly all of them told me that Austrians do not want another anschluss. (One Conservative leader in Graz did admit to a post-1945 anschluss movement in Styria, though.) But while in Vienna most respondents, in following up the "of course no anschluss" comment, remarked that "Austrian state consciousness" is now strong, the provincials generally emphasized that it was well grounded "among the youth." A top Conservative in Salzburg said that state consciousness was a problem among the older people.

When a provincial respondent wished to stress approvingly the

9. No interviews were carried out in Lower Austria, which other evidence indicates is more like Vienna than like the other Länder. The seat of the Lower Austrian government is in fact Vienna. This dates from the time when Vienna and Lower Austria constituted one Land.

development of Austrian state consciousness since 1945 he usually related it to economic viability (*Lebensfähigkeit*) in the manner of the pragmatic national elites and, like them, was content to accept this as an adequate foundation for a stable political community. As in Vienna, it was characteristically the top leadership who spoke of political community in these terms. The Conservative governor and Socialist lieutenant-governor of Tyrol, the Conservative governor of the Vorarlberg, and the Socialist mayor of Graz in particular underlined the connection between economic viability and state consciousness. It was rather surprising that Governor Wallnöfer of Tyrol brought up the subject when asked to comment on the success of the Tyrolean citizenship education program. "Since 1945 people have believed in the economic viability of Tyrol and of Austria," he declared. "Jobs abound and people feel secure in their jobs." To this able pragmatist it was clear that the best teacher of good citizenship is the full stomach.

In Vienna most of the respondents who rejected the cultural nation concept did not at the same time emphasize their Germanness. Some of them insisted that Austrian culture is universal and cannot be given a national label. By contrast, the provincials readily said that they were German in a cultural sense. One Vorarlberger reminded me that Hitler was an Austrian, not a German. Some of my respondents, especially those in Salzburg, Styria, and the Vorarlberg when asked whether there was much discussion of the Austrian nation in their area, replied: "Of course you must know that this is a center of Pan-German (deutschnational, Liberal) sentiment."

Many of the provincials with whom I spoke backed up their statements about the German character of Austrian culture with an ethnic reference, something that I heard only rarely in Vienna. As the Socialist lieutenant-governor of Tyrol said to me, "We belong to the Bayuvar tribe (Bayuvarischer Stamm) just like the Bavarians and we do have a common language with the Germans." (This man added, though: "But Americans are never thought of as English, are they? Just so in Austria, we are not Germans.") More typically, a respondent would generalize: "All Austrians as far west as the Arlberg are Bayuvaren. The Vorarlbergers are Alemannen (another of the ancient German tribes)." Only one public official, the

Conservative governor of Tyrol, explicitly rejected the ethnic myth and pointed out that Tyroleans were a mixture (*Mischung*) of people from east, west, and all over. But he said this in the context of a discussion of Tyrolean individuality rather than as an acceptance of the Austrian nation idea. The press officer of the Vorarlberg state government told me about problems of integrating the large number of new people who have been flocking into the prosperous Vorarlberg industries in recent years. They come not only from Vienna and the "underdeveloped" areas of Austria like Carinthia but from Greece and Turkey as well, and some of them, to hasten their assimilation in their new home, "become super-Alemannen." (The tribal myth dies hard in Austria.)

Geography was frequently invoked by my provincial respondents in explaining their hesitations about the idea of an Austrian nation and their feelings of affinity for German culture. "We lie so close to the border" said the governor of Salzburg, a Conservative. A leading Socialist member of the provincial legislature used an identical expression. To an American this does not seem a significant point. Residents of Buffalo or Detroit certainly do not feel they are Canadians because they live in border towns. Nor would residents of El Paso say they are Spaniards or Mexicans, despite their proximity to an Hispanic cultural area. The vast political and economic bulk of the United States lies at their backs and draws them into their own country. A glance at the map, however, shows that *no* part of Austria is more than a hundred miles from *some* international boundary. The entire country is a borderland, facing outward toward six different states and five different language areas. Salzburg lies only seventy-five miles by autobahn from Munich, a major center of the Western European trade on which it depends for its livelihood. Vienna, the historical center and modern political capital of Austria, is more than three times that distance to the east, and the roads running east from the city cross a strictly controlled Iron Curtain into Czechoslovakia and Hungary. It is no wonder that a shared language combined with a bustling trade, open communication across the border, and the East-West political polarization lead Salzburgers to turn more readily to Munich, and then to Germany, than to Vienna and through it to Austria.

To Styrians and Carinthians, living in a borderland means something different. Instead of signifying a special affinity to the people across the line, it means mounting a border watch against them. Styria and Carinthia face south, toward what is now Yugoslavia, and for centuries their people have seen themselves as bastions of German culture in a sea of Slavs. The tradition originated in the medieval or Renaissance empire and was modernized during the last quarter of the nineteenth century by Pan-German nationalists like demagogue Georg von Schönerer. It took political form during the years immediately after 1918 when German-speaking inhabitants formed home guard units to fight Slovene regulars and guerrillas who were trying to push Slovenia's border northward. Similar Yugoslav pressures, combined with insurrectionary activity in local islands of Slovenian culture, began again in 1945 and lasted until 1960. Thus long experience in intertwining the defense of Austrian territory with the defense of German culture has made it difficult for Styrians and Carinthians to appreciate the idea of an Austrian cultural nation, which they identify with Vienna (where the idea originated), which, in turn has always been seen by the people of the western and southern Länder as a polyglot and a heavily Slav place.

Though they don't refer to their state as a border territory or speak of a border watch, Tyroleans have problems with the idea of an Austrian cultural nation for reasons similar to those of the Styrians and Carinthians. Despite the facts that the Tyrol lost its southern region to Italy by Allied decree more than fifty years ago and that the cession was confirmed both by Hitler and by the triumphant Allies of World War II, the people north of the Brenner Pass will not let go. As far as they are concerned, the Tyrol is still one country, one community. They adamantly affirm this in such things as the map of Tyrol, which every citizen receives along with his young citizen's book when he comes of age. The map is titled *Das Land Tirol* ("The State of Tyrol"), and it shows both north and south as one unit, defined by a heavy orange line. An unobtrusive dotted black line runs across the map close to the center, but only in the legend does one learn that this is the "Austrian state border."

Given a progressive Italianization, economically and culturally, of the southern region plus the unwillingness of the northern region

to "let the south go," Tyroleans live in a continous atmosphere of
siege. Innsbruck walls are prominently painted with enormous graf-
fitti demanding "self-determination for South Tyrol," "freedom for
South Tyrol." And the papers constantly carry accounts of terrorist
activities against Italian authorities and of interminable negotiations
between Vienna and Rome on questions of cultural autonomy for
the South Tyroleans. While the battle is in part defined as a defense
of parochial values, which we shall examine shortly, it is also, seen
as a defense of German culture. The ease with which one falls into
the "Italian versus German" frame of reference is demonstrated by
the comments of a member of the state legislature from Innsbruck
who is known as a leading spokesman on the South Tyrolean question. This man had just finished telling me that there was a strong
Austrian state consciousness in Tyrol and that one could find it
especially in areas where Germans from the Federal Republic are
buying up large lots of land. There is, he said, a concern for the
alienation (*Fremdung*) of Tyrol vis-à-vis the Germans. Guests are
welcome, but Tyroleans wish to be lords in their own house. Moreover, Tyroleans smart under the arrogance of German tourists,
whom they have come to call *Bifke* (beef faces). Austrians who
work and live in Germany are always happy to come back to the
homeland, and they continue to think and feel as Austrians, he
claimed. But when we turned to a discussion of the South Tyrol
question, his specialty, the legislator opened the subject with the
spontaneous remark that "in 1918 the South Tyrol was a purely
German land" (*rein deutsches Land*). He caught himself at this
point and hurriedly changed the phrase to "had a purely Austrian-
Tyrolean character." But this was artificial. The German language
is one of the chief things that has been under attack, and it is a
major vehicle of other cultural values. The focus on things German
is accentuated by the further fact that numerous right-wingers from
West Germany have gone to the South Tyrol to make common
cause with the local people in the blowing up of bridges and other
terrorist activities, all in the name of defending German culture.
In Innsbruck a large contingent of students from the Federal Republic keeps up a running verbal war on the South Tyrol question, again
in the name of things German. There does not seem much room
for an Austrian cultural nation in such a context.

Though nearly all the provincial respondents denied that there was any discussion of the Austrian nation in their areas, either among the public at large or among intellectuals, to parallel the "much overworked" polemic carried on incessantly in Vienna, they nevertheless expressed a great sensitivity to the subject. A young Conservative functionary in Innsbruck who was reluctant to answer many of my questions about various other aspects of Austrian politics closed up altogether when I mentioned the Austrian nation theme and began waving his finger at me in a reproving fashion. When he finally opened his mouth to talk he spoke on an entirely different subject. A professor in the America Institute at the University of Innsbruck, who had asked me to contribute to an Austrian-American journal that he edits, became quite embarrassed when he heard what my research dealt with. "Oh that one's a hot potato around here," he remarked, and he quickly dropped his request for an article.

A Conservative newsman complained about Chancellor Klaus, who, as we have seen, has been very circumspect about the Austrian nation; the reporter claimed that in advancing the cause of a national holiday for Austria Klaus heated up the controversy. Another Tyrolean respondent mentioned in passing that there had been a warm discussion in the state legislature about whether one should speak of tomatoes as *Paradeiser* (an old Austrian word) or *Tomaten* (the word used in West Germany). There have also been student scuffles in Styria and in Upper Austria provoked by discussion of the Austrian nation. Governor Lechner of Salzburg said that "the debate about an 'Austrian nation' is foolish. Austria is indeed a political community (*Staatsvolk*) but culturally and ethnically we are with Germany. There is no more anschluss feeling—but we have and we want to keep good relations with Germany." To quote a leading Socialist member of the Tyrolean legislature: "We feel as Austrians, and no one wants anschluss again. But why have a discussion over whether we are a nation? Why irritate the Germans and produce all kinds of complications? Discussion is not needed. Austrian consciousness is there. Why manufacture a tinder box (*Zündstoff*)?"

It is not fully clear to me what motivates this provincial anxiety about the Austrian nation. Presumably there is some worry about trade with Germany and about tourism, which is 75 percent German. There may also be a feeling of net cultural loss if too great a separation of things Austrian from things German is accomplished, given the feelings of cultural dependence that we have described. A problem for the proponents of the Austrian nation idea is the paucity of new, specifically Austrian contributions to the arts, literature, and science.

By contrast, German productivity in all these areas continues undiminished despite the loss of political power and territory. I think this is what one respondent in the Burgenland, a state where German, Slav, and Hungarian culture meet and where the German language is a ticket to social, political, and economic status, had in mind when he said, "I come from where Liszt was born. Just after World War I the Hungarians but up a placard in his memory, even though Liszt spoke French. Then in 1926 the Germans put up a placard." Adding a statement that disputes like this about nationality are ridiculous, he ended with what appeared a non sequitur: "We don't need the idea of an Austrian cultural nation. I don't want to lose our connections across the [German] border."

Strong regional attachments as well as German feeling militate against the acceptance of the Austrian nation theme by provincial political elites. The typical hierarchy of allegiances was succinctly expressed by Dr. Fritz Prior, Conservative lieutenant-governor of the Tyrol, who told me that "alongside our regional consciousness (*Landesbewusstsein*) we have an Austrian consciousness which is based on the concept of federalism. We are partners in a federal state." Dr. Hans Huebmer, press officer for the government of Vorarlberg, stated that "the Vorarlberger is first and foremost a Vorarlberger. His heart has three loyalties—*Heimat Vorarlberg, Staat Österreich, Deutsche Kultur*." [10]

My respondents characteristically explained the strength of *Heimatbewusstsein* with references to events from the pages of local history. I noticed this in the Länder where regional sentiment is strongest. Sometimes the emphasis was simply on a tradition of autonomy. "You know that from the eleventh century onward Styria was an independent duchy," Governor Josef Krainer declared. "We

10. Interviews with Fritz Prior and Hans Huebmer, Innsbruck, July 14, 1966, and Bregenz, August 5, 1966.

have a strong feeling of local pride." This is a reference to the fact that as one of the crown lands, whose existence as a duchy predated its acquisition by the Habsburgs, Styria was always governed by the Habsburg emperor acting as duke of Styria, rather than by an appointed Imperial governor.[11]

In Tyrol the emphasis is on their ancient yeoman democracy, which Tyroleans see as something that sets them apart from eastern Austrians. As Conservative Governor Eduard Wallnöfer put it, "Our democracy is 700 years old. The peasants were free landowners here when other Austrians were serfs." An editor of the Innsbruck Catholic newspaper *Volksbote* used virtually the same words, as did a functionary of the Conservative Workers and Clerks Association in Salzburg. Governor Wallnöfer also mentioned regional differences in the conduct of public business, saying that Tyroleans stress democratic discussion while elsewhere the voice of authority or of expertise carries the day without comment from the legislative floor. My Salzburg respondent illustrated yeoman democracy with the western custom of bearing arms, which the Viennese "don't understand."

The yeoman heroism of Andreas Hofer, who rallied Tyrolean farmers against the troops of Napoleon in 1809 is celebrated today as though the war had been fought yesterday. Pictures of Hofer are everywhere, and there is an enormous statue in bronze on the slope of Bergisel, a battle site just outside Innsbruck. The official anthem of Tyrol sings of his martyrdom, and his name is invoked by politicians in the way Americans hail Washington, Jefferson, and Lincoln. Memories of two world wars are shunted aside, but the freedom battles of 1809 are remembered daily, especially in the schoolroom. The *Volksbote* editor explained the significance and relationship of Hofer to the idea of an Austrian nation. (Twice, in 1805 and 1809 the Austrian emperor bought peace from Napoleon with the cession of Tyrol, after 450 years of union between Tyrol and Austria. The second cession followed a gallant war of liberation in which Tyroleans, with their own arms, had driven out the French and Bavarian enemy, and the emperor in a special manifesto had sworn that his "loyal county of Tyrol, including the Vorarlberg, should never again be separated from the body of the Aus-

11. Interview with Governor Josef Krainer, Graz, June 6, 1968.

trian imperial state" and that he would sign "no other treaty of peace than one which binds this region indissolubly to my monarchy.")[12] A hundred years later, in 1909, another emperor, Francis Joseph, came to Innsbruck to celebrate the centenary of Hofer's fight and to make amends to the Tyroleans. But the Tyroleans, who in 1809 viewed the events of that time as a treacherous imperial sellout, to this day harbor feelings of animosity against Vienna. Moreover, the freedom war has a contemporary parallel in the ironic similarity between the second cession of 1809 and the loss of South Tyrol in 1918. In breaking up the historic Land, Napoleon joined part of the South Tyrol to the kingdom of Italy. And it was in Mantua, an Italian city, that Hofer was executed by his captors. In 1918 as well as in 1809 Vienna was unable to help.

Conceptions of differences in moral character between Tyroleans and Viennese—democratic openness versus servile double-dealing —probably derive from historical traditions of the kind outlined above. A young Conservative party functionary in Innsbruck, for example, complained to me about what he considered the devious way in which Franz Hetzenauer, former minister of justice from the Tyrol, had been dropped from the government by the national leadership of the Volkspartei. "We Tyroleans," my respondent said, "are self-willed, honest, and open (ehrlich und direkt). The Viennese are dishonest. They say yes and mean no. We say no and mean no." Apart from the question of the validity of such stereotypes, it apparently did not occur to the man that the chancellor and Conservative party head at the time of Hetzenauer's dismissal was neither a Habsburg nor a Viennese bureaucrat but a Carinthian baker's son who had served as governor of Salzburg before becoming federal chancellor. Myths, especially when they are spun out of the stuff of history, can bear more weight on judgment than the power of reflection, even among political elites.

In some cases my respondents invoked geographical myths to explain parochial sentiment. A Socialist functionary, who is also a member of the upper house of the Austrian parliament from Carinthia, described his Land as a "closed unity," cut off from the rest

12. The Wolkersdorfer Handbillet of Emperor Francis I of May 29, 1809, reproduced in Wolfgang Pfaundler, ed., Tiroler Jungbürgerbuch (Innsbruck: Inn-Verlag, 1963), p. 65.

of Austria by high mountains and therefore very different from Inner Österreich (minimally, Lower Austria, Vienna, and the northern portions of Upper Austria, though sometimes a more inclusive concept).[13] Another respondent spoke of the Carinthian's love of the particular, the individual as a derivative of the mountainous geography: "All our valleys, the Lavanthal, the Drauthal etc.—each has its own special characteristics." In the face of so much isolation, and the pluralism of even little Carinthia, how can one discover a single nation among the nine Länder of Austria? As I listened to these two earnest men I thought of my own impression of Klagenfurt as a thriving commercial crossroads, not an isolated Alpine hamlet. Again, historical myth rather than contemporary reality seemed to govern as my respondents pondered the "Austrian nation."

Some of the provincials with whom I spoke evidenced a disposition to free themselves from the various parochial myths we have been describing. A Socialist functionary in Innsbruck said that he found Tyrolean patriotism—one could almost call this Texas-like phenomenon Tyrolean nationalism—to be ridiculous.[14]

The Conservatives get all worked up about it—movements for the reinvigoration of the old folkways, clubs of all kinds. But the SPÖ is not interested in these things. The worker says, "We are Austrians. We *must* build Austria, or we will be sucked up by the Germans." We require an Austrian consciousness in order not to be taken over economically by the Germans.

But even this man, in commenting on the progress of the negotiations on South Tyrol, fell into the standard speech. Italian pressure, he said, "has begun to decline vis-à-vis the Ger—— (he hesitated), the Austrians, the South Tyroleans."

Those who still believe in the myths indicated that those myths are losing much of their former power to set the Länder against Vienna. This seems to be a function of the growing federalization of real power and influence within the two major political parties,

13. One respondent said, however, " 'Inner Austria' is only one place: Vienna."

14. One ardent respondent did in fact tell me: "There is not an Austrian nation, but there is a Tyrolean nation."

by contrast with the constant centralism during the First Republic. Animosity toward Vienna is decreasing, said the Conservative lieutenant-governor of Tyrol, "as our relations are established on a sound federal basis." As cultural officer he also heartily approved the youth exchanges between the capital and the Länder. His predecessors, he noted, were much more antagonistic to Vienna than he (a man in his early forties.) Governor Wallnöfer of Tyrol told me that while Tyroleans grumble a great deal about Vienna, this did not mean anything for Austrian unity. After all, Tyrol had been with Austria for 600 years.[15] Governor Krainer of Styria expressed the same thought in different language. The Socialist lieutenant-governor of Salzburg spoke enthusiastically of the federalization of the SPÖ after the disastrous election of 1966—at which time personnel changes were made in the national leadership, a new committee of party chairmen of the Land organizations had been put together to advise the party central committee, and there had been efforts to bring younger people into the higher party councils.

One might suppose that the diffusion of power and authority within the two major parties combined with a limited reallocation of functions between Vienna and the Länder might also de-ideologize the concept of federalism. In the past this emotionally loaded word has been a sign of deep division between Vienna and all the provinces. Defusing it would be a large step in the direction of Austrian unity. In prosperous, highly industrialized Salzburg, whose governor has risen to the post of chancellor, I found that this had in fact occurred. The present governor told me that he was trying to rid the concept of its emotional overtones and find a pragmatic, common-sense rule for the division of functions and authority between Vienna and the land. A young official of the land Conservative party organization said:

> You have to distinguish between what people want and what is politically practical. Salzburgers are not as easily fired up by the mere idea of federalism as the Vorarlbergers are, not so emotional as they. One must look at the matter in hand and judge it pragmatically. You can't just yell "federalism" if a particular

15. Interviews with Lieutenant-Governor Fritz Prior and Governor Eduard Wallnöfer, Innsbruck, July 14, 1966, and July 25, 1966.

matter is better managed in Vienna—for example, construction of power works. On the other hand, there are things that best can be done at the Land level, and still others by the Gemeinde. We should think in terms of the [old Christian Social] principle of subsidiarity, but make decisions from case to case, not on the basis of slogans.

In this interview in particular I heard echoes of the consensualist Austrianism, which mixes idealism with pragmatism, that I discovered among the younger party functionaries in Vienna. Like most of those people, this man was in his early thirties. Nevertheless, he did not embrace the concept of the Austrian nation, as they did.

The decay of ideology within the Länder, signified by generally good feeling and good working relationships between the two major parties at the Land level, also bodes well for Austrian unity. Coalition government still prevails in the Länder, but it has not produced a political stalemate as it did at the federal level in 1965. The Vorarlberger press officer told me that "on local issues (*Landesinteressen*) there are no party boundaries, ideologically speaking. The relations between the ÖVP and SPÖ are very good." The Conservative lieutenant-governor of Upper Austria spoke in the same terms: "The two parties are not deeply divided in provincial affairs. Each one simply promises to do a better job than the other. Issues between the parties are on a practical level. Ideology is now something that we leave to the intellectuals." But it has not always been so. My respondent grew up in a mining town in the 1930s and recalls being stoned by Socialists as he walked to church with his father. At that time the workers were ideological Marxists and were not interested merely in bread-and-butter questions as they are today.

A Socialist functionary in Innsbruck told me that the older and more ideological Socialists are in the central apparatus in Vienna. The provincial functionaries tend to be younger and more reformist in their bent. "The ÖVP and the Catholic church know more about Marxism than we do," he said. Karl Kunst, Socialist lieutenant-governor of Tyrol, noted various important areas where there are no substantial differences between the two major parties. In contrast to the battle that proceeds continuously at the national level,

Tyrolean Socialists and Conservatives have no differences over educational policy. While teachers are, for the most part, Conservatives, Kunst finds them "very progressive." Unlike the University of Vienna, the University of Innsbruck is not a bone of contention between the parties, he said. "In general," he remarked, "the *Lager* mentality is not so great here." Herr Kunst takes the pragmatist Karl Renner rather than the dogmatist Otto Bauer as his own model. And he approves of synthesizers like Günther Nenning, whom the pragmatists among the national leadership have virtually read out of the party.[16] Similar approval of Nenning was voiced by a leading state legislator in Salzburg, who said: "We need such people to provoke discussion and stimulate new ideas. You need some pike in every carp pond."

A young Socialist functionary in Klagenfurt, explaining why Carinthian farmers as well as workers vote Socialist, remarked at one point that the "SPÖ is tolerant, not dogmatic." And he noted that more and more elections tend to turn on personalities. The Socialist lieutenant-governor of Salzburg expressed approval of Bruno Kreisky, head of the Socialist party, "because he is a practical person and not dogmatic." In the next breath this same man told me that he was against the de-ideologization of politics, however. When we went on to discuss the matter, it turned out that he was calling for idealism, in the manner of the consensualists we have treated earlier, rather than a return to divisive ideology. "We need a new Marx, new ideals," he said. "Marxism must not be a simplistic doctrine as it was before. And we must combine it with a scientific approach. Idealism is something we need to develop in the youth, but in conjunction with practice. In the past the ideals were simply taken as something abstractly given." I had found another consensualist in the provinces (a man in his early forties). But like the consensualist Conservative functionary mentioned earlier, he did not embrace the Austrian nation concept. "We are Austrians," he said. "Whether we call ourselves a nation or not doesn't matter." The debate among the Viennese intellectuals he found irrelevant. "These theoretical flights are academic. We speak

16. Interview with Lieutenant-Governor Karl Kunst, Innsbruck, July 27, 1966.

German, as they do in Switzerland, and they don't have any debate about the Swiss nation." [17]

Several Socialist provincial respondents expressed approval of the party's decision to go into opposition after losing the 1966 election and they told me that they had been in favor of this course immediately after the election results were known. One said, "We were the first to say openly, 'Let's have a one party government' which, as you know, is the normal form of parliamentary democracy." "The Tyrolean SPÖ was for going into opposition," the secretary of the Land party organization there told me. "In the past all the decisions have been made at the top of the party hierarchy. We wanted to try the new form to see whether it wouldn't result in more meaningful political activity and influence for the middle and lower functionaries of the party." Here was evidence that the equalization of power and influence within the parties, the decentralization of party power, goes hand in hand with the consensualist unification of Austrian politics. For only in a basically consensualist context would Socialist "young Turks" in the provinces have made a bid for power and status by taking their party out of the national government. Yet, paradoxically, most of these people had no interest in "the Austrian nation."

In summary, what is the status of the Austrian nation idea today among Austrian political elites? At the tops of the two major parties we find pragmatic politicians who take pride in Austria as a stable and prosperous political and economic community that they themselves have created by rational politics out of the problematic opportunities offered them by history. Their Austria rests on the material values of economic well-being, political peace, and personal freedom, and they are reluctant to embrace what some consider the spiritually and morally higher, and certainly the emotionally warmer, idea of Austria as a cultural nation. They fear that to press the issue might not complete the nation-building task but rather destroy what they have built by re-kindling the flames of dying political religions, which in the past have been destructive in Austrian political life.

17. Interview with Lieutenant-Governor Karl Steinocher, Salzburg, June 17, 1968.

Beneath this top echelon of about two dozen persons is a vast, many-tiered middle range of elites, seated both in Vienna and in the Länder. In Vienna the old ideological attitudes (on the Con-servative-Socialist dimension, not on the Pan-German-Austrian di-mension) persist in this group alongside the pragmatic views of those at the top. The attitude of the pragmatists toward the Aus-trian nation is similar to that of their like-minded superiors, while the ideologists manipulate the concept as a weapon in their partisan battles.

Most of these men, both at the top and in the middle ranges, and no matter what their ages, are what we might call "old Austrians," men whose political thought and behavior are heavily conditioned by the past—the past of partisan ideological battles, political dis-memberment, poverty, economic breakdown, and anschluss. But among the middle-range elites in Vienna we also find some exam-ples of a "new Austrian"—a man young enough to have few per-sonal recollections of this past and to have escaped indoctrination in its spirit, unlike others of his age group. These "new Austrians" represent the beginnings of a consensualist Austrianism which com-bines a practical regard for the material values of established po-litical nationhood—peace, prosperity, freedom—with an idealism nourished by the thought of Austria as a cultural nation. They are democrats, pragmatists, idealists, and, above all, Austrians by na-ture and education. They are the first citizens of an Austrian nation that is a complete nation in all senses.

Going out from Vienna into the middle ranges of the political elites in the Länder we find a very pragmatic, anti-ideological men-tality on the Conservative-Socialist dimension, combined with a political concept of Austria at all levels. Like their pragmatist coun-terparts in Vienna, these men reject the Austrian cultural nation idea for fear of its divisive potentialities, but also for other reasons, both rational and nonrational. A heightened awareness of the im-portance for them of trade with West Germany and a sense of cul-tural dependence on Germany, especially in the areas that orient to Munich by virtue of the communications network, are among the rational grounds. Among the nonrational are a host of Pan-German and parochial ethnic, historical, and geographical myths that continue to be propagated at home and in the schools. The

Pan-German myths are fortified by the realities of twentieth-century cultural conflict with Yugoslavia and Italy. We have seen, however, that in many cases these myths and slogans seem to lead a verbal life of their own but to exert little influence on practical politics. As power and authority are decentralized within the parties and within the formal institutions of government, the community of the Länder with Vienna grows apace and the old divisive watchwords become merely ritualistic tribal pieties.

Some beginnings of a consensualist idealism are found among the youngest of the provincial elites with whom I spoke. As with the Viennese consensualists their idealism is combined with a "natural" Austrianism. But unlike the Viennese Austrianism, this is an unreflective Austrianism that contains no cultural reference that can be intellectualized. It is simply a given emotional fact, a feeling of togetherness. None of the provincial consensualists with whom I spoke accepted the concept of the Austrian cultural nation. Indeed, most of them probably did not know what the expression meant.

7. CULTURAL MINORITIES:
CROATIAN ELITES

In the last chapter we described the ideas and attitudes of German-speaking elites. Minority groups speaking other languages were mentioned only to indicate how their presence has affected the national conscionsness of the dominant German-speaking Austrians. In this chapter we shall consider how elites of the largest of these minorities, the Croatians of the Burgenland, think about Austria and the Austrian nation. We are dealing here with a politically integrated group that has inhabited the Burgenland for over 450 years and has never been feared as a political or cultural aggressor by its German-speaking neighbors. Consequently we make no claim that the attitudinal patterns found among the Croatians obtain also for the Slovenians in the south, who have played a far different political role.

The 1961 Austrian census showed a Croatian population in the Burgenland of slightly more than 28,000 persons, 10.4 percent of the total population of Austria's easternmost and second smallest Land. The percentage has been gradually declining since 1910, when the ratio stood at 15 percent. Croatians form a majority in forty villages and towns and a minority in eight others.

Croatian settlement of the Burgenland began about 1515 and continued in waves during the sixteenth and seventeenth centuries, until about 1650. Fleeing north from Turkish marauders who had invaded their Croatian homeland, the settlers were welcomed to the Burgenland by local magnates whose towns had already been devastated by the Turkish armies. The areas in which the immigrants settled were at the time administered as part of the Austrian crown lands, and there the new arrivals found that they enjoyed more rights as farmers than they had in the kingdom of Hungary, of which Croatia was then a part. (The Burgenland was soon thereafter incorporated into Hungary, however.)

Today Croatians are fully integrated into the Austrian polity. They do not have a political party of their own and do not form a bloc within any of the established Austrian parties. Normally they divide their vote almost 50-50 between the two great parties, much as occurs throughout Austria. Cleavages are largely along economic lines. The well-off and the rural people vote Conservative, the poor and the industrial workers Socialist. In the Land elections of 1968 an unusually high percentage (60 percent) of the Croatian vote went Socialist.

Cultural integration is also occurring as industrialization proceeds, and its recently increased pace has caused a deep rift in the Croatian community. One faction consists of the more prosperous farmers and trades people, especially those who live in the isolated villages of southern Burgenland, who are alarmed at their dwindling numbers as more and more people leave rural occupations for the cities, where they must come to terms with a German-speaking majority. They also find the German-speaking, urban culture invading their home towns, brought in by modern mass communications and industrial products. These people are fiercely determined to preserve their language and the old folkways and customs of the Croatian people. The church is one rallying point for the achievement of these aims, and the Croats have created others—a Croatian cultural association, numerous folk music groups, a cultural exchange program with Yugoslavia. Conservative on economic grounds, they also use the local ÖVP party organization for their cultural ends.

The other faction consists of the industrial workers and day laborers, many of whom commute back and forth to work in Eisenstadt and Vienna from rural villages. They are transported by the firms that hire them. On weekends they may also till a field or two in their Croatian home towns. A majority of these people want to be assimilated because they feel that their minority language relegates them permanently to a low-class station. Unable to speak German well, and only with a heavy Croatian accent, they lack access to higher education and good jobs. In addition, they experience much of the snobbery and social ostracism in Vienna that Negroes do in American culture. Socialists by virtue of their occupational status, they use the Socialist party to pursue their assimilationist goal.

At present the assimilation question turns on the language of instruction in the public schools. Since the Burgenland was joined to Austria in 1920 by the Treaty of Trianon (it had for hundreds of years before been part of Hungary), the Croatian minority has enjoyed the right to have Croatian used as the language of instruction in the public schools. The school law of 1937 had provided for instruction in Croatian in areas more than 70 percent Croatian and for a mixed German-Croatian approach in schools between 30 percent and 70 percent Croatian. Suspended during the anschluss, the right was restored by the State Treaty of 1955. The assimilationists argue that a right should not be made into a legal duty, as the treaty now provides. They want parents to have the freedom to choose either German or Croatian as the language of instruction for their children and not be compelled to have the children grow up speaking only Croatian. The local Socialist party is pressing for revision of the law in this direction. The Conservatives want to maintain the status quo, fearing that if the language is lost the entire cultural heritage will soon be forgotten; thus the local Conservatives have come out against a change in the law.[1]

During June 1968 I interviewed five Croatian cultural and political leaders, among whom were representatives of both of the factions that have formed over the question of assimilation. One of the Conservatives was an elderly (about seventy) priest who is the chief spiritual and cultural leader of the community. He has written a history of the Croatian villages and has published a collection of Croatian folksongs. Another was the young (about twenty-five) secretary of the Croatian Cultural Association. Both men live in Eisenstadt, a German-speaking city and the capital of the Burgenland. A third was the Cultural Association's president, a school principal in Trausdorf an der Wulka, one of the villages with a Croatian majority located near Eisenstadt. The other two respondents were Socialist politicians who represent the forces of assimilation. Each is the mayor of a town with a Croatian majority in

1. Much of the foregoing background material is taken from a report on the Croatian school controversy, "Neues Vaterland—seit 1515," in *AZ-Sonntag,* June 2, 1968.

roatians in the Burgenland

SOURCE: *A–Z Sonntag*, Vienna,
ne 2, 1968. With permission.

mmunities with a Croatian Majority

Parndorf
Neudorf
Hornstein
Oslip
Steinbrunn
Trausdorf
Sillingtal
Wulkaprodersdorf
Siegendorf
Zagersdorf
Klingenbach
Drassburg
Baumgarten
Weingraben
Grosswarasdorf
Kleinwarasdorf
Kroatischer Minihof
Nikitsch
Nebersdorf
Kroatisch Geresdorf
Unterpullendorf
Grossmutschen
Kleinmutschen
Frankenau
Rauhriegel-Allersgraben
Mönchmeierhof
Rumpersdorf
Althodis
Podgoria
Weiden
Podler
Zuberbach
Dürnbach
Schachendorf
Schandorf
Spitzzicken
Stinatz
Neuberg
Güttenbach
Heugraben

ommunities with a Croatian Minority

1 Kittsee
2 Pama
2 Sigless
3 Antau
9 Kaisersdorf
3 Hackerberg
7 Kroatisch Tschantschendorf
8 Reinersdorf

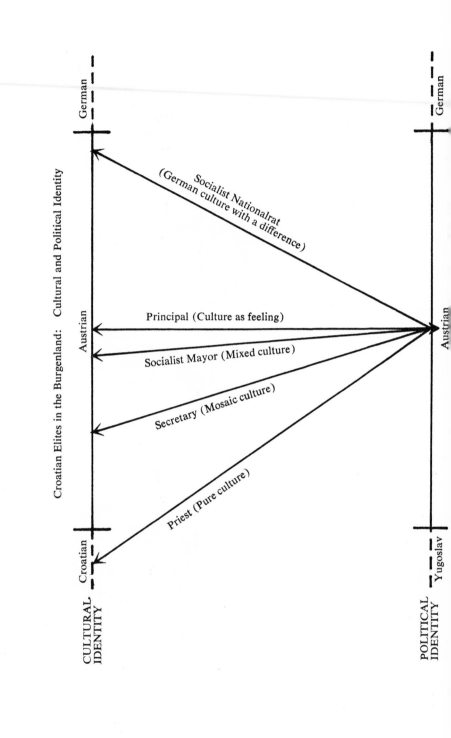

Croatian Elites in the Burgenland: Cultural and Political Identity

CULTURAL IDENTITY

German

Austrian

Croatian

POLITICAL IDENTITY

German

Austrian

Yugoslav

Socialist Nationalrat (German culture with a difference)

Principal (Culture as feeling)

Socialist Mayor (Mixed culture)

Secretary (Mosaic culture)

Priest (Pure culture)

the immediate vicinity of Eisenstadt. One of them is also a member of the federal parliament, where he has led the legal fight for revision of the school law.

How do these Croatians, the one group preoccupied with preserving Croatian culture and the other with assimilation into the German-speaking urban culture surrounding them, stand on the Austrian nation issue? There were no sharp differences on the question discernible either within or between the two groups. Two of the three antiassimilationists, who wish to preserve Croatian culture, and one of the two assimilationists readily accepted the idea that Austria is a cultural as well as a political nation. On neither side was the Austrian nation concept viewed as a threat or a "hot potato." One assimilationist and one antiassimilationist avoided using the term *nation* in any of its senses, though they did not explicitly repudiate such usage, and both of them, and especially the antiassimilationist, obviously thought warmly of Austria as a political community to which they are happy to belong.

There were, of course, nuances of difference in the replies of the respondents to my questions about the Austrian nation, and they are revealing ones. Let us deal first with the cultural nation concept by placing the responses along a scale at one end of which we designate a "pure Croatian" position and at the other end a "pure German" position. The polar positions (which are purely ideal points) exclude any idea of Austria as a cultural nation. The midpoint is the "pure Austrian culture" position and the bars on either side of it define a range of Austrian cultural attitudes. This range does not exclude the ideas of Croatian nation and German nation, and may itself be derived by combining these ideas in various ways. (See the accompanying chart.)

Toward the "pure German" end of the Austrian culture range we find, paradoxically, our most pronounced antiassimilationist, the priest, and our most pronounced assimilationist, the Nationalrat, occupying the same position. The priest told me that "Austrians are a different *Volksstamm* than the [other?] German *Stämme*. Austrians have their own special manner (*Eigenart*)." This way of talking about Austria was particularly popular in the most German-oriented western Länder, especially Salzburg and Tyrol. It designates the Austrian as a special kind of German. The reference is both cultural and ethnic. That this was the good father's intention was confirmed by other of his statements. In talking about the problems of conserving Croatian culture in the Burgenland, the priest always referred to non-Croatians as Germans, not Austrians. For example, he said that the workers who commute to Eisenstadt and Vienna "spend much of their time in a German milieu. They marry German girls. Their children speak German, and Croatian culture is lost. The denationalization process was set in motion not by the Germans but by the new way we earn our daily bread." As the priest sees it, Austrian culture is German culture, and as a Croatian he does not want to be absorbed into it. He himself speaks German with an accent.

When I asked the Nationalrat about the Austrian nation idea he replied by recounting the political history of Austria in capsule form from 1918 on, emphasizing the disillusionment that Austrians had felt with the anschluss with Gross Deutschland, which he described as desired by the SPÖ for economic reasons only. "Even the local Nazis were disenchanted by the degree to which Germany had swallowed Austria up." When I asked how Croatians fit into Austria he replied: "None of the Croatians want to be Yugoslavs; they want to be Austrians. They *feel* Austrian, and they *are* Austrians. We speak Austrian-German. But we are not Germans any more than Americans are English or Italians and French-speaking people in Switzerland [are] Italians or Frenchmen. They are Swiss." When talking about the assimilation question he said: "The villages are now becoming mixed. Germans are coming in. Croatians intermarry with the Germans. . . . When they become Germanized, however, they feel that they are Austrians, not Germans." Then he added an historical note: "In the German Army during World War II there was always a distinction made between Germans and Austrians. In the occupied lands the people always acted differently toward the Austrians than they did toward the Germans." Nevertheless, he later said: "Austria is too small to develop a culture of its own. We are intricately tied into German culture. Look at the German command of the publishing business, for example." When speaking of the relegation of Croatians who speak German poorly to a second-class social and economic status, he remarked in passing that "German culture is also much higher than Yugoslavia's, and their economy is more highly developed."

Most of these statements were intended by the Nationalrat to distinguish Austrian from German, to avoid leaving the impression that he made a simple identification of the two. What is interesting, however, is that as a Croatian-Austrian he saw this identity problem as one that had to be explained. This indicates that he *does* see a close affinity between Austrian and German. His point of reference in explaining things Austrian is not Croatian but German culture. He differs from the priest in that he does not separate himself personally from the idea of "Austrian as a kind of German." Rather, he identifies himself this way.

None of the other three respondents, all of whom apply the nation concept to Austria, used the "Austrian-as-a-kind-of-German" frame of reference. On the antiassimilationist side, the Cultural Association secretary said: "Yes, there is an Austrian nation, but like the old empire it is an amalgam of minorities." When asked, "Do you see Austria as a cultural nation?" he replied: "It is a fact both politically and culturally, but it must be understood as a mixture, a mosaic." The word *mosaic* probably better conveyed his intention than did the word *mixture,* for he wished to stress the autonomy of the elements in the amalgam, the pluralist character of his concept. He then reminded me that Paula von Preradovic, who authored the Austrian federal anthem, was of Croatian stock, after which he launched into a detailed discussion of Croatian culture and the way it is nurtured today. He stressed that the intellectuals who collect local traditions and songs for publication in anthologies "write only in Croatian." In contrast to the priest, with whom he shares a passionate love of Croatian culture, he does not feel that he must defend this culture by separating it from Austrian culture. Instead, he wants to incorporate his heritage into that culture as a vital part of Austrian life.

On the assimilationist side the responses of the Socialist mayor were more like those of the secretary than those of his colleague in the assimilation battle, the Nationalrat. When I asked him whether he accepted the idea of Austria as a cultural nation, the mayor said: "Yes, because our customs are very like those of the

German towns around here. It is mostly the marriage customs that
are different. Vienna and the Burgenland are mixtures. We don't
depend upon and defend Germandom (*Deutschtum*) as they do
elsewhere in Austria." As an assimilationist, he did not insist, as
the secretary did, on the autonomy of Croatianism within Austrian
culture, but he was happy with the idea of a true mixture. The
point is that he saw the Austrian nation as a new and different
substance. It was not "a kind of German culture" in which he saw
himself being absorbed by learning to speak German; rather it came
across as something revealing both German *and* Slavic origins.

The fifth respondent, the president of the Croatian Cultural Union and a school principal, showed himself much more moderate
in his hopes and expectations for preserving Croatian culture than
did the priest or the secretary. His own style of life indicated a high
degree of integration. I was surprised to find this man living in a
very modern house furnished with modern furniture of no distinctive flavor. There was a new car in the garage, and when the president's daughter popped her head into the room, she spoke a perfect,
accentless German. When talking about the assimilation question
the president did not seem to lament the process the way the other
two did. And when discussing the work of the Cultural Union he
said: "There has indeed been a revival of the old customs—but
only for shows, special performances." He obviously thought of his
work as the preservation of an interesting museum piece, not the
revival or defense of culture as a whole, which was the frame of
reference of the other antiassimilationists.

His moderate expectations had an effect on his concept of Austria. He told me that "wanting to remain Croatian or not is not
related to the question of what Austria is." He then went on to
explain how the dominant characteristic of the environment deter-
mines what people are today. World culture today is urban and
industrial, he said, and Austria is an urban and industrial state. In
speaking specifically about the Austrian nation question he said:
"Austria is our fatherland. The population is Austrian in its mentality. Austria is both a cultural and a political concept. It is easiest
to realize that we are Austrians when we travel abroad. . . . When
we see another Austrian car we feel our unity, a special bond (*ver-
bunden*). We all belong together." At no point in the interview did

the president refer either to German or Croatian elements in something called the Austrian nation. Though expressly stating that Austria was both a political and a cultural concept, he did not suggest a single identifying element of that culture that could be considered unique. We may surmise that he had none in mind and that "Austria" meant to him that segment of modern urban culture in which he happened to live, which is united by feelings of togetherness with no basis in any obvious uniqueness. And being Croatian was not a matter of culture, in the broad sense at all; it was a hobby.

The cultural nation concept thus produced a certain variety of responses among the Croatians whom I interviewed. These differences are obviously related to such factors as age, class status, and degree of integration into the German-speaking environment. The last factor seems of special importance. The old, unassimilated conservative intellectual, brought up in a Burgenland that was part of Hungary, sees only Slavs and Germans, no Austrians. The young, unassimilated conservative intellectual, raised in a Burgenland that is an integral part of the Second Austrian Republic, sees Slavs and Germans who are also Austrians. The middle-aged (fiftyish) Socialist politician whose position as Nationalrat keeps him constantly in touch with German-speaking Austrians, whose language he sees as the key to social and economic success for the underprivileged Croatians of his constituency, sees Austrians as the kind of Germans that the Slavs in Austria wish to become. His objective is to have his constituency *become* assimilated. The younger (fortyish), almost fully assimilated Socialist politician whose position as mayor of a town whose Croatian population has had access since the 1920s to education in the German language and who are bussed daily to nearby Eisenstadt as professional people and officials sees Austrians as a people of mixed Slavic and German characteristics. The middle-aged (mid-fifties), half-assimilated school principal who presides over a Croatian school attended also by a minority of German-speaking children has abandoned ethnic group and language cultural references and become a modern man who sees Austrians as modern men who live, and therefore feel, together.

The scale on the political nation dimension runs from "pure Yugoslav" at one end to "pure West German" at the other. In this category the responses showed much greater uniformity; they all clustered around the "pure Austrian" position at the line's center. None of the respondents, as free, relatively prosperous persons of Catholic belief whose ancestors have from time immemorial been a part of Austria, has any interest in anschluss with Yugoslavia. "Yugoslavia maintains an office to defend the cultural interests of Slavic minorities abroad, but no one here in the Burgenland has the slightest interest in Yugoslavia as a state," the Socialist mayor declared. "Croatians have always been good Austrians and good Catholics. We never experienced discrimination in the Burgenland," he added. "We have been here for 400 years," said the Socialist Nationalrat. "None of the Croatians want to be Yugoslavs. They want to be Austrians." The school principal said the same: "We came here 400 years ago and we have no attachment to the old homeland. Austria is our fatherland." And the old priest: "We are happy not to be Communist-controlled today. We have great freedom here. As a national minority we can develop as we wish." The Cultural Association secretary, the youngest of the respondents, found it unnecessary to make any kind of disclaimers about political allegiance, vis-à-vis either Yugoslavia or Germany. And the Conservative school director found it unnecessary to make any disclaimers about Germany, as did the Socialist mayor. Only the Socialist Nationalrat felt it important to do so. "We speak Austrian German. But we are not Germans any more than Americans are English or Italians and French-speaking people in Switzerland are Italians or Frenchmen." And then he went on to explain the Austrian desire for political independence as a function of disenchantment with the German rule during the anschluss period.

The most extensive positive statement about Austrian political independence was made by the old priest. "We *must* interest ourselves in the Austrian state," he said, "otherwise we shall be drawn into the German sea. But the Germans are surrounded by Slavs and Russians, who make up two-thirds of the population of Europe. The Austrians will find that *they* need us Croatians to help them conduct their foreign trade with the East and also in diplomatic posts."

Again, as with the cultural dimension, the moderates on the assimilation question display what we may call the most natural Austrian position. The extreme antiassimilationist viewed the Austrian state (he did not say *political nation*) as a pure utility, a rational instrument for the preservation of Croatian cultural values. The extreme assimilationist thought back to a period when Austrians wanted to be politically a part of Germany and derived his political Austrianism at least in part from the negative experience of actual anschluss. The other three respondents simply took their political Austrianism for granted, as something naturally "given."

In summary, how shall we describe the position of Croatian elites on the question of the Austrian nation, and how does that position compare with that of German-speaking Austrians? This is a difficult question to answer with the data we have on hand, for several reasons: the small number of respondents; the fact that all of these live either in German-speaking Eisenstadt or in one of the nearby Croatian towns rather than in the more isolated southern villages; and the fact that only two of the five were of the *political* elite. Nevertheless, an impressionistic comparison which may be of some value can be made.

On the cultural question, the majority of Croatian respondents were more like consensualists in the middle ranges of the Viennese elites than like those in the Länder. Three of the five expressly accepted Austria both as a political and a cultural nation, something that I have otherwise found almost exclusively in Vienna. Two of these three, one an intellectual but the other a practicing politician with mostly administrative concerns, were able to specify a content for the cultural nation, though one of them, like the provincial consensualists, had only a feeling about the cultural nation.

On the political side, the resemblance was to the "natural Austrian" position of the young Austrians I interviewed both among the Viennese and among the provincial middle-range elites. But in the Burgenland this position does not seem to be only a function of age but also of the long separation of the Croatian minority from its Slavic homeland, its liberal treatment by two Austrian republics, and its noninvolvement, as a language minority, with Pan-Germanism.

8. NATIONAL CONSCIOUSNESS
IN THE POPULATION AT LARGE

In a democratic age, elite opinion is intimately tied in with the opinions of the man in the street, influencing and being influenced in turn by that opinion. Many if not most of the elite personalities whose views were discussed in chapter 6 answered this writer's questions by predicting what the man in the street thinks, or can be brought to think, about the Austrian nation issue. Which of these respondents best understood his constituents—the pragmatist in Vienna who opted for the restricted concept of political nation, the Viennese idealist who called Austria a cultural nation, or the provincial who found the word *nation* unsuitable for Austrians and who preferred to talk about state consciousness? If there are regional differences on the question similar to those found among elites, do they follow the pattern of elite opinion or do they diverge from it? Is elite opinion ahead or behind that of the masses? What differences do age, sex, occupation, and party affiliation make in national consciousness?

To answer these questions we must go directly to the man in the office, the factory, or the farm. But does the average man have an opinion on questions as subtle and abstract as the difference between a political and a cultural nation? His time is consumed in making a living, raising a family, and finding a little leisure for amusement and personal renewal. Knowing this, some of the elite respondents told me that the question of national consciousness does not arise for the man in the street, he does not think about it. But these were also the people who told me that extended public discussion of the nation problem could have no positive effect and might prove dangerously divisive—implying that the man in the street does, or at least can be made to think about these things.

It seemed meaningful to question the average man directly about the Austrian nation, as well as to seek indirect measurements of the level of his national consciousness, because of his special experience. The average Austrian, either personally or through a close relative, has experienced a fourfold political collapse and reconstruction of total proportions in the last fifty years—territorial dismemberment and a revolution from monarchy to republic, the establishment of a "Black" dictatorship, absorption into "Greater Germany" accompanied by a "Brown" dictatorship, and lastly the separation of the Austrian Länder from Germany and the reconstruction of the republic. Implicit in each of these upheavals was a new definition of political identity, a new answer to the question about the Austrian nation. And with each upheaval came a vast shift in the political vocabulary, the jargon and slogans that the average man was expected to learn and use—"Long live the emperor," "Long live the republic," "German-Austria," "The Second German State," "Red-White-Red until dead," "One Reich, One Leader, One People," "Year Zero," "Long live Austria, long live the republic," and so forth. In this context it seemed reasonable to expect that the average man would have some thoughts about the Austrian nation question.

Opinion surveys show that in fact he does. In this chapter the findings of five recent surveys, some of which deal comprehensively with the question of national identity and others of which touch on special facets of the subject, will be discussed. All were done between the years 1956 and 1966.[1]

The earliest study was done by Dr. Walter Fessel's Institute for Market and Opinion Research (Vienna) during April 1956, a year after the State Treaty (see table 6). The word *people (Volk)* not *nation (Nation)* was used in the survey, and *Volk* used to mean the same as *Staatsvolk,* which is close to the concept of political nation. The 1894 Brockhaus gives as the meaning for *Volk:* "the totality of citizens"; and the source contrasts it with *Nation,* which is defined as the "hereditary tribal, speech, customs, and cultural community." The 1957 Brockhaus, however, equates *Volk* with *Nation* and describes it as "constituted by a common spiritual and

---

1. A sixth survey was carried out by the Austrian Gallup Institute after this chapter was completed. It indicated a continuation of the trend toward the emergence of an Austrian national identity reported in the earlier polls. Ten percent more of the Austrian people thought that Austrians are a nation or are developing into one than did so in 1966. The poll results were reported in *Kurier,* December 8, 1971, p. 2. See citation in Kurt Steiner, *Politics in Austria* (Boston: Little, Brown, 1972), p. 156.

Table 6. Fessel Survey of National Consciousness (1956),
by Sex and Age

In April 1956 the following question was asked of a representative cross section of the Austrian population: "It is repeatedly debated as to whether we Austrians are Germans or not. Are you personally of the opinion that we are a group within the German people, or are we a uniquely Austrian people?"

	By sex (%)			By age (%)		
Response	Men	Women	Total	18–39	40–59	60 and older
Austrians are a unique people	47	54	49	44	48	65
Austrians belong to the German people	50	38	46	51	48	26
No opinion	3	8	5	5	4	9

Source: Survey by Dr. Walter Fessel, Institut f. Marktforschung (Vienna), reported in "Querschnitte der öffentlichen Meinung," in R. Stiefbold et al., eds., *Wahlen u. Parteien in Österreich*, vol. 2 (Vienna: Öst. Bundesverlag, 1966), p. 584. Representative national sample. With permission of Dr. Fessel.

cultural development and, usually, by a common speech; increasingly connected with these things is the striving for political unity (state)." We cannot be sure, therefore, in what sense the respondents understood the word. The results show that not quite half the Austrian rank and file were ready to accept an Austrian identity. But if the respondents thought that they were being asked to choose in a total sense between being Austrian and being German, while they actually felt themselves to be both, the results cannot be said to reveal the true state of the Austrian mind.

That this is likely—that Austrians at the time wished to have a double identity—is apparent from the results of a youth survey done by Dr. Fessel in 1959 (see table 7). The sample of Austrian youth polled evidently was beginning to develop some kind of special Austrian identity, and seeing the word *Volk* in the second statement, the respondents probably thought that they were being asked if they were part of a unique political nation. But in the third statement, seeing the word *Germans* used without qualification, they were equally sure that in a general cultural sense they were nevertheless Germans. Hence the almost identical affirmation of the two statements. The Austrian identity was, however, strongly enough formed to produce a rather firm no to the anschluss question.

Table 7. Fessel Youth Study (1959): Attitudes Toward Nationalism

Scale: 1 = positively true
2 = probably true
3 = don't know; no opinion
4 = probably false
5 = certainly false

Statement	Mean value	Standard deviation
"The interests of a people (the nation) come before all others."	2.35	1.57
"The Austrians are not Germans but a unique people."	1.70	1.15
"The Austrians are Germans."	1.74	1.89
"Austria and Germany should be united."	4.07	1.25

SOURCE: Dr. Walter Fessel, Institut f. Marktforschung, *Jugend Studie*, 1959/60, table 48. National sample. N = 150. By permission of the Österreichische Volkspartei.

These two surveys, especially the second, seem to indicate the beginnings of a specialized Austrian identity among the general public during the late 1950s. However, both seem to establish a continued German cultural feeling. In 1963 a poll was conducted by Dr. Manfred Koch, a German psychologist who also used the facilities of the Fessel Institute (see table 8). The poll was obviously designed to measure cultural identity in the traditional sense. If all the responses from 100 to 60 were put together as a largely German position, and all from 50 to 0 as a largely Austrian position, the ratio would be heavily in favor of the German position—51 percent to 41 percent.

Additional surveys on the subject were carried out during 1964 by the Social Science Study Society, a Socialist-sponsored survey research organization in Vienna, and during 1966 by the Gallup Institute in Vienna on behalf of this writer. The report on the 1964 survey indicates that those who conducted the poll intended a political rather than a cultural definition of nation and presumably this was conveyed to the sample interviewed. They did not say how they defined political nation, however (see table 9).

It will be noted that the percentage of the sample who thought Austrians constitute a nation was about the same as the number who had responded this way in the 1956 survey. But only 15.34 percent said that Austrians were not a nation, less than half the number who in 1956 had said that they belonged to "the German

Table 8. Koch Survey of National Consciousness (1963)

Percentage frequencies of answers to the so-called thermometer question: "Here are two antithetical views. At about what point between them would your view fall?"

100 = Austrians are precisely as German as the other German *Stämme*, e.g., Bavarians, Swabians, etc.

0 = Austrians are in no sense German, but a unique nation.

Degree of similarity	*Percentage of answers*
100	28
90	8
80	7
70	5
60	3
50	11
40	2
30	4
20	4
10	3
0	17
No position	8

SOURCE: Manfred Koch, "Das Deutschenbild der Österreicher," in *Bericht über den 24. Kongress der Deutschen Gesellschaft f. Psychologie* (Göttingen: Verlag f. Psychologie), table 2, p. 336. Random survey with structured interview; N = 2,000. With permission.

Table 9. SWSG Survey of National Consciousness (1964)

This poll was concerned with the following problem: Many people say that Austrians are a nation. Others say Austrians are not a nation. Still others say Austrians are slowly beginning to feel that they are a nation. The respondent had to decide which view, in his opinion, was correct.

	FPÖ sup-porters %	*KPÖ* sup-porters %	*ÖVP* sup-porters %	*SPÖ* sup-porters %	*No party* %	*Total* %
Austrians are a nation	22.02	50.00	52.45	55.72	37.50	47.37
Austrians are not a nation	53.21	21.87	11.41	8.67	16.67	15.34
Austrians are slowly beginning to feel that they are a nation	20.18	17.19	22.01	23.80	24.74	23.04
Don't know	4.59	10.94	14.13	11.81	21.09	14.25

SOURCE: Sozialwissenschaftliche Studiengesellschaft, "Das Nationalbewusstsein der Österreicher," *Die Meinung* (Vienna: Spring, 1965), p. 10. Representative national sample. N = 2,500. With permission.

Volk." And 23.04 percent said that Austrians were gradually beginning to feel that they are a nation. It is possible that if there had been a transitional category in the 1956 survey, some of the German identifiers would have chosen this alternative.

The first two surveys, in 1956 and 1959, showed the emergence of some kind of Austrian identity, but its nature was not clear. The third showed that, whatever the character of that identity, in 1963 a majority still thought of themselves as Germans in a traditional cultural and ethnic sense. The fourth survey of 1964–65 seemed to show that when *nation* was used with specific reference to political community, a large majority (70 percent) expressed an existing or developing Austrianism.

In the 1966 Gallup Institute survey an effort was made to pose the questions so that both cultural and political identity were revealed at the same time (see table 10). The first alternative was designed for those who subscribe to the maximal or cultural nation position, à la Hurdes; such persons have a deep attachment to Austrian cultural separateness and are usually anti-German. The second and fifth alternatives were designed for those who retain a traditional cultural identity as Germans but who also have a warm attachment to the Austrian political community. The expression *Staatsnation* was not used in these two because this could be read to mean only a very restricted rational and pragmatic acceptance of the Austrian state. The two statements implied and the elite interviews have confirmed that there is an unfocused, emotional Austrianism which arises *out of* the experience of the Second Republic as a successful political enterprise but spills over from specific political reference into a sort of general cultural feeling. (Consider, for example, the feelings of the Croatian school director in the Burgenland who spoke of the warm emotions he has on seeing an Austrian license plate when traveling abroad, or the patriotic excitement engendered by Austrian victories in international soccer, skiing, or ice-skating competitions.) It seems clear this sort of feeling can coexist with attachment to German culture, if the latter is defined in the more traditional linguistic and "high culture" sense. It is primarily a political identity, but with cultural or quasi-cultural overtones. Hence the expression *Austrian nation* was used here in an unqualified sense and paired with the idea of German cultural

Table 10. Gallup Survey of National Consciousness (1966), by Sex, Age, and Vocation

QUESTION: "Many people say that the Austrians are a unique nation. Others maintain that Austrians are a part of the German nation. Between these two views there are also many shades of opinion. What do you think?"

Response	% of entire population	% by sex		% by age			% by vocation				
		Men	Women	Up to 30	Up to 50	Over 50	Workers	Farmers	Prof. & self-employed	Officials	Pensioners
Austria is a completely unique nation and not a part of the German nation	35	33	36	40	30	36	39	33	31	16	43
Although Austria belongs to the realm of German speech and culture, Austria is a unique nation	29	33	26	28	32	27	29	34	29	25	25
Although Austria is an independent state, Austrians belong to the German nation	11	12	11	11	11	11	8	12	13	19	9
Although Austrians are a political nation and stand up for the independence of the state, they still belong to the German nation	9	0	9	6	11	9	9	8	12	12	7
Although Austria belongs to the realm of German speech and culture, Austrians are beginning slowly to feel that they are a unique nation	8	9	7	7	10	7	5	7	10	21	6
Other	8	3	11	8	6	10	10	6	5	7	10
Number of cases	2,500	1,135	1,365	654	797	1,049	732	644	312	261	551

SOURCE: Österreichisches Gallup Institut (Vienna), Report of special survey for W. T. Bluhm as part of omnibus survey, April 1966, p. 12. National random sample. N = 2,500.

NATIONAL CONSCIOUSNESS IN THE POPULATION AT LARGE   227

identity. The fourth alternative was for people with a very restricted Austrian political identity, and the third for those with a purely German identity.

The 35 percent of the sample who opted for the maximal Austrian, non-German position in 1966 is double the number found in favor of that position in the 1963 thermometer poll. (This may have been because the word *nation* was used here without ethnic reference.) An additional 37 percent opted for the extended political nation identity. This means that 72 percent expressed a political Austrianism with a cultural extension running from partial to total.

One discrepancy is to be noted between the findings of the last survey and the results of some elite interviews. Altogether, 81 percent of the respondents in the survey were prepared to apply the word *nation* in some sense to Austria, while the provincial elites, including those with evident Austrian feeling, almost universally rejected the word as an inappropriate label. This is consistent with the findings of other scholars, such as Stiefbold and Powell, to the effect that, because of their inbreeding, Austrian political elites at the middle ranges tend to be more ideological in the traditional sense than either top leaders or the man in the street. Mass opinion seems to have changed faster than elite opinion in the matter of the Austrian nation. That the general usage of *nation* is changing is indicated in a 1965 article in *Die neue Front* entitled "The Changing Meaning of 'National,' " which we cited in chapter 5.

What similarities or differences in the comparative Austrianism of the supporters of the various political parties are revealed by the surveys discussed above? Only three of them—the Fessel survey of 1956, the SWSG poll of 1964–65, and the Gallup study of 1966 —report a breakdown by party (see tables 9, 11, 12). As the accompanying tables show, in each of these the Socialists scored higher than the Conservatives, with differences varying from 3 percent to 14 percent, depending on the wording of the particular question. This is a reversal of the pattern of national feelings in the two major parties during the First Republic, when the Conservatives were the most Austrian-minded party and the Socialists largely Pan-German. But since the largest percentage-point differences between the parties are found on questions that seem to measure cul-

Table 11. Fessel Survey of National Consciousness (1956),
by Party and Occupation
(In percentages)

By party	Austrian people[a]	German people[a]	No opinion[a]
ÖVP supporters	55	42	3
SPÖ supporters	66	30	4
Other or no party	22	74	4
By occupation			
Professionals & self-employed	32	61	7
White-collar workers	48	48	4
Blue-collar workers	62	32	6
Agricultural occupations	56	37	7

[a] See table 6.
SOURCE: Same as for table 6; p. 585. Representative national sample.

Table 12. Gallup Survey of National Consciousness (1966), by Party
(In percentages)

Response	ÖVP	SPÖ	FPÖ	DFP	KPÖ	No party	No answer
Austria is a completely unique nation and not a part of the German nation	30	44	16	19	2	36	35
Although Austria belongs to the realm of German speech and culture, Austria is a unique nation	31	30	21	27	1	38	25
Although Austria is an independent state, Austrians belong to the German nation	12	6	30	27	–	7	12
Although Austrians are a political nation and stand up for the independence of the state, they still belong to the German nation	10	8	23	19	–	7	7
Although Austria belongs to the realm of German speech and culture, Austrians are beginning slowly to feel that they are a unique nation	13	7	6	7	–	6	4
Other	4	5	4	1	–	6	17
Number of cases	766	742	129	84	3	167	609

SOURCE: Same as for table 10; p. 13. National random sample. N = 2,500.

tural rather than purely political allegiance, both parties now appear to stand quite close together as equal supporters of the political community.

What about the other parties? Only two of the surveys give percentages for the Freedom party, and only one of them for the Communists.[2] It is to be remarked, in view of the widespread Pan-German image of the FPÖ, that in the SWSG poll as many as 42.20 percent of the Freedom party respondents adopted either the full Austrian or the transitional position, and in the Gallup poll 66 percent took one or another of the various Austrian positions. In the SWSG survey the Communists showed a majority for the Austrian or transitional positions but scored 7 percent lower than the Conservatives and 11 percent lower than the Socialists. This should be seen in comparison with the fact that the Communist leadership has ardently championed the full Austrian nation idea from 1945 to the present. The difference between the views of Conservative elites and followers and Socialist elites and followers is thus much less than the difference between the views of Communist elites and followers on the nation question.

Region proved to be a crucial factor for distinguishing attitudes about the Austrian nation among political elites. Only two of the surveys, the Fessel poll of 1956 and the Gallup study of 1966, published mass data on this dimension (see tables 13 and 14).

The most accurate comparison of the two polls is achieved by grouping together the three alternatives of the 1966 survey that emphasize Austrian feeling and place allegiance to things German in the "although" category or leave them out altogether, and by amalgamating the statistics for the three Austrian alternatives. In the earlier survey Vienna, Lower Austria/Burgenland, and Tyrol/Vorarlberg showed the strongest Austrianism; Upper Austria/Salzburg the least (13 to 18 percentage-point difference); and Styria/Carinthia held a middling position, which might be assignable to the first group if the standard deviation is taken into account. The comparison shows a considerable increase in Austrianism between 1956 and 1966 for every region, with the increase most marked in the least Austrian and least marked in the most Austrian areas.

2. There were only three Communists in the Gallup sample; thus no percentage ratio could be computed for that party in the 1966 survey.

Table 13. Gallup Survey of National Consciousness (1966), by Region
(In percentages)

Response	Vienna	Lower Austria/ Burgenland	Styria/ Carinthia	Upper Austria/ Salzburg	Tyrol/ Vorarlberg
Austria is a completely unique nation and not a part of the German nation	33	42	40	30	20
Although Austria belongs to the realm of German speech and culture, Austria is a unique nation	35	26	26	25	39
Although Austria is an independent state, Austrians belong to the German nation	7	6	10	25	8
Although Austrians are a political nation and stand up for the independence of the state, they still belong to the German nation	10	7	10	8	11
Although Austria belongs to the realm of German speech and culture, Austrians are beginning slowly to feel that they are a unique nation	6	11	4	6	18
No reply	9	8	10	6	4
Number of cases	642	576	554	497	231

SOURCE: Same as for table 10; p. 132. National random sample. N = 2,500.

The overall picture presented by the comparison thus shows a rapidly developing consensus on identity among the Länder over the ten-year period.

A special aspect of the dynamic toward consensus is revealed by separating the transitional (#5) responses in the 1966 poll ("Austrians are beginning slowly to feel that they are a unique nation") from the other two pro-Austrian alternatives. This indicates that in the areas of least marked Austrian sentiment—Upper Austria/Salzburg and Styria/Carinthia—conversion to the Austrian position

Table 14. Fessel Survey of National Consciousness (1956), by Region
(In percentages)

	Austrian people[a]	German people[a]	No opinion[a]
Vienna	69	24	7
Lower Austria, Burgenland	52	39	9
Upper Austria, Salzburg	33	63	4
Styria, Carinthia	35	62	3
Tyrol, Vorarlberg	53	45	2

[a] See table 6.
SOURCE: Same as for table 6; p. 585. Representative national sample.

during the ten-year period in question was both quantitatively and qualitatively the most pronounced. In the first of these areas 90 percent and in the second about 80 percent of the change was to one of the two most pronounced Austrian positions, with only 10 percent and 20 percent of the shift, respectively, moving into the transitional category. Tyrol/Vorarlberg and Lower Austria/Burgenland, which moved from the second into the most Austrian grouping showed the highest percentage of "emerging Austrians" by giving the largest number of "slowly beginning" or transitional responses.

If we add responses to alternative #4 (emphasizing cultural community with Germany but accepting the political nation label for Austria) to the category of pro-Austrian responses, we find an Austrian consensus of over 80 percent in each of the regional groupings except Upper Austria/Salzburg, where the figure is 69 percent. This is consistent with the predictions of elites in both Vienna and the Länder about the extent of state consciousness today.

There seems to be a discrepancy, however, between the results of the 1966 poll and the elite predictions about the balance between those who accept the full Austrian (political and cultural nation) position, those who affirm the political nation position but reject the cultural concept, and those who are "Austrian conscious" but unwilling to apply the nation label in any of its senses to Austria. The elite interviews indicated that acceptance of the cultural nation concept was confined to Viennese intellectuals and a small segment of the middle range of political elites who live and work in Vienna. The rest of the country, with the exception of Salzburg (where

serious identity problems for the older generations were stressed),
was seen as "Austrian feeling" in a political sense. Only Viennese
politicians thought "political nation" an apt expression for this
feeling, however; others preferred "state consciousness," "Austrian
feeling," or "Austrian-mindedness." If the poll's findings are valid,
the elites would not seem to be in touch with the groundswell of a
multidimensional Austrianism at the grass roots. The high percentages for Styria/Carinthia and for Upper Austria/Salzburg are particularly remarkable. These areas, in which overall Austrianism is
supposedly weakest, showed a larger or as large a percentage of
all-out Austrians as Vienna, which is in the first grouping vis-à-vis
Austrian enthusiasts.

There appears to be another discrepancy between the elite interviews and the 1966 survey results in the findings about acceptance
of the nation label in any sense. The interviews in the western
Länder indicated a general rejection of the concept, yet only 11
percent of the national survey sample repudiated it, and there were
no significant differences in the quantity of these responses from
regional group to regional group. This may, however, be due to
the wording of the response alternatives rather than to mispercep-
tions by elites. The only response alternatives in which the word
"nation" was not applied to Austria contained no positive Austrian
affirmation, but simply admitted the fact of legal independence. It
is likely that this forced acceptance by "Austrian-minded" and
"state conscious" people who otherwise might have shied away
from the word.

The 1956 Fessel survey and the 1966 Gallup survey presented
a breakdown according to sex (see tables 6 and 10). The 1956
results showed a majority of women in favor of the Austrian alternative and a majority of men for the German. By 1966 there was
no significant difference between men and women on the question
of the Austrian nation. On each of the Austrian alternatives but
one the responses of men and women fell within 3 percentage points
of one another, and for alternative #2 the difference was only 7
percent, with the men showing a slightly stronger Austrianism than
the women. Putting the three pro-Austrian alternatives together
gives a difference of 6 percent in the same direction. However, 3
percent more women than men opted for the most-Austrian alter-

native, #1, but the difference falls within the standard deviation.

The two-alternative 1956 survey showed blue-collar workers as the most Austrian among occupational groups with farmers second. White-collar workers were third, and well behind, at the bottom of the scale, came self-employed people and professionals. The 1966 poll showed quite a different picture (see tables 10 and 11). Most comparable with the pro-Austrian alternative of the 1956 survey are the three pro-Austrian alternatives (combined) of the 1966 poll. Comparison indicates an increase in the Austrianism of all groups, especially among the urban middle class, and a notable diminution of the range of differences among all the groups. An enormous growth of 38 percent—more than double the 1956 figure—is found among the professional and self-employed groups. The smallest increase is among farmers—only 6 percent.

These results should be viewed in conjunction with the findings of the 1966 poll about the intensity of Austrianism among the various occupational groups. Pensioners and others living on an income, not surveyed in 1956, were the Austrian maximalists; next came workers, followed by officials and white-collar workers, and trailed by professionals and self-employed individuals. These three categories were all in the same range. At the bottom of the scale on this alternative were the farmers, a full 15 percent behind the urban middle classes. The line on the imaginary graph flattens out, however, for those who selected the second Austrian alternative, with the differences among occupational groups reduced to between 4 and 9 percent. When the three emphatically Austrian alternatives are added together, the line flattens still more, with the differences among four of the groups reduced to between 1 and 4 percent and with the farmers only 8 to 12 points behind. This should be compared with the variation of between 6 and 30 percent among groups shown in the 1956 survey. When the minimally Austrian, political nation alternative is added in, differences among four of the groups disappear almost altogether and the farmers are only 7 to 8 points behind. The result is little different from the national average for the population as a whole. The third Austrian alternative, which measures current change ("slowly beginning to feel that they are a unique nation") showed the highest percentages among the various groups which scored lowest on the first alternative, with farmers showing the greatest disposition to evolve further in an Austrian direction.

The occupational breakdown presents good evidence that modernization—urbanization and industrialization—strongly supports the Austrian national idea when tied in, as it is today, with economic success. The 1956 survey showed a comparative picture of the Austrianism of occupational groups that differed from that of the 1930s primarily in the reversal of the workers' position from Pan-German to the most Austrian. The urban middle classes, however, remained low on the scale, with a majority of them espousing a German rather than an Austrian identity, much as they had done throughout the First Republic. By 1966, however, this group had experienced a remarkable conversion to Austrianism, placing in the same range as the previously most-Austrian groups. The farmers, almost alone during the 1930s as carriers of the Austrian idea (though of course large numbers of them were also Pan-German, depending on the region in question), by 1956 slipped to second place, and in 1966 to the bottom of the scale, well behind all other groups. That the economic miracle of the decade from 1955 to 1965 had much to do with the newly found Austrianism of the urban classes seems a not improbable conclusion and appears to bear out the intuitive psychology of the pragmatic politicians about the causes (at least the short-run ones) of national feeling. That farmers have evolved less quickly to an Austrian position and have lost their comparative status in a radical way (moving from first down to last) is probably attributable primarily to the fact that of all economic groups farmers have profited least by the economic miracle and in many areas are a very marginal group. That this most traditional class is today in the process of developing more Austrian feeling than the other groups may be the result of a growing urban feedback into the farming community which, unlike the old-style farm, is no longer isolated from the culture of the city. The rural "old Austrians" may be learning a new kind of Austrianism from the urban "new Austrians." The upshot of all these changes is a degree of consensus among social and economic groups on the national identity question that is unparalleled in Austrian history.

Age is another important factor to investigate in our exploration of popular patterns of identity in Austria. On this topic we have data from two of the surveys we have been discussing and also some information from a special youth study done by the Fessel Institute in 1959–60 (see tables 6 and 10). The most complete and most comparable age data are in the 1956 and 1966 surveys. In 1956 the most-Austrian group was in the 60-year-plus bracket, the next in the 40- to 59-year-old bracket, and the last among the people from 18 to 39. It is not surprising that in this survey the youth should have been found the least attached to Austria. In 1956 the entire population from 18 to 39 years of age had been born between 1917 and 1938. This means that a large proportion of them had grown up during the chaotic First Republic when Pan-Germanism was becoming increasingly popular. The oldest of this group were 21 when the anschluss took place, and the youngest had just come into the world. Nor is it surprising that their parents, mostly 40 to 59 years old, should have had similar attitudes in 1956. The oldest of these people were born in 1897, were 21 when the Habsburg Empire went to pieces, and 41 at the anschluss. None of these people had had happy experiences with republican govern-ment in Austria during their politically formative years. The grand-fathers of 1956, born from around 1876 to 1896, for the most part remembered the empire as colorful and generally prosperous, and their Austrianism is no doubt a carryover from their old *Kaisertreue* of this early happy period, translated into national patriotism.

The 1966 survey shows a very different constellation of Austrian sentiment by age group. The youngest (in this survey "up to 30" rather than "18 to 30") are now the most Austrian-minded and the oldest the least, though on the basis of the combined results for the three most emphatic Austrian responses, the oldest and the youngest are only 5 percentage points apart. All groups have much higher scores than in 1956—ranging from 10 to 30 percentage points. The youngest group in this survey overlaps by only two years the youngest group in 1956, and, unlike that sample, all of them have spent their formative years in the Second Republic. (The oldest of them were born in 1936, just two years before the anschluss and were only 9 in 1945 when Nazi educational influ-ences were substantially eliminated from Austrian schools.) If these are "natural" Austrians, their fathers, the group from 31 to 50, who were between 21 and 40 at the start of the economic miracle, have doubtless developed their Austrianism out of material satisfactions greater than any they had earlier enjoyed. The oldest group one would suppose would not only rank lower, as it does, but very much lower than the other two on the Austrian scale, which it does not. It includes the formerly Pan-German fathers of the 1956 survey along with an offsetting remnant of the "old Austrians." Apparently this group, too, could be swayed by the economic well-being it has enjoyed in the Second Republic, which surpassed what most of them knew during the seven brief years of anschluss with the Third Reich—to which they had looked for salvation of all kinds. That the youngest are "natural" Austrians is attested by the fact that they scored highest on the first pro-Austrian alternative, which distinguishes Austrians in a comprehensive way from Germans. That the second group has learned its Austrianism is indicated by the fact that it scored lowest of the groups on the first pro-Austrian alternative, highest on the second, which acknowledges Austrian nationality along with Austrian participation in German speech and culture, and highest on the dynamic alternative ("slowly beginning to feel they are a unique nation"). The relatively high acknowledgment of comprehensive Austrianism by the oldest age group is probably mostly attributable to the fact that this group is partially populated by "old Austrians," for whom Austrianism was also a natural state of mind, and possibly also to the radical disillusionment with German rule experienced by some of this group during the anschluss period.

Indirect Measurements

What indirect measures of Austrian national consciousness have been obtained through the resources of survey research? The SWSG poll involved a number of such measures. For instance, one question, responses to which tend to substantiate our suppositions in the paragraphs above about a close connection between the development of Austrian consciousness and the results of the economic miracle, was: "When, in your opinion, have Austrians had it the best?" (See table 15.)

Another indirect measure that substantiates our findings from di-

Table 15. SWSG Survey of National Consciousness (1964):
Responses to Question "When Have You Had It Best?"
(In percentages)

Period	FPÖ sup-porters	KPÖ sup-porters	ÖVP sup-porters	SPÖ sup-porters	No party	Total
Before 1918	4.59	1.56	12.23	0.92	4.69	5.04
After 1918	0.92	4.69	0.27	2.77	2.08	1.91
After 1934 under Dollfuss and Schnuschnigg	1.83	–	3.26	0.37	1.30	1.43
1938 after the anschluss with Germany	44.96	–	1.09	1.84	3.91	5.32
1945 after the collapse at the end of WW II	1.83	15.63	3.26	2.40	4.43	3.68
1955 after the withdrawal of the allies	13.76	12.50	17.66	16.79	17.97	16.90
Only during the last few years	30.28	57.81	57.88	72.88	59.89	61.90
Don't know	1.83	7.81	4.35	2.03	5.73	3.82

SOURCE: Same as for table 9; p. 9. Representative national sample. N = 2,500.

rect questioning was obtained by the SWSG with a question about where people preferred to live (see table 16). A resounding majority voted for Austria. On the party breakdown, both major parties voted overwhelmingly for Austria. Only Freedom party members made Germany their first choice.

Belief in Austria as a nation capable of sustaining a vital culture was also measured. Those interviewed were asked to respond true or false to the following statements: "Austria is a forgotten museum

Table 16. SWSG Survey of National Consciousness (1964):
"Where Do Austrians Wish to Live?"
(In percentages)

	FPÖ Supporters	KPÖ Supporters	ÖVP Supporters	SPÖ Supporters	No party	Total
Switzerland	11.93	15.63	14.13	13.47	24.22	16.43
Germany	55.96	10.94	8.97	8.30	13.54	13.50
Austria	27.52	59.37	73.10	75.09	52.34	64.42
No opinion	4.59	14.06	3.80	3.14	9.90	5.65

SOURCE: Same as for table 9; p. 9. Representative national sample. N = 2,500.

piece. In Austria one can still find old and genuine culture. Austrians are politically without character. In Austria one can still live pleasantly (*gemütlich*). Austria's charm is known throughout the world. If Austria did not exist she would have to be created." To all except the last statement 65 percent to 86 percent of the respondents gave an overwhelmingly pro-Austrian response. Only 36 percent said that Austria ought to be created if she did not exist, however, although only 31 percent negated the proposition. Thirty-three percent did not know.

A healthy majority of 64 percent favored "protest against the desecration of the flag" when asked what action they would take if they saw foreigners rip down an Austrian flag. This indicates the development of a considerable degree of national pride, though only 12 percent said that they would protest with fisticuffs.

In response to a question as to what the respondents would do if Austria were divided up among neighboring states as it had been in 1918, 41 percent indicated that they would engage in some sort of defensive or protest action. The alternatives of this kind included partisan warfare, strikes, underground activities, and emigration. Twenty-two percent said that they would do what the majority did, and 18 percent said that they would do nothing. Only 1 percent said that they would agree with dismemberment and 18 percent gave no answer or a nonstandard response.

An indirect measure of the quality of Austrian national consciousness is found in the results of both the SWSG poll of 1964–65 and the Koch survey of 1963, which employed questions dealing with the affinity of Austrians for other European peoples (see tables 17 and 18). Koch found that 44 percent of his sample thought Germans to be the most congenial among ten alternatives. The SWSG study found the same pro-German percentage in a seven-alternative list. Koch found, in addition, that only 3 percent of his sample were actively hostile to Germans. He judged this to be "because they feel most closely related to them. The relationship is seen as existing in the areas of speech and of history," especially as a result of the World War I alliance. But Koch also measured for Austrian national pride and found an overwhelming positive response on this dimension—87 percent. As objects of national pride the respondents mentioned such things as the beauty of the

Table 17. Koch Survey of National Consciousness (1963):
Sympathy with Other Peoples

Percentage frequency of answers to the questions: "To which of these nations do you feel most sympathetic? . . . least sympathetic?"

Most sympathetic		*Least sympathetic*	
Germans	44	Italians	34
Swiss	22	Czechs	27
Scandinavians	11	Yugoslavs	11
Dutch	10	Hungarians	7
English	6	French	6
French	5	English	4
Hungarians	3	Swiss	3
Czechs	2	Germans	3
Yugoslavs	2	Scandinavians	1
Italians	2	Dutch	1
All the same	4	All the same	7
No position	7	No position	9

SOURCE: Same as for table 8. Random survey with structured interview. N = 2,000.

landscape, international goodwill and love for Austria, the winter Olympic games, Austrian sports prowess, a history of achievement in music, hospitality to strangers who come as guests, Austria's democratic constitution and freedom under the law, the beauty and fame of Vienna. Special qualities of personality and moral values seen as distinctly Austrian were also mentioned by Koch's respondents, all of which we have discussed in an earlier chapter under the heading "The Austrian Man" (*der österreichische Mensch*).

Koch's findings and those of the SWSG about an Austrian

Table 18. SWSG Survey of National Consciousness (1965): Responses to Question "To What Nation Are You Most Sympathetic?"

	Percentage
German nation	44
Swiss nation	25
Dutch nation	9
Czech nation	2
Hungarian nation	3
Italian nation	2
Yugoslav nation	1
No opinion	14

SOURCE: Sozialwissenschaftliche Studiengesellschaft, "Das Nationalbewusstsein der Österreicher," pt. 2, *Die Meinung* (Vienna: Fall, 1965), p. 2. Representative national sample. N = 2,500. With permission.

affinity for Germans support the belief that the national identity concepts of the average man, as we have argued above (see p. 225), do not make the Austrian cultural nation and German cultural nation exclusive concepts. It is possible and usual for the man in the street to identify strongly as a German in cultural matters and still be an enthusiastic Austrian, not only politically but culturally as well, although the cultural referents may be of a rather primitive variety. Language is for him the chief cultural bond with Germans, while other cultural landmarks are more Austrian than German. This would explain why the 1966 survey drew so few responses in favor of a purely political Austrianism, when some elite interviews, especially those in the provinces, had led me to expect that this would be a dominant theme.

Summary

In summary, what do our measures of popular attitudes toward the Austrian nation show? By 1956, 49 percent of the Austrian population had developed a strong Austrian consciousness, one probably more vital and widespread than had existed in any year from 1918 until then. It was a product of disenchantment with Germany after the anschluss and of sufferings as a part of the Third Reich during World War II. Most noteworthy was that by that year the Socialist working class had become loyal Austrians, in large part because of the vested interest that they had acquired in the state from participation in the government coalition, as well as from the harsh experiences of the anschluss years.

The period from 1956 to 1966, when pragmatic politicians from both Conservative and Socialist camps cooperated to produce, with Marshall Plan aid, an economic miracle, brought a marked growth in Austrian feeling among all groups and a strong diminution of differences among them on the identity question in its broader definition. Supporters of the two major parties have been and continue to be the chief carriers of the Austrian nation idea, but even the majority of the Pan-German Freedom party members fall within the "Austrian" consensus.

Austrian youth, born and raised in a period of peace and prosperity, display a "natural" Austrianism, which they simply accept as a fact of life, but they retain a certain cultural identification as

Germans as well. The middle-aged people, despite the discontinuity of present with earlier identities, have become strongly Austrian, also as a function of peace and prosperity, but more self-consciously and probably more superficially so. The urban middle classes, once carriers of the Pan-German ideal, have for the same reasons undergone a similar identity shift, though both they and the middle-aged retain a strong cultural identity as Germans. Farmers, once the most enthusiastic Austrians, are now the least enthusiastic, but only in a relative sense and with the additional qualification that they continue to evolve an Austrian identity in greater numbers than other economic groups, probably as a result of new urban influences on farm life.

The mushrooming of Austrian consciousness, however, has not resulted in the development of a parallel antagonism to Germans, which arch-Austrian ideologues believe necessary for the establishment of a stable national identity. The average Austrian, enthusiastic patriot though he is, likes Germans more than any other European people and feels a certain cultural bond with them, though he sees Austria as a unique cultural and political nation.

In short, survey research shows that the Austrian nation concept is a well-established psychological fact, both as a political and to a degree as a cultural reality. How *stable* a fact it is, however, may depend on the continuation of the present "fair weather" and on the direction and rate of a variety of currents in the complex dynamics of political, social, economic, and cultural change.

9. THE AUSTRIAN NATION TODAY

The Tradition of the Incomplete

Willy Lorenz, an aging Viennese publisher and publicist and a member of the last imperial generation, has written of the tragic incompleteness that he sees as characteristic of Austrian life since the early days of the empire. He finds it everywhere, in Austrian music, architecture, literature, politics, and even technological invention. Schubert's Eighth, the famous "Unfinished Symphony" is one example; the beautiful Monastery Church of Klosterneuburg, which one of the Habsburgs planned as a second Escorial, is another; Francis Joseph's unfinished Ringstrasse and New Hofburg Palace are others. Lorenz reminds us of the military hesitation to move on Berlin after the victory of Kunersdorf in 1759, which effort, if successful, might have altered the whole course of European history by skotching Hohenzollern competition at the outset. The failure of the Archduke Charles to follow up his victory over Napoleon at Aspern in 1809, and Francis Joseph's timidity after Solferino in 1859 and after the disaster at Königgrätz in 1866 are other political examples. The unfinished masterpieces of Robert Musil exemplify the tragic flaw in literature. Lorenz also shows that if they had been able to raise the capital to exploit their technical discoveries, Austrians would today be known as inventors of the modern steamship screw, the typewriter, and the sewing machine.

The tradition of tragic incompleteness is rooted, Lorenz believes, in the Austrian character—in a penchant for pessimism and lack of self-trust.

> There is a deeply tragic flaw in the Austrian soul. It consists in this, that the Austrian has no self-confidence, no trust in his own capabilities, and thus the talents which have been bestowed on him are developed only imperfectly and in small measure in comparison with their potential. . . . So often the Austrian has

had only to take one last small step to complete his work. But he almost never takes that last step. It almost always comes to that. And so he remains the complete unfulfilled.[1]

Why this pessimism and lack of self-confidence? Lorenz thinks it may come from a "transcendentally rooted timidity of the Austrian to grapple with the course of events in the world, because he might disturb some plan better than his own. Gladly he excuses himself for being in the world at all." Entering an occupied room the Austrian always asks, "Am I not disturbing you (stör' ich nicht)?"[2]

The unfinished character of Austrian life is not uniquely Lorenz's observation. The theme has been developed by other Viennese literati seeking to understand and express the characteristic qualities of Austrian life in order to teach Austrians a lesson in self-improvement. One such person is Hans Weigel, a Jewish émigré whose love of and fascination for the Vienna in which he was raised brought him back there to make his home after the war. In his book, Flucht vor der Grösse [Flight from Greatness], published in Vienna in 1960, Weigel takes as his theme the characteristic failure of promising Austrian intellectuals to live up to their promise—a failure that he attributes to the "incomplete development of their capabilities" (p. 16). Typically, they allow their talents to flower too early, and their works then turn out to be mere fragments, says Weigel. Of Schubert, the author writes that he lacked "an awareness of his uniqueness, lacked self-knowledge." He didn't work his music over; he simply wrote it down as it flowed out of him (pp. 22–23).

Other, darker things accompany lack of self-understanding, according to Weigel. In the work of Ferdinand Raimund, one of the greatest of the nineteenth-century Austrian playwrights, who is still read and performed today, Weigel finds evidence of a "flight into schizophrenia." He "wanted to be Schiller and Shakespeare, so that he could not be completely Ferdinand Raimund." He was good at comedy, but he wanted to write tragedy. It was a way that led to self-destruction, and Weigel sees Raimund as standing at

1. Lorenz, AEIOU, p. 29.
2. Ibid., p. 30.

the beginning of a line of Austrian writers who manifest the same tragic penchant. "With Raimund's biography begins the gallery of the 'eternal brides,' which Grillparzer, Nestroy, and Lenau continue. Seen from the end, and as a whole, it reveals an almost fanatic, demonic propensity to maneuver one's life from the beginning into a closed corner. . . ." And then he generalizes: "Self-destructiveness thus appears as the Austrian cardinal virtue" (p. 45).

In his sketch of the life and work of Johann Nestroy, whose bittersweet comedies in *Wienerisch* are still the delight of Austrians —one sees them constantly on the Viennese and provincial stage, on television, and even in the movies—Weigel describes the playwright as "modest, shy, inhibited, in no way extraordinary, quiet, kind, ready to teach; he was defenseless, anxious, given to depression" (p. 94). He writes of him as a poet who "looks at man unsparingly, mercilessly in his entire *Fragwürdigkeit*. He flies from this knowledge and realization into the world of apparently uncomplicated, comfortable buffoonery . . . and hides himself from the history of great world literature in pieces written in the local dialects of neighborhoods outside Vienna's Ring (Vorstädte) which oblige him to remain in the world of transitory everydayness" (p. 86). Weigel is writing about Nestroy and also about the Austrian people.

Weigel comments at length on Nestroy's *Lumpazivagabundus*, a play of the *Vormärz*, the fragile period of conservative calm presided over by Metternich between the imperial military debacles of the Napoleonic Wars and the Revolution of 1848. Much loved today by Austrians, and especially by the Viennese, it is frequently performed on the stage and has also been made into a film. Its tone is one of bitter alienation, but in a charming *Wienerisch* manner. Weigel calls it "the great 'NO!' the great question mark, which strikes triumphantly through all the inadequacies [of the humble personae of the drama]. . . . It is a promethean protest against the higher powers" (p. 80). He calls it "an apocalypse in three-quarter time" in the manner of the singing and dancing of "Oh du lieber Augustin" during the plague days (p. 83). The play "streams scepticism, bitterness, fatalism, but presents these things in a comfortable, droll, gay manner; the man of the *Vormärz* saw himself upon the stage. The Austrian found himself strengthened as he turned to enter the present by not thinking about tomorrow" (p. 84). Here Weigel is also speaking to the Austrian of our day, who feels so at home at a performance of *Lumpazivagabundus*.

Against Franz Grillparzer, whom Austrians universally acclaim as their greatest poet and playwright and compare favorably with Goethe, Weigel directs his major attack. He describes Grillparzer as a psychological wreck and writes of the man's "incomprehensible self-alienation, self-estrangement, his monstrously brilliant self-hatred in which he allowed his greatness to be throttled" (p. 105). He wrote no really great tragedies, says Weigel, but in his own life he experienced the greatest of tragedies. "He had both within himself and in his external advantages all the possibilities for fulfillment as author, as man, as husband. It took a life of more than eighty years to dig under and bury their realization. He was a tenacious, unerring fanatic of self-destruction" (p. 105).

The schizophrenia that Weigel finds characteristic of the Austrian political mentality is epitomized by Grillparzer. "One can bring Grillparzer forward as a witness to substantiate every pro and every contra. . . . One can put together an Austrophile and an anti-Austrian anthology out of quotations from Grillparzer. . . . Grillparzer—who said in 1830 that a republic is better than this 'abominable stability system,' who later defended Radetzky and acclaimed him in an elegy, although he was of the opinion that despotism had destroyed his life" (p. 131). "Austrian—that is for him in a 'civil and political sense obviously the worst thing one can become.' On the other hand Austria is 'a goodly land, so worthy that a prince would gladly be her vassal.' " " 'Long live Austria! Habsburg forever!' are the lines that end the drama of King Ottokar; in this 'Habsburg forever!' Grillparzer legitimates and confirms retrospectively and freely that despotism which caused the destruction of his literary life, as he himself has attested" (p. 132). "Flight from greatness into the tormenting, the tormented, the petty, the mediocre. . . . In the history of the human spirit the Austrian Franz Grillparzer deserves no chapter, only a footnote printed in small letters, because it was not in battle with the world that he won victory and suffered defeat, because it was only against himself that he fought, it was only himself that he pulled down, wounded and killed" (p. 139). With these words Weigel sums up Grillparzer—and the Austrian people.

Weigel's critique of the Austrian mentality is merciless. He analyzes into a moral absurdity Grillparzer's most famous lines, the "song in praise of Austria" which appears in the midst of the Ottokar drama, at the pronunciation of which "the Austrian public reverts to the classroom and docilely applauds." The line that triggers the applause was never thought through grammatically to a conclusion, Weigel says disdainfully. Grillparzer has the speaker say:

> It's possible that in Saxony and on the Rhine there may be folk who more in books have read: But the needful things that please our God, the clear glance, the open and the upright mind. . . .

"Well, what is to be made of these things?" asks Weigel.

> There stands forth the Austrian before them all. . . .

"And how does he behave?" Weigel asks. "Does he at least speak his opinion, draw from his clear glance and upright mind the consequences? No. The action consists only in that the Austrian steps forward before them all. . . ."

> Thinks his part, and lets the others talk!

"The Austrian Grillparzer refuses to draw the grammatical, personal and artistic consequences of his premise," says Weigel. " 'The only needful things that please our God, the clear glance, the open and the upright mind. . . .' He says nothing about what he attempts or does not attempt with the glance and mind. The great, deep, self-destructive Grillparzer flaw yawns wide, right between 'mind' and 'there.' The Austrian Grillparzer steps forward before every man, before every matter, every claim, every conflict, every allurement from outside. But he fails to act; he doesn't even talk but lets the others talk. He thinks his part. He resigns. He cops out. He flies from reality into possibility:

> A possibility towers over all the broad expanses,
> The real shows itself merely in confined space

At the beginning he sees the end, and hesitates" (p. 113).

Lorenz and Weigel have not described *Austrian* character. They have only accurately described what *used* to be leading traits of *Viennese* character. Who would deny that Raimund, Nestroy, and Grillparzer were symbolic men who embodied the uncertain, the melancholy, the neurotic mentality of the imperial elites that, in their time, were in fact leading Austria to her self-destruction; first psychological and moral collapse, then political catastrophe? The death of great empires is not unheralded by internal decay. That Sigmund Freud should have evolved his theories of mental illness not in New York, Paris, or London but in Vienna in the last years of this enormous collapse and the chaos of its aftermath does not appear to be a happenstance.

One can still see vestiges of social neurosis in Vienna today: the sudden flare of rage over some trifle in the midst of stolid taciturnity on the crowded streetcar; the house-ordinance placards in the entryways of apartment houses that read, "NO NOISE OF ANY KIND in the courtyard or hallways. The courtyard is not a play yard." A similar sign is posted in the waiting room of the cable car station at the foot of the Raxalpe, Vienna's "house mountain," just two hours away by car. In the wide expanses of Schönbrunn Park on a Sunday afternoon if a two-year-old cries out in a fit of temper, as two-year-olds will, people wheel around and scowl at the culprit and say, "Sssss. . . ." Then there are the eternal slander trials recounted daily in the newspapers, usually occasioned by insults uttered in heat. Alongside all this there are the hearty greetings, warm smiles, twinkling eyes, and droll remarks in *Wienerisch* that one meets in the delicatessen, the Tabak-Trafik, or the candy store. There is also the relaxed *Gemütlichkeit* and good fellowship of the *Heurigen*.

Another trace of the neurotic and melancholy past is found in the myths that the Viennese constantly retell about themselves as a group and about one another as individuals. For example, there is the pessimistic upper-middle-class lady who worries about the Russians just across the Czech border. There is nothing that can be done to stave off ultimate tragedy, "because, you know, we have no self-confidence, we Austrians," she says. Perhaps she had been reading Weigel. Then there is the middle-aged party bureaucrat who in his comments about many well-known Austrian politicians began: "Oh that one is a regular psychological case, a real split personality!" Then he would go on to describe the nature of the man's schizophrenia. These notions also exist among young intellectuals. A young Socialist who is anything but a melancholy and passive pessimist but rather an ebullient, go-getting entrepreneur who knows how to make his way in the world and is busy doing it, said: "You know, sometimes I find this Austrian split personality in myself; I'm not always sure who I am."

Then there is the academician in his late twenties whose shy and impassive face hides a Nestrovian drollness and humor and who advises me to read *Der Herr Karl* if I want to get a good idea about the flavor of Austrian life today. *Der Herr Karl* is a brief volume of cabaret pieces by two talented Viennese entertainers and playwrights, Helmut Qualtinger and Carl B. Merz.[3] The skits are political and social takeoffs which the authors perform in the cabarets of Vienna and in Germany as far noth as Hamburg. "What is rotten in the Austrian state (and in the world)," says the Foreword, "they place on the pillory and deliver over to the scorn and laughter of the public." The authors are described as "joke makers, who mean it seriously. . . . Their joy in the attack breathes the spirit of Nestroy; they are jugglers of speech, masters of the witty word, and artists in their handling of the Viennese dialect."[4] Qualtinger, who is an actor as well as writer and entertainer, has appeared as the leading figure in the film version of Nestroy's *Lumpazivagabundus.*

The manner and message of *Der Herr Karl* is typically Nestrovian, droll, sarcastic, alienated. In the lead skit "Herr Karl," an aging Viennese ne'er-do-well, soliloquizes about his life before an imaginary young person while "dogging it" on his job—putting groceries on the shelves of a store where he is employed as a stock boy. He has lived out his life enjoying as many humble private pleasures, particularly those of the table and the bed, as possible and sans commitment to anything in the public world. A resigned observer of the inevitably unhappy course of that world, he has manipulated it as far as possible to protect himself from its sporadic storms and maximize his private pleasures at its expense.

3. rororo Taschenbuch Ausgabe (Munich: Georg Müller, 1964).
4. Ibid., p. 2.

Here is his comment on the burning of the Palace of Justice in Vienna in 1927, which climaxed one phase of the exhausting conflict between "Blacks" and "Reds" that prepared the way for the "Brown" takeover of 1938:

> That was an awful time. So upset. People were angry, exasperated, fanatic. Nobody could tell which party was the strongest. It was impossible to decide which way to turn, which side to join. . . . And then came the historic year '26, and the burning of the Palace of Justice. It was '26. . . . I'm sure of it. An uncle of mine died that year . . . didn't leave me anything . . . and then there was the thing about the palace. . . . It was '27. And they marched. . . . I don't know exactly *what* was wrong. . . . Anyway there was a fire . . . an awful fire . . . a beautiful blaze . . . ! I really love a good fire. We all ran over and took a look. . . . I like to look at a fire. . . . When I see a fire and hear the "TAAAA-TUUU" I run over to it. I love to see the crowds of people standing around . . . staring into the flames . . . a regular natural spectacle!

More bitingly Nestrovian is Herr Karl's comment on his own political maneuvers.

> Up to '34 I was a Socialist. But that was no kind of a business. You couldn't make a living at that. . . . If I was one today . . . but I'm past that stage now. . . . I've reached, shall we say, a certain maturity. I've got those things straight now. . . . Yeah, well, in the '30s . . . you know how they were. No, you really don't. You're much too young. But you really don't have to know about them. . . . Those are things that don't need to be stirred up again. Nobody likes to remember them . . . nobody in Austria. . . . Later I went demonstrating for the Blacks . . . for the Heimwehr . . . got five shillings for it. . . . Then I went over to . . . the Nazis . . . got five schillings there too. . . . Yeah, . . . well, Austria was always unpolitical. . . . I mean, we're not political people . . . but a little money is something else, not so?

He then goes on to recount how he made out as a petty Nazi official during the anschluss, making Jews scrub anti-Nazi slogans off the sidewalk, posting maxims like "Good health is a duty" and "other such educational sayings" in the hall of the municipal apartment where he lived. "Others got rich then," he comments. "But I was a victim. . . . I was an idealist." When the Russians and then the Americans got to Vienna he learned how to get along with them as well.

This is the way the Viennese comment on themselves, on their past and their present mentality. But Lorenz's "unfinished symphony," Weigel's schizophrenia and self-immolation, and much of "Herr Karl's" opportunism are a vestigial remain rather than a reflection of today's reality. They belong in a class with all the scare talk about impending strikes and even the renewal of civil war were the Conservatives to try to "go it alone" after winning a legislative majority in the 1966 elections. The Conservatives went it alone, and people closed their eyes and stuffed their fingers in their ears and waited—but the blowup never came, and they have since relaxed with the new system, even though there is still a certain longing for the coalition.

The Mentality of the New Elite:
The "Modern Man" in Power

Conservative Reformers like Klaus, Withalm, and Maleta are anything but resigned, uncertain, or melancholy men; nor are Socialists like Kreisky, Czernetz, and Gratz. And their opportunism is not the cynical immoralism of a Herr Karl but the rational realism of ambitious, democratic politicians playing the democratic game to win, an ambition that the democratic system requires to make it work.[5] Their pragmatism is active, hard-hitting, but also cool, calculated, prudent. They maneuver for advantage, but they know what the limits of power are and they observe them, as we have seen in our examination of the current evolution of the political system. As we have already noted, a new breed of leaders among the up-and-coming young men in both major parties displays a consensual idealism happily fused with a cool, pragmatic sense with which they combine an optimistic and ebullient spirit. These

5. On this point see Richard Neustadt, *Presidential Power: The Politics of Leadership* (New York: John Wiley & Sons, 1960).

are just the opposite of the neurotic qualities we have been discussing. And these men seem to be the wave of Austria's future.

In the Länder outside Vienna I was impressed with the energy, rationality, practicality, balance, and optimism of the political leaders I met, especially the younger ones. I found neurotic characteristics in few, at least in the hierarchies of the two major parties. I still remember with pleasure and amazement my interview with the busy Socialist Nationalrat and mayor of the Croatian town of Steinbrunn in the Burgenland. He exuded energy and obviously enjoyed his bustling life of many roles. I met him at one office where he was directing his subordinates in the execution of several different tasks while constantly answering two telephones. To find greater quiet for the interview we went to another of his offices but were still interrupted there by the telephone, which he answered each time succinctly and with authority. The Nationalrat told me with great pride of his achievements and those of his party in building a more modern Burgenland in the brief span of years since the withdrawal of the Russian occupation troops. He was particularly proud of the magnificent new central water supply system for the northern Burgenland, in the building of which he had played a significant role. That project, which was supposed to have taken twelve to fifteen years to accomplish, had been completed instead in seven. By 1965, forty-seven towns with a population of 90,000 had been tied into the supply system. In 1951 only 6 percent of Burgenland homes had received water from a central public supply system. The water supply network was to be one of the chief cornerstones in a grand plan for the economic development of the area and for its promotion as a tourist attraction.

There was the same sort of bustling, enthusiastic creativeness in Carinthia, another of Austria's formerly backward areas. Take the young typesetter, far better-spoken and read than education for such an occupation would imply, who is now working full time as youth secretary of the local branch of the trade federation. After our conversation about the Austrian nation concept we joined his pretty wife for a delicious luncheon she had prepared to serve in the dinette of their small but modern and beautifully furnished apartment. Driving back to town we stopped at the sports stadium so that my respondent and host could preside over the closing of a trades federation youth competition and see to the awarding of prizes. The head of a youth center for the training of electrical apprentices, a friendly man in his forties, rode into town with us from the stadium. He was bursting with enthusiasm about the experimental program of his center which combined staggered shifts of five months each of on-the-job training and formal instruction. Experimental exchanges with centers in other Länder in specialized training and sports were also part of the program. It was the only program of its kind, he told me. That morning I had also spoken with a delegate to the Federal Council, the upper house of the national legislature, about the development of Carinthia under his party's (Socialist) leadership. His eyes glowed as he told me about the party's plans and accomplishments in the fields of electrification, education, hospital buildings, and tourism. Ninety-eight percent of the Land was now electrified, he told me, whereas only 30 percent had been when the Socialists assumed power. Everything was "biggest and best"—the biggest power station in Austria; one of the highest dams; a brand new modern university under construction, which would offer political science and economics (instead of the traditional public law offering); new hospitals—with more beds than in any other Länder, in proportion to the Land's size; and 12,500,000 overnight tourists in 1967, compared to 300,000 in 1936.

It is the same story among the social and economic elites. I was surprised and impressed by the informality, openness, vigor, and friendliness of the head of a leading Austrian publishing house, the Molden Verlag. Fritz Molden looked in no way like a worried or fawning *Hofrat* but rather like a young American tycoon who has just established a successful business and has yet grander and more ambitious plans on the drawing board. When I left his office I asked the secretary how to address a letter of thanks to him—was it "Herr Doktor," "Herr Direktor," or what? She replied that her boss always signed himself simply "Fritz P. Molden" and liked to be addressed in that manner. Hans Igler, director of Austria's leading private bank, the Schöller Bank, and a man who has served as economic adviser to the chancellor of the republic, as executive chairman of the nationalized industries board, and as director of the Marshall Plan aid program struck me as a man of precisely the same stripe and mentality—hearty, informal, hard-working.

All this is evidence of the emergence in the Austrian political elite of a new race of "modern men," men of the kind described by Daniel Lerner in *The Passing of Traditional Society*,[6] men with the kind of ideas and personality structure that seem to go peculiarly well with the effective operation of the modern, liberal democratic nation-state. We could also describe them as bearers of the "civic culture," the cluster of ideas and personal traits which Gabriel Almond and Sidney Verba see as the psychological underpinning of a functioning democratic system. Lerner's list of modern characteristics includes (1) acceptance, even love of change and innovation, with which goes physical and social mobility, ambition to make one's way in the world, self-realization; (2) rationality, in the sense of a calculating, utilitarian outlook; (3) a "rationalist and positivist spirit" which views the future as "manipulable, not ordained"; (4) empathy—a "capacity to see oneself in the other fellow's situation," an ability to enlarge one's identity by identifying "personal values with public issues"; (5) a desire to participate in the larger public world rather than remain confined in a parochial situation; (6) a fondness for the urban setting, for an urban way of life; (7) a sense of well-being and happiness amidst mundane values. Moreover, as Lerner sees it, the modern man needs and possesses a "transpersonal common doctrine formulated in terms of shared secondary symbols—a national 'ideology' which enables persons unknown to each other to engage in political controversy or achieve 'consensus' by comparing their opinions." [7] The respondents discussed above possess most of the first seven of these modern qualities in a preeminent degree. As we have seen in chapter 6, in the eighth area there is some ambiguity and considerable retention of traditional patterns of thought—but also much progress in the development of a healthy national identity. So far as the average man is concerned, it is precisely in the most modern areas of Austria that national consciousness has increased most rapidly, as we saw in the last chapter.

6. See Lerner, *The Passing of Traditional Society*, pp. 47 ff.
7. Ibid., p. 50.

The Present State of the Austrian Nation

Returning to the hypotheses with which we began this book, we find that the experience of republican Austria bears out the speculation of Etzioni. Political integration has been achieved without an underpinning of cultural homogeneity (i.e., without general assent to the idea of an Austrian cultural nation in the traditional and extended sense of "culture"). We find that Etzioni is also right in suggesting that political culture should be separated from culture in general in talking about the psychological or moral concomitants of successful political integration. In Austria there is plainly agreement on a "limited set of values and symbols directly related to unification, including legitimation of the new power center, a sense of identity, shared political rituals, and the like," what we have called consensual democracy and an identity as a political nation in the extended sense. Actually the cultural aura surrounding Austrian political identity is somewhat broader than a purely political culture. But it does not embrace culture in general and is plainly combined with a continued widespread feeling of Germanness.

The experience of Austria also seems to bear out the thesis of the functionalists that political loyalties follow economic interests. The demonstration of Austrian economic viability and the development of a mature industrial economy that can produce affluence, perhaps more than any other factors, account for the present strong Austrian attachment to the state. In addition, we have shown that the structural evolution of the polity from contract to consensus was intimately related, as a dependent variable, to social and demographic changes which were the concomitants of the completion of industrialization.

The Second Austrian Republic appears today to be very stable. But we have no way of predicting with certainty that it will be stable tomorrow. The Austrian cultural nationalists prophesy that it will not be stable in the face of a severe economic setback, since it was primarily economic well-being that begot the present situation.

On the other hand, there are those who argue that to foster the ideal of a specific Austrian culture would create an old-fashioned nationalism that would be retrogressive in the face of events that point toward the integration of small political units into ever larger ones. Otto Schulmeister, editor of *Die Presse,* speaks of Austria as a "Piedmont of hope for Europe." A leading Conservative has been quoted as saying, "What do we need with a national foundation (*Nationalstiftung*)? We are about to enter Europe." In other words, it is argued that in a day of movement toward regional integration, it is not necessary to complete integration in particular small areas by creating a background of cultural homogeneity. Complete cultural integration might hold back necessary regional union. I believe this position has some merit.

Some of the older people (those over 40) who seek to promote the idea of an Austrian cultural nation say of those who talk about the uniting of Europe in this fashion that they use the idea of Europe as a coverup for a crypto Pan-German expansionism, since a united Western Europe would be dominated by Germany. Many of them deeply hate the Germans because of the anschluss experience. Some Socialists feel that Austrian participation in an extensive Western economic integration would endanger the position of the nationalized industries. And they worry about the effect of such a development on Austrian relations across the Iron Curtain and on Austria's status as a neutral. They, and some Conservatives who entertain the same worries, combine their Austrian cultural nationalism with a broader Europeanism which embraces Eastern Europe as well. Nostalgic recollections of the empire probably account for an interest in closer relations with the East on the part of some of the older Conservative cultural nationalists. Another factor in Viennese cultural nationalists' attitudes toward Austrian participation in a purely Western European economic union is an adverse estimate of the relative position of Vienna and eastern Austria in such a unit. It is undeniable that western Austria is already closely tied into the German market and has shown greater economic vitality than the eastern Länder. And, as we have seen, the balance of political power, population, and wealth is shifting increasingly westward, away from Vienna. The concentration of Austrian cultural nationalist elite opinions in Vienna is no doubt connected with this general situation.

This writer has not gained the impression that all those who talk glowingly about Austrian integration into Western Europe and who restrict the idea of Austria to the "political nation" are either neo-Nazis or crypto-German nationalists. However, some of them certainly are. Austria has recently negotiated a special arrangement with the European Economic Community, because her European Free Trade Association membership alone does not guarantee long-run economic security. Eventually she needs to be integrated into some larger economic unit in a fashion that would not be incompatible with political autonomy and neutrality.

The success of the Austrians in creating at least a present state of political integration on the basis of economic achievement seems to call into question the current non-Western and especially African emphasis on the creation of a cultural nation as the basis of political stability. We have seen that of all the states in Europe, Austria, in the beginning of her nation-building experience, has much in common with the emerging states of the non-Western world. Coleman and Rosberg are no doubt correct when they say that "the problem of 'territorial' integration stems from the persistence—indeed, the paramountcy—or 'primordial' attachments or ties; that is, individuals identify themselves much more strongly with historical groups defined in terms of kinship, religion, language, or culture than with the civil order of the new states. . . . The essence of the problem is . . . the welding together of a mélange of peoples of widely varying primordial attachments into a new and larger 'territorial community.' " We may doubt, however, on the basis of the Austrian experience, that such welding requires, as many African leaders believe, "the formation of single-party dominant regimes" which self-consciously try to fashion a national political culture.[8] The Austrian attempt to do precisely this via the Fatherland Front failed miserably. Instead, it was a contractarian approach that worked.

The value of contractarianism—rational conflict management—for political integration is perhaps the chief lesson that this case study of Austrian nation building teaches. As Eric Nordlinger has

8. James S. Coleman and Carl F. Rosberg, eds., *Political Parties and National Integration in Tropical Africa* (Berkeley: University of California Press, 1964), pp. 687–88, in Welch, *Dream of Unity*, pp. 344–45 and comment by Welch, p. 345.

pointed out, the literature on political development and nation building has largely overlooked the important relationship between the two.[9] It was contractarianism above all else—the 1945 abandonment by Austrian elites of ideological politics for rational problem solving, cooperatively undertaken across the lines of the hostile *Lager,* that developed the positive potential of the year 1945. The integrating situation without an integrating intention would have remained barren. The conflict management procedures of the Great Coalition were the harrow by which this intention had its fructifying effect.

The obvious rejoinder to this is that the Austrian contractarians did not operate in an international vacuum to produce political integration via the economics of affluence; they worked in a rather special and perhaps unique context—which involved the fact and the memory of a seven-year anschluss followed by Marshall Plan aid which was in turn followed by strong international support for a separate Austrian state. Integrating intention sans a propitious situation would have been equally sterile. I do not conclude, however, that the Austrian experiment must remain unique. The dictatorships and civil wars of the years since independence may be shock treatments that will affect emerging peoples much as anschluss and war affected the Austrian nation. And the international situation is not something given, like a mute fact of nature; rather, it is reducible to an intention, the intention of the leaders of the great powers. Hopefully they, as well as local elites in the developing states can learn to adopt such a contractarian approach in the use of their power and resources. If the Austrians could do so, why can't others?

9. Nordlinger, *Conflict Regulation,* p. 3. See also chapter 2, n. 37.

INDEX

Broda, Christian, 119
Burgenland: dissolved during anschluss era, 47*n*; Russian occupation of, 53, 86; population movements, 83, 87, 88; National
Assembly elections, 95, 96; national consciousness of elites, 198;
national identity of Croatian
elites, 208–19; national consciousness of general public, 229–32
Burschenschaften, 154, 170
Busek, Erhard, 188
Business Federation (Wirtschaftsbund), 106
Butschek, Felix, 145–46
Bystricky, Josef, 140

Carinthia: parochialism, 4–5, 200–
01; British occupation, 53; population growth, 83, 84, 88; economic development, 84; National
Assembly elections, 95, 96; national consciousness of elites, 195;
national consciousness of general
public, 229–32
Catholic church, 124–25, 162–67
Chin, Robert, 6
Christian Social party (Christlich-
soziale Partei): origins and Great-
Austrian ideology, 16, 20; seizure
of power in *1934*, 34–35. *See also*
Austrian People's party
Churchill, Winston, 50
Citizenship education, 134–36, 138,
139, 140, 141, 143
Coalition, Grand. *See* Grand Coali-
tion
Coleman, James S., 256
Communist Party of Austria (Kom-
munistische Partei Österreichs—
KPÖ), 130, 169, 229
Consensual idealists, 188–90, 203,
204, 206, 207
Conservatives. *See* Austrian People's
party
Contractarianism, 63–66, 256–57
Core Group (Kernkreis), 58, 111,
112, 115, 148, 152, 184, 187. *See
also* Austrian People's party
Corporative State, 34–45

Coudenhove-Kalergi, Barbara, 157
Croatian elites, 208–19
Cultural nation concept: defined,
8–9; in nineteenth-century Austrian nation building, 14; in the
thought of Ignaz Seipel, 18, 26–
28; during the First Republic,
42; Conservative leaders' views
(*1945*), 63; Socialist leaders'
views (*1945*), 63; in People's
party program (*1947*), 64; in
Communist theory, 131; views of
Felix Hurdes, 133; in citizenship
education program, 134–36; Austrian Union views, 137; Ernst
Kolb's views, 138; Heinrich
Drimmel's views, 138–39; Reichenau Conference, 141; literary
debate about, 143–48; Austrian
National Institute and Walter
Jambor, 149–52; Kurt Skalnik
and *Die Furche*, 152–53; Freedom party on, 156; the press and,
156–62; Catholic church and, 166–
67; Günther Nenning's view,
175; top party leaders' views, 179,
180–81; views of middle-range
party leaders, 184; views of local
party leaders, 192, 193, 195, 196;
views of Croatian elites, 213–17,
219; views of general public, 223,
225. *See also* Austrian nation concept; Political nation concept
Czernetz, Karl, 119, 180, 181, 182

Democratic Progressive party (Dem-
okratische Fortschrittliche Partei
—DFP), 97
Deutsch, Julius, 60
Deutsch, Karl, 7
Diem, Peter, 76*n*
Dolberg, Richard, 136
Dolezal, Günther, 137
Dollfuss, Engelbert, 11, 34–40, 162
Drimmel, Heinrich, 138–40, 142,
147

Economic development: during the
First Republic, 82, 85–86; during